THE BLACKENING OF EUROPE

VOL. III

CRITICAL VIEWS

CLARE ELLIS

THE BLACKENING OF EUROPE

VOLUME III. CRITICAL VIEWS

ARKTOS
LONDON 2025

ARKTOS

Arktos.com fb.com/Arktos arktosmedia arktosjournal

ISBN

978-1-917646-78-9 (Paperback)
978-1-917646-79-6 (Ebook)

Editing

Constantin von Hoffmeister

Layout and Cover

Tor Westman

CONTENTS

PART V

Critical Views

PART V

Critical Views

'A city cannot be constituted from any chance collection of people, or in any chance period of time. Most of the cities which have admitted settlers, either at the time of their foundation or later, have been troubled by faction.'

— Aristotle

'What causes a people's demise is neither the use of bombs nor military operations, but ethnic flooding. The primary and most effective weapon of war has always been embodied by an invasion of foreign populations, naturalisations, and a gradual seizure of power by foreigners.

Ethnic homogeneity is the condition for civil peace and prosperity. As rightly noted by Aristotle, the peaceful and economically viable coexistence of ethnically different populations on a single territory is generally impossible. It leads to incessant conflicts, followed by a civil war in which the invaders attempt to replace the natives.'

— Guillaume Faye

'World harmony need not be threatened by the cultural differences which exist and the sense of superiority that most people feel for their way of life. The danger arises when one culture sees itself as possessing a way of life that is superior and suitable for all the world's peoples and seeks to impose its way of life on others.'

— Byron M. Roth

INTRODUCTION

EUROPEANS, known as Whites, are experiencing population decline. Europeans are already a minority in the world, making up about one billion of the world's 7.7 billion inhabitants, or less than 13 percent of the total population. Since the 1960s, Europeans have seen a steady decline in births, such that today, they have one of the lowest fertility rates in the world. The total fertility rate (TFR) must be 2.1 for a population to completely replace itself through births. The European Union's TFR is around 1.6, while the global average is 2.5, with Africa having the highest TFR in the world at 4.7.

Along with the decline in White births, about sixty years ago European elites sanctioned a population-changing practice that has now become quintessential to the cosmopolitan project of the European Union: large-scale non-European immigration. Because of these two trends—decline in fertility rates and the introduction of mass-immigration—the populations of many cities and towns throughout the EU are now majority non-European. Indigenous Europeans are minorities in these areas. If these trends continue, by the end of this century non-White peoples will come to represent the absolute majority population of entire European countries. When this majority-minority shift occurs, there will be an unprecedented transfer of political power from European peoples to non-Europeans, essentially signalling the end of European sovereignty over their ancestral homelands.

Clearly, indigenous Europeans are becoming demographic and political minorities in their homelands. However, this downfall is not just the result of declining fertility rates and large-scale non-European immigration, but also, and very importantly, the result of political ideologies that accompany these two trends. The EU project, including efforts to form a Euro-Mediterranean Union, is a politically constructed cosmopolitan project founded on demographic engineering, anti-nationalism, the erasure of ethno-national identities, the creation of multi-ethnic societies, and the separation of political authority and sovereignty from indigenous Europeans. The EU project, accompanied by neoconservative policies, has opened Europe to large-scale non-European immigration (legal and *illegal*), widespread socio-political problems associated with violent and nonviolent forms of political Islam, and leftist-Third World alliances that are hostile to European power structures and identities. The great majority of ethnic Europeans are being drowned by a Europhobic Euro-Arab Dialogue, by leftism, by the rapidly growing demographic of Muslim and non-European immigrants, and also by Zionists and neoconservatives that laud a deracinated, liberal, Judeo-Christian identity for Europeans and label ethno-national European identities and anti-immigration sentiments among Europeans as racist and a new form of Nazism. In sum, while they are still the majority of their national populations, indigenous Europeans and their traditional political and cultural institutions and identities are undergoing processes of erasure — stigmatized, marginalized, deprived, and replaced — by mandated immigration*ism*, multicultural*ism*, and other ideological methods of dispossession and forced diversification (cosmopolitan*ism*, cultural Marx*ism*, Islam*ism* etc.) while their resistance is criminalized.

Is the EU cosmopolitan project a form of genocide? What international laws and rights are being violated? Is it creating the conditions for civil war? We provide answers to these questions in this volume. But before we delve in, it is important to summarize what was discussed in Volumes I and II, revisit the Eurabia thesis, and evaluate established neoconservative critiques of the EU project.

In Volume I: *Ideologies and International Developments*, we began with an examination of the early-20th-century European-integration models of Pan-Europa, the United States of Europe, and Eurafrica and found that these early plans involved: the joint exploitation, by Europe, of the resources and land of the African colonies; a new culturally united Europe led by a spiritual aristocracy (Judaism); and a new European identity stripped of its distinct ethno-national characteristics. Drawing most notably from the influential socialist ideas of Richard von Coudenhove-Kalergi, we found that at this time the unification of Europe was perceived as the first step toward the eventual unity of humanity under a World Federation in perpetual peace. Fabianism and cultural Marxism furthered this goal. Both these ideologies have been integral to: the progressive transformation of Europe into a denationalized and open European Union (including the promotion of Euro-Mediterranean integration); the creation of the new European and world citizen; and the gradual development of a new world order based on cosmopolitan ideas of perpetual peace, initiated by the wealthy socialist classes, and exacted by changing the system from within by infiltrating educational institutions, government agencies, and political parties.

We then examined other influences that had direct bearing on further European integration and the cosmopolitan project. We found that post-WWII international institutions, namely the Atlantic Charter, the United Nations, and the Universal Declaration of Human Rights, established a new global order and effectively opened European nations to large-scale non-European immigration. Moreover, there were certain developments and conflicts in the Middle East (i.e. the creation of Israel and Pan-Islamism) that provided the geopolitical context for an additional integration model: Eurabia. Of particular concern was the 1970s oil crisis that triggered the formation of the Euro-Arab Dialogue, a cultural, political, and economic cooperative partnership that promoted the importation of Muslim migrants and Islam into Europe. Official documents from the 1980s into the 21st century also demonstrated additional strategies for intra-European, Eurafrican, Euro-Arab, and Euro-Mediterranean political, economic, and cultural integration.

We then scrutinized the four ideologies that have been essential to the creation of the present form of the European Union: cosmopolitanism, social liberalism, neoliberalism, and neoconservatism. Contemporary cosmopolitanism is fixated on transforming the world according to universal socialist ideals and values and is intimately involved with the creation of a new socialist-capitalist class that is dependent on cheap Third World labour. Influential cosmopolitan Jürgen Habermas promotes the idea that mass-immigration will transform European nations into ethnically diverse liberal democracies. He wants to use immigrants and the universal principles of rights to overturn national self-determination and the plurality of sovereign-states and decouple European majority ethnic groups from their ethno-cultural political identities. Furthermore, while Canadian multiculturalist William Kymlicka promotes group rights for ethnic minorities and non-European immigrants, he does not grant the same rights for ethnic Europeans.

Social liberalism has roots in Marx's theories of historical materialism and the end of capitalism, applies social science methods (social engineering) to make European societies more liberal, and views moral authority and judgments through the lenses of relativism and emotivism. Neoliberalism has an economic basis in deregulation, privatization, and reduced funding for social services. It transfers political power from the political authority of the state to the economy and judiciary; corporations and a small wealthy elite control the economy, and by extension society and local politics. Debt and dependency are incurred because of the interventionist and coercive opening of foreign markets to the capitalist world economy and transnational corporations and the international financial elite gain increasing power over the global economy and over life itself. Neoconservatism is rooted in neoliberal economics, has left-wing origins, has a predominantly Jewish composition, is devoted to the security of Israel at the expense of America, and is based on Democratic Peace Theory and the notion of the 'end of history'. It advocates pre-emptive war and intervention, and the use of military might to achieve American global leadership, spread American freedom and democracy, and prevent any potential or actual rivals arising as a global superpower to challenge American hegemony.

We now turn to Volume II: *Immigration and Islam*. We demonstrated that immigration into Europe has been predominately from Muslim countries in Africa, Asia, and the Middle East since the 1960s. Net migration into the European Union is now around 1.5 million a year and many cities are increasingly non-European in composition. Due to aging populations and below-replacement fertility rates, net migration (which has been increasing since the 1990s) is the main source of population growth for the five key European countries that were profiled: Belgium, the United Kingdom, France, Sweden, and Germany. Between 10 and 20% of the populations of these five nations are now foreign-born. In addition, most residency permits granted to immigrants are for family reasons rather than employment.

With reference to experts and analysts, we then discussed the origin of Islam, the revival of political Islam in the 20th century, militant Islamist movements such as the Taliban, al Qaeda, and ISIS, the differences between violent, non-violent, and participationist Islamists, and Islamist channels of operation in Europe. We addressed Islamist declarations of the demographic conquest and Islamization of Europe, and evaluated the proposition that Islamism represents a Gramscian counter-hegemonic ideology and movement against the power structures of the West. We also analysed Muslim demographics in the European Union. We found that Islam is the fastest growing religion in Europe, that around 7% of the EU population is Muslim, that Sharia law is having an increasing impact on the political landscape, and that many of the largest cities have significant Muslim populations (with many areas turned into 'Sharia-controlled areas' leading to 'White flight' and 'Jewish flight'). Statistics and demographics in the five key European countries mentioned above also revealed that Muslims have low educational levels, high welfare consumption, high unemployment rates, and high incarceration rates compared to national and other immigrant groups. There are also increasing problems with the radicalisation of Muslims in schools, social media, mosques, and prisons, and significant support for radical Islam in Europe.

We showed, through statistical analysis, that since at least the late 1980s a majority of Europeans have opposed political Islam and Muslim enclaves in Europe as well as large-scale population changes brought about by global mass-immigration. But there has been no effective action taken by political elites. In fact, there has been an increase in immigration and more statements that political Islam belongs in Europe. And what about the 2015/2016 migrant crisis? It revealed not just the open-door policy of EU elites and the flouting of asylum laws, but more importantly, it reflected a mass exodus of young Muslim men who used the Mediterranean Sea and land routes for clandestine entry into Europe. The vast majority (over 90%) of irregular migrants during this time came from Muslim majority countries in Africa, the Middle East, and South Asia, many of which were safe or safe third countries. Over 60% were not genuine asylum seekers, and some were terrorists.

Despite these facts, elites argued that the migrant crisis could be used to solve economic and demographic (and political) issues in Europe. But a critical evaluation of demographic data (education and employment levels, language abilities, etc.) of recent asylum seekers and first and second generation non-European immigrants cast serious doubt on their claims. As did the actual and estimated costs of the migrant crisis for individual European nations, for the European Union as a whole, and for Europeans as individuals, including social and security costs, such as migrant crime waves, the 2015 New

Year's Eve mass-sexual assaults in Germany and elsewhere, and the hundreds of lives that were lost and the hundreds more that were wounded in the Islamist terrorist attacks in Paris (2015) and Brussels (2016). These incidents, and many others, revealed the failure of costly integration and counter-radicalism strategies and the actual crisis of non-European migration into Europe in general. More importantly, they exposed the disgraceful behaviour of EU bureaucrats and other elites who lied about and denied the ethnic nature and extent of these crimes, blamed the victims, and censored media and police reports for political ends.

And now we turn to Volume III: *Critical Views*. We begin with a detailed account of the Eurabia thesis, which is foundational to the present form of the European Union. We then turn to a discerning evaluation of Muslim immigration, Islamism, multiculturalism, and left-wing ideologies in the EU as presented by neoconservative authors Bat Ye'or, Melanie Phillips, and Bruce Bawer. We summarize their views and then critique and refute some of their central arguments, including:

- Islamist aggression against Israel and the West is a metaphysical conflict between good and evil
- An Israel-West neoconservative alliance against Islam and Leftism is necessary
- Palestinianism is a Nazi-Jihadi fascist alliance between Europe and the Arab countries
- Europe needs mass-immigration
- Europe should adopt American assimilationism (liberal individualism and monoculturalism)
- Europe must rid itself of ethno-nationalism.

Referring to international laws, rights, and other official documents, we then define some central terms, such as self-determination, discrimination, persecution, genocide, indigenous rights, and the aim and basis of the European Union. In an effort of assessment, we then consult the research of several scholars and experts on demography and ethnicity and apply the aforementioned laws, rights, and legal terms to various aspects of the EU cosmopolitan project. The central argument is that EU elites, pro-immigrant open-border leftists, Third World oppositionists, anti-European immigrants, Islamists, and neoconservatives (the liberal Right) share a common ground: the negation and undermining of ethnic European demographic majority rule and national homeland sovereignty. These groups knowingly use immigration and the recent flows of irregular migrants into Europe, as well as discriminatory measures, hate propaganda, and exclusionary ideologies that condemn indigenous Europeans who oppose their goals, to elicit regime change in Europe. Such a project dismisses the will of European peoples, renders them political and demographic minorities in their own homelands, increases the likelihood of civil war, and violates numerous international laws that serve to protect the rights of distinct ethnic peoples from any form of genocide.

14. THE EURABIA THESIS AND AN ANALYSIS AND CRITIQUE OF THREE CONSERVATIVE VIEWS

14.1 The Eurabia Thesis

HISTORIAN Bat Ye'or (Gisèle Littman) is the most important scholarly proponent of the Eurabia thesis. She is the thinker behind Melanie Phillips's *Londonistan* (2006) and Bruce Bawer's *While Europe Slept: How Radical Islam is Destroying the West from Within* (2006). She has also exercised considerable influence on many of the most important authors who warn us about the Islamization of Europe, including Daniel Pipes, Niall Ferguson, Robert Spencer, and Bernard Lewis. The major work of Bat Ye'or is *Eurabia: The Euro-Arab Axis* (2005/2011), to which we now turn.

In this book Ye'or explains that the Euro-Arab Dialogue (EAD) was established by the European Economic Community (EEC) as a response to the oil embargo of 1973. The EAD was centred on a multilateral economic forum that aimed to strengthen economic, financial, technical, and cultural co-operation between the Nine of the EEC and the twenty Arab League states. The EEC perceived that such cooperation would bring about economic benefits for Europe from 'expanded oil, commercial, and industrial markets', which included the 'massive sales of arms, as well as of industrial and nuclear equipment'.[1] The EEC also founded the European Parliamentary Association for Euro-Arab Cooperation (PAEAC) with the aim of cultivating cultural, economic, and political cooperation between Europe and the Arab-Muslim world. A PAEAC meeting in Strasbourg, June 1975, recognized the 'historical contribution of Arab culture to European development' and discussed 'the contribution that the European countries can still expect from Arab culture, notably in the area of human values'. The provision of the 'means', created by the Arab countries, to enable Arab immigrants 'to participate in Arab cultural and religious life' in their respective European host countries was also deliberated, and included the propagation of Islam and the Arab culture throughout Europe.[2]

To a large extent these discussions were stimulated by a study on the conditions of Euro-Arab cooperation submitted to and accepted by the PAEAC by Belgian member, Tilj De Clercq. He wrote that '[a] medium and long term policy must henceforth be formulated in order to bring about economic cooperation through a combination of Arab manpower reserves and raw materials, and European technology and "management"'.[3] In fact, according to Ye'or, ever since the first General Commission meeting in Luxembourg (1976) 'every EAD meeting passed resolutions in support of Arab immigration, labor, and employment in Europe', resolutions that were reaffirmed in subsequent meetings. In other words, while Europe expanded its markets and transferred its technology to the Arab world and received a guarantee of oil supplies, it itself received Arab manpower through large-scale immigration from Muslim countries—immigrants who were perceived as 'builders of the future Euro-Arab alliance: "Eurabia"'.[4]

---

1 Ye'or, *Eurabia*, 70. For more information on the Euro-Arab Dialogue, see Volume I.

2 Cited in Ye'or, *Eurabia*, 66.

3 Declercq citied in ibid, 64.

4 Ye'or, *Eurabia*, 93, 164.

This EAD plan for the 'implantation of homogeneous ethnic communities' into Europe, which resulted in the rapid growth of Muslim communities, necessitated the need for addressing the living and working conditions of these Muslim immigrants. Several immigration policies were enacted by the EEC, like the 1978 Damascus Declaration, which gave immigrants the right to retain their cultural traditions and not integrate into the secular European culture of their host nation. Other policies, such as from the Hamburg Symposium (1983), have given immigrants the opportunity to 'enjoy all the political, cultural, social, and religious rights of the host country'. In addition, Arabs have called for 'special privileges' for Arab immigrants, including equal work opportunities, and have demanded that host countries 'provide immigrants with vocational training, freedom of movement, suitable living conditions, and financial aid should they decide to return to their homeland'. Muslims have also insisted on the 'partial incorporation of *shari'a* into European civil law'; Ye'or claims that since the early 1980s Islamic Sharia Councils have been founded in Europe and have created 'a parallel unofficial Islamic legal system'.[5]

Even the selection, by Europe, of source countries for immigrants have not escaped Islamic scrutiny and external Arab demands, as illustrated in the early 2000s, when the EU was on the brink of enlargement by the admission of ten Eastern European countries. The Arab States of the Mediterranean were concerned that such enlargement would affect them financially as well as affect their status as 'Western Europe's privileged source of immigration'. In response to these fears, in February 2003 the Euro-Mediterranean Study Commission (EuroMeSCo) issued a report which stressed that the main sources of immigration into the EU would primarily be from Muslim countries (Turkey, the countries to the east of Central and Eastern Europe, and the Mediterranean Arab countries). Then, in October 2003, the High-Level Advisory Group of the European Commission issued a report

5 Ibid, 95, 75, 137, 106.

that predicted that Arab Muslims along with the Muslim populations of Bulgaria, the Balkans, and Turkey, and the Turkish Muslim populations in Germany and Austria, would contribute to the 'diversification of European Islam'.[6]

On top of these developments, Ye'or points out that host populations have been required to 'satisfy' and adapt to the 'religious, cultural, and social requirements' of Muslims immigrants. This accommodation has been actively promoted by Eurocrats via their 'sociopolitical directives', which have pervaded all European institutions and include: the whitewashing of Islamism (divorcing it from terrorism, jihad, and geopolitical goals), the propagation of Islamic culture and religion, and support for the 'Arab perspective' regarding Islam and the Islamic world. These Eurocrat directives have been 'wholeheartedly embraced, applied and monitored by European leaders, intellectuals, and activists', such as by the socialist finance minister of France and 8th president of the European Commission, Jacques Delors, who stated that 'Islam is a component of Europe's value system, and this fact must be acknowledged in order to prevent the exclusion of Muslims'. Such propaganda has been grounded in idealistic notions about respect between cultures and religions and the enrichment of human knowledge through cultural diversity, as well as involving pernicious concepts such as 'the Andalusia utopia', 'Islamic cultural superiority', 'Christianophobia' and 'European self-guilt'.[7]

The indoctrination of indigenous Europeans to accept the social and political goals and ideologies of the EAD, especially the presence of Islam in Europe, is being accomplished by what Ye'or calls 'a gigantic machinery' that has been 'planned and ordered at the top of Europe's political, cultural, and economic establishment' and executed through 'various legal, cultural and political frameworks': the Damascus (1978) and Barcelona (1995) Declarations, the Hamburg Symposium (1983),

6 Ibid, 140–141, 233–234.

7 Ibid, 94, 103, 77, 143, 161.

the European Institute for Research on Mediterranean and Euro-Arab Cooperation (MEDEA, 1995), the Euro-Mediterranean Partnership (EUROMED, 1995), the Euro-Mediterranean Foundation for the Dialogue of Cultures (Anna Lindh Foundation, 2004), the European Neighbourhood Policy (2004), and the Union for the Mediterranean (UfM, 2008). Ye'or writes that the Anna Lindh Foundation 'seems to be designed to condition the minds of Europeans and mold them according to guidelines imposed by the Euro-Arab network' and has aimed

> to retain exclusive and totalitarian control on everything written and taught about the Mediterranean area in EU schools and universities. The report outlines a program to control the intellectual life, thoughts and activities of the whole Partnership area through guidelines given to the press, the schools, the universities and NGOS; through the arts, films, publications, and political pressure; and through the expurgation of history, reworking of school syllabi and other means — all in order to *create a new mankind* according to the Dialogue's standards "in the spirit of and in support of the EU's neighbourhood policy".[8]

Ye'or well knows that indigenous European populations have been 'betrayed and misled by their own leaders' through the political, educational, and media systems as well as through various cultural activities. She also knows that with the EAD and its further developments, 'identities are to be destroyed in order to dissolve diversity into a uniform anonymous humanity .... differences are submerged into a collective Us'. Yet the first process of this engineering of collectivity is the erasure of the differences of Europeans from Muslims by the promotion of the cultural, political, and religious identity of Muslims over and above that of Europeans. For example, while Eurabians denounce 'the Crusades, the Inquisition, imperialism, and European colonialism' and suggest that Europe owes 'a moral debt to the Arab Palestinians and to the Muslim world', there is no acknowledgment

8 Ye'or, *Eurabia*, 239, 129, 243, 236–237 (my emphasis).

of the 'moral debt' owed to Christian Europe for the historical jihad expansionism of Islam. Leftist Eurocrats attribute the sources of Islamist rage and terrorism to 'circumstantial situations like "poverty," "underdevelopment," "humiliation," or "frustration"—for which the West and Israel bore responsibility'. Here the aggressor is transformed into the victim. The history of European civilization has also been distorted to fit in line with the social and political goals of the EAD, such as the claim that the Greek scientific heritage of Europe was actually transmitted from the Arab-Muslim world. Denying the central relevance of the ancestral foundations of Greek, Roman, and Judeo-Christianity, as well as lesser progenitors, such as European pagan and tribal heritages, and also denying the fact that Greek civilization was taught in the Byzantine Empire and Italy and was transmitted to Western Europe in the eleventh century, this view of history promotes the idea that Islam 'is the only relevant ancestor of modern European civilisation', a view that is prevalent in textbooks.[9]

The ideals of the Barcelona Declaration and the epitomes of the European leftists, whether clerics, educators, or politicians, are not practiced by Muslim countries and the Arab League states. The EU has claimed 'that it promotes democracy, the rule of law, respect for human rights, and fundamental freedoms with the Arab countries through the Barcelona Process', but 'none of these goals has been attained in the African, Middle East, and Asian dictatorships'. Although the EAD is 'a political dialogue based on observance of essential principles of international law…in accordance with the United Nations Charter and the Universal Declaration of Human Rights (UDHR)

---

9 Ibid, 143, 235, 187, 199. Since 1981, Ismail Raji al-Faruqi, founder of the influential International Institute of Islamic Thought (IIIT, which states on its website that it is, among other things, 'the voice of the Muslim intellectual tradition in the West'), has challenged Western philosophy and education, perceiving them as contrary to Islam. He and IIIT have stressed the 'reIslamization' of science and the *Islamization of Knowledge* to 'fill the vacuum created when Western civilization will finally collapse'. See: International Institute of Islamic Thought, 'About Us'. https://iiit.org/en/about-us/.

as well as other obligations under international law', the 1990 Cairo Declaration of Human Rights (CDHR) supersedes the UDHR for Muslim countries (and the Arab League), conforming to Sharia rather than human law. What this means is that the rights of Muslim immigrants in the West are incomparable to the rights of European immigrants and indigenous non-Muslim populations in Muslim majority countries; in fact, the persecution of minorities that occurs in Muslim majority countries is considered justifiable under the CDHR and is whitewashed by the European media, government officials, and educational institutions. More importantly, mass-immigration from Europe into Muslim countries on the same scale conducted by Muslim countries into Europe 'would never be tolerated'.[10]

The ideologies of cultural relativism and 'political correctness' have also been imposed upon European populations by the Eurabian elites. For example, in addition to the false portrayal of European history, Europeans who have 'functional relations with the immigrants', such as 'civil servants, medical staff, members of the police force, social workers, and others', have been required to undergo 'special training and educational courses' that sensitize them to the requirements and sensibilities of Muslim immigrants. Any criticism of Islamic history, Islamic doctrine, large-scale Muslim immigration, and the demographic colonization of Europe is also strictly prohibited. Since the 1980s anti-immigration sentiments arising from European natives has been consistently labeled as 'xenophobic', 'right wing extremist', 'racist', 'Arabophobic', 'Islamophobic', and even associated with Nazi anti-Semitism by 'universities, books, and the media' as well as by politicians and other influential public figures, such as 'the EAD's agents and executives'.[11]

10 Ibid, 246, 244, 106, 198–200, 106–107, 237. European mass-immigration into Middle Eastern Muslim countries is not necessary; Muslim immigrants are considered as surplus population, manpower that Europe 'requires', whereas no such surplus population exists in Europe.

11 Ye'or, *Eurabia*, 97, 103, 252.

A consequence of this hostile and elitist subversion has been what Ye'or calls 'the mutation of European civilization' or 'a hybrid culture: Eurabia'. With the support of the European elites and the legal system and the gagging of native dissent, over the past fifty years millions of Muslims, who have been perceived as 'builders of the future Euro-Arab alliance', have immigrated to Europe with no intention of integrating into the host culture and society; they have brought their cultural norms and habits with them, have rejected the secular liberal culture of Europe in favour of their own, and have utilized the legal system to protect their interests, all of which has created a volatile situation of social fragmentation and separatism within Europe at the expense of indigenous Europeans and their ways of life.[12]

14.2 Bat Ye'or

The Eurabia thesis is grounded in an extensive amount of evidence and exposes the pernicious influences of Islamism, multiculturalism, and left wing ideologies in the EU. Ye'or provides a persuasive critique of the growth of Muslim communities, the promotion of Islam in European nations, and the denunciation (by EU bureaucrats and intellectual elites) of the concerns of European peoples about such developments. However, there are several aspects of her argument that are problematic. What follows is a critical examination and refutation of some of the main themes presented in *Eurabia: The Euro-Arab Axis* (2005/2011).

14.2.1 Franco-German Reconciliation, European Integration, Euro-Mediterranean Union, and Anti-American Strategy

Ye'or claims that after losing its colonial empire from the onset of decolonization (late 1940s) and Algerian independence (1962), France under Charles de Gaulle (and others, such as Jacques Chirac) sought

12 Ibid, 102, 164.

to regain influence by leading the unification of Europe and by initiating cooperative partnerships with the Arab and African Muslim worlds. French elites wanted a 'Franco-Arab alliance' whereby France would 'build a community with all the Mediterranean countries', especially 'with a Muslim federation extending over North Africa and the Middle East'. Ye'or claims that this Franco-Arab cooperation 'coalesced with de Gaulle's greatest ambition'—the unification of Europe. This union of Europe rested upon the restoration of good relations between France and West Germany, and these two countries collaborated with each other to undertake a long-term geopolitical plan that sought the integration of the European and Arab Mediterranean countries into 'a single interdependent economic bloc' (Eurabia) that would act as 'an international counterweight to America'.[13]

In contrast to Ye'or's claims that France was a leading mastermind in the creation of Eurabia, certain French governments have attempted to stop labour immigration and family reunification over the years, through various laws and acts, such as the Chirac and Barre governments, the first Pasqua Law (1986), the Second Pasqua Law (1994), the Debre Law, and so on.[14] Furthermore, none of the ideas that Ye'or originates in France and Germany were new or confined to these countries. As detailed in Volume I of this work, the integration of Europe became popular in the nineteenth century on both sides of the Atlantic and reached a high pitch in the interwar and initial post-WWII era in the twentieth century among many leading politicians and public figures in Europe, the United Kingdom, and the United States.

The notion of European alignment with the Mediterranean countries to the south (and east) as an integrated geopolitical bloc to counter America was an idea that was first disseminated by the Austrian geo-politician and activist Richard Coudenhove-Kalergi in the form

13 Ye'or, *Eurabia*, 39–41.

14 Also see: Kofman, Rogoz, and Lévy, 'Family Migration Policies in France'.

of Eurafrica and Pan-Europa and was supported by a wide-range of leading European and American elites from the 1920s onwards. European integration and Euro-Mediterranean alignment were part of a long-term socialist vision of a world federation of humanity, whereby the world, in an effort to maintain the balance of powers and attain perpetual peace, would be divided into five political blocs that would be lawfully ordered on a global scale. Franco-German reconciliation was indeed a first step towards European integration and a Euro-Mediterranean union, and an attempt to create a disarmed and peaceful Europe, but it was an idea that did not originate in post-WWII France but instead came out of the pre-WWI Atlantic peace movements and the interwar Pan-European movement. Aristide Briand, the French foreign minister, and Gustav Stresemann, the Germany foreign minister, were both greatly influenced by the ideas of Kalergi, and in 1926 they were awarded the Nobel Peace Prize for their efforts at Franco-German reconciliation. The alignment of West Germany and France in the extraction and production of coal and steel, as declared by the European Coal and Steel Community (ECSC) in 1951 (Treaty of Paris) led by Jean Monnet, finally cemented reconciliation between these two countries, but it was not confined to France and Germany; the Benelux countries and Italy also signed and belonged to this community. The Friendship Treaty (Elysee Treaty), a peaceful cooperation between Germany and France that has lasted ever since its inception in 1963, embodies Kalergi's ideas of Franco-German reconciliation and initial European integration.[15]

In sum, in her analysis Ye'or neglects the long history behind European unification with the Mediterranean areas, the ideas of a world federation based on five major world political blocs and the balance of powers, as well as the historical notions of peace, disarmament, anti-nationalism, and cosmopolitanism. All of these influences arose long before the leftism of the 1960s, have not been confined to

15 Rompuy, 'Acceptance speech on the occasion of the Award of the European Prize Coudenhove-Kalergi 2012: "Peace and the European idea"'.

France and Germany, have been endorsed by America, and have been central to European unification and to various Euro-Mediterranean partnerships.

14.2.2 Oil Embargo Not a Threat but a Pretext for European Plan of Political Reversal

Ye'or asserts that the Arabs used the 1973 oil embargo as a weapon to gain leverage over international foreign affairs regarding the Middle East conflict. But, she also alleges that Europe, particularly France and Germany, 'panicked' and succumbed to the oil threat by endorsing the Arab perspective 'toward Israel' in exchange for guaranteed oil supplies and access to Arab markets. She also claims that America knew that the oil threat was empty because the Arabs 'would have been powerless without Western technology' and without oil and natural gas revenues, and that Americans 'proved', through their policies, that this interdependent relationship between the Western and Arab Worlds meant that 'there never was an oil threat'.[16]

In addition, Ye'or asserts that because 'there never was an oil threat' and because Europe did not use its political leverage to remain 'politically autonomous' but instead, motivated by 'fear...greed and misplaced ambition', established the Euro-Arab Dialogue and other cooperative partnerships with the Arab world, the oil embargo was really 'just a pretext for a political reversal already planned by France and Germany'. This Franco-German 'planned reversal' was the integration of Europe through common political and economic strategies toward core issues such as foreign policy in the Middle East, and a Euro-Arab integration that aimed towards the creation of a geopolitical bloc that would rival America.[17]

As previously mentioned, the integration of Europe as a geopolitical bloc that also utilized the Mediterranean countries in an effort

---

16 Ye'or, *Eurabia*, 48, 101, 230.

17 Ibid, 230, 162, 225, 40.

to counter America was not new or confined to a Franco-German collusion. Although the oil embargo of 1973 was a new factor that prompted the increased need for a common European foreign policy in the Middle East, particularly regarding the peace process, this foreign policy had already been in development since at least the time of Kalergi, and especially since the Suez crisis, when the Arabs began to explicitly reveal their ideological aspirations (Islamism) and geopolitical powers (via oil and pan-Islamic nationalisms) and threaten Europe's interests in the region.

Although Ye'or attempts to convince the reader that the oil embargo was an 'empty threat', which may have been applicable to America as it had its own oil supplies, this is just not true for Europe. Europe was dependent on a large amount of its oil supplies from the Arab oil-producing countries and its biggest port, Rotterdam, was completely embargoed, which affected all the European nations (including Britain, which was not embargoed at all). The effects of rising oil prices per barrel and the reduction of oil supplies to Europe by 25 percent resulted in massive inflation and unemployment, hardly facts that render the threat of the embargo 'empty'. How would America (and Israel) have secured or guaranteed a vital energy resource for European industry if Europe had not established a dialogue with the Arab League and continued to be at the mercy of the oil embargo? How would they have prevented Arab hostility towards Europe? Why does Ye'or not mention the Soviet threat[18] and the role this played in the European 'appeasement' of the Arabs and the development of the Dialogue?

One of the main reasons why the EEC entered into the Dialogue with the Arab League states was to avert the possibility of another

---

18 The Soviet Union declared its support for the Arab nations and the oil embargo. See: Christopher C. Wren, 'Moscow Angrily Denying Role in Arab Oil Embargo'. *The New York Times*. December 6 1973. https://www.nytimes.com/1973/12/06/archives/moscow-angrily-denying-role-in-arab-oil-embargo-western-curbs-noted.html.

embargo in the future and to secure long-term guarantees of oil from the oil-producing countries in the Arab world. In fact, in 2014 a meeting of pro-Israel American neoconservatives aired on Horowitz Freedom Center TV revealed that America itself was dependent upon Middle Eastern oil, and even admitted that America relies on terroristic Islamic groups such as ISIS for the continued existence of the American military.[19] What is important here, is that by denying the reliance of Europe and America on Middle Eastern oil, Ye'or can then gain credibility for her accusations against Europe—that the Europeans began the Dialogue and continue it with the Arabs because they are first and foremost anti-semitic and want to destroy Israel. Such accusations are unfounded. European elites have in no way fully endorsed the Arab perspective on Israel. While they have said they recognize Palestinian rights and nationhood, a statement which has aimed at placating Arab hostility and has not been enforced, they have not been opposed to or sought the destruction of Israel as a nation-state or the Jews and Israelis as a people; rather, they have requested that Israel abide by UN Resolution 242[20] by withdrawing from former Arab lands that were taken by force in 1967 and going back to the armistice lines of 1949.

14.2.3 Politics and Policy on Israel and a Nazi-Jihadi Alliance

According to Ye'or, the project of Euro-Mediterranean integration has roots in ideas advocated by Adolf Hitler, as represented in his 1941 vision: 'the common interests of a unified Europe within an economic

19 'Pro-Israel American Conservative: Thank God for ISIS...US Will be in Middle East Forever', YouTube video (Horowitz Freedom Center TV).

20 United Nations Security Council, *Resolution 242* (1967) of 22 November 1967. https://unispal.un.org/DPA/DPR/unispal.nsf/0/7D35E1F729DF491C85256EE700686136. Also see Volume I, chapter 3 for more information about conflicts in the Middle East and how they influenced Euro-Arab cooperation.

zone completed by the African colonies'.[21] She argues that this plan has otherwise manifested in the Euro-Arab Dialogue of 1974 and the successive developments towards a Euro-Mediterranean union that came after, which she considers anti-Zionist. She claims that a Nazi-Jihadi fascist alliance between Europe and the Arab countries, a 'Euro-Arab Nazism' in the form of Palestinianism,[22] constitutes the EAD partnership and characterizes the construction of Eurabia. She explains that through the EAD the European heads of state developed, for the first time, a common European foreign policy that was aligned with the Arab League's policy on Israel. She thinks this shared policy also involves a 'common political will' of 'collective hostility' toward Israel, which has been revealed through EAD Declarations that recognized the rights and national identity of Palestinians and urged the withdrawal of Israel from the 'occupied territories' of post-1949. Therefore, according to Ye'or, Europe has endorsed the Palestinian Liberation Organisation's (PLO) 'ideology, strategy, propaganda, and phraseology' and constructed '[a]n entire war policy for the delegitimization of Israel'.[23]

Ye'or also thinks the supposed Nazi-Jihadi Euro-Arab alliance is the re-emergence of the same alliance of the 1930s era and poses an existential threat to Israel: 'As Judaism was the target of Nazi ideology, so Israel's very existence is a central target of Euro-Arab policy'. She further claims that 'anti-Zionist dogma' that links 'Zionism with racism' has been spread far and wide by EAD inspired 'radio, television, the

21 Adolf Hitler as cited in Ye'or, *Eurabia*, 148.

22 Palestinians are transformed into victims and Israelis into Nazis; put simply, it is 'Palestinian victimology'. See chapter 14 in Ye'or, *Eurabia* for further definition.

23 Ye'or, *Eurabia*, 181, 184, 52, 89, 56, 86, 73. Ye'or claims Palestinian Liberation Theology, the Muslim-Christian dialogue, counters the Jewish-Christian rapprochement of Vatican II (1960s) and harnesses the same currents, the 'traditional anti-Semitism', that led Theodor Herzl to found Zionism and which also 'led to the *shoah*'. Ibid, 177, emphasis in original. See *Eurabia*, chapter 14, 'Palestinianism: A New Eurabian Cult — Manipulation of Jewish History'.

press and the UN educational publications'. She also blames Europe for internationalising the Arab-Israeli conflict by its public support of the Arab position and its more radical of leaders, Arafat and the PLO, and accuses Europe of using the conflict 'as a tool against America to strengthen EU influence and interests in the Islamic world, while working for the disintegration of Israel'.[24]

As previously mentioned, the EAD and the European Union have not aimed at the destruction of Israel or the elimination of her people, but rather have requested Israel withdraw to 1949 armistice lines. This shared foreign policy of Europe was essentially part of a strategy to gain European unity and was an effort to appease the Arabs' conditions for dialogue and economic partnership and has not been enforced. In addition, the drive towards European unification and its use and development of Euro-Mediterranean partnerships have been in development since the late nineteenth and early twentieth centuries and have been endorsed by leading figures in both Europe and America.

For Ye'or to claim that Hitler and National Socialism are connected in a vital way to Euro-Mediterranean unification, and therefore the destruction of Europe from massive Muslim immigration and subsequent colonisation, is to entirely miss the significant role and lasting impact Kalergi et al. have had on this engineering project. The socialism of Hitler was ethnic and national, whereas the socialism of Kalergi was cosmopolitan and international. The Palestinian Third-World socialism of Eurabia is the socialism of Kalergi, the Frankfurt School (cultural Marxism), and Fabianism. It is a socialism of anti-nationalism, open borders, and miscegenation, policies that do not bode well for both the European indigenous peoples and Israelis alike, for they aim to destroy ethnic nationalism, meaning the loss of national and ethnic sovereignty, political power, and identity.

---

24 Ibid, 115, 23, 59, 180, 46–47, 42, 156, 87, 113.

It was Kalergi-Fabian-Frankfurt School socialism that gave rise to the EAD, not the National Socialism of Hitler. Although both Hitler and Kalergi did not intend for Third World immigration into Europe, it was Kalergi who advocated the settlement, exploitation, and Europeanization of Africa (and the Arab world if necessary) while also imagining a mixed European race of the future, a 'Euro-Asian Negroid' that would be spiritually overseen by a Jewish elite. He wrote in *Practical Idealism* that Jews are the predestined spiritual leader race of Europe and the world:

> Instead of destroying Judaism, Europe, through an artificial selection process and without having the intention, ennobled it and educated it to be the leading nation of the future .... this people... became Europe's spiritual aristocracy.... a new aristocratic race by God's [the Spirit's] grace just at the time when the feudal nobility fell into decay.[25]

14.2.4 Palestinianism and the Andalusian Myth

Ye'or claims there is a 'hidden war against Israel' in the forms of Palestinian Liberation Theology and Replacement Theology. These are socialist developments arising from Latin America, Third Worldism,[26] Islamic supremacism, Liberation Theology of the Church, and from 'European pro-Palestinian lobbies' that have, according to Ye'or, sought

25 Kalergi, *Practical Idealism*, 50. Translation by Landgraf. To note, this citation is taken from Chapter 10, titled '*Judentum und Zukunftsadel*' or 'Judaism and Future Nobility'. Original German text: 'Statt das Judentum zu vernichten, hat es Europa wider Willen durch jenen künstlichen Ausleseprozeß veredelt und zu einer Führernation der Zukunft erzogen. Kein Wunder also, daß dieses Volk, dem Ghetto-Kerker entsprungen, sich zu einem geistigen Adel Europas entwickelt. So hat eine gütige Vorsehung Europa in dem Augenblick, als der Feudaladel verfiel, durch die Judenemanzipation eine neue Adelsrasse von Geistes Gnaden geschenkt.' Also see: Volume I.

26 According to Ye'or, Third Worldism is a solidarity movement that arose in the 1970s among 'clergymen, intellectuals, and politicians in favour of massive Muslim immigration to European countries'; Ye'or, *Eurabia*, 47. Also see Volume I.

'to create a Euro-Arab population that would fight in Europe for Arab causes against Zionism and "American imperialism"'. Ye'or asserts that 'Palestinianism provides the moral justification for the elimination of the State of Israel' and it is intertwined with 'a new Christian reading of the Bible, in line with the Qur'an, that would expel Israel from its biblical identity as well as its patrimony'. It is a reassertion of 'traditional European anti-semitism' ('contempt for the First Testament') within the context of Palestinian-Israeli relations. However, according to the Islamist component of Palestinianism, Biblical figures (Abraham, Jesus et al.) are viewed as Muslim prophets, Islam is viewed as preceding Judaism and Christianity, and Jerusalem is viewed as having always been Islamic. In other words, because Judaism and Christianity came out of Islam (are 'outdated expressions[s] of Islam'), Abrahamic civilization is Islamic, which means that Europe and Israel are Islamic at their roots and thus subservient to Islam (replacing both Judaism and Christianity with Islam). According to Ye'or, this 'Islamization of the Jewish sources of Christianity' and the de-legitimation of the 'biblical identity' and 'patrimony' of Israel aims to give legitimacy to the Islamist claims over the Holy Land, Al Quds/Jerusalem, as well as the Christian lands of Europe.[27]

Europeans who also delegitimize 'Israel's sovereignty over the Old City of Jerusalem' because of 'theological Judeophobia [denying the centrality of Judaism to the origin of Christianity] and subservience to Islamic threats' are dhimmis according to Ye'or. She explains that dhimmitude denies difference of the 'Other', the other people of the Book, their roots, historical belonging, and identity, which reduces them to mere 'amnesic collections of individuals' that are vulnerable to 'manipulation' and that 'seek their survival by flattering their oppressors'. She asserts that 'European dhimmitude' is defined by 'policies of submission, humiliation, and services, blended with anti-semitism and anti-Americanism'. Europeans who are not 'proud' of their

27 Ye'or, *Eurabia*, 59, 46–47, 177–178, 194, 180, 215–216. Also see chapters 14 and 16 in *Eurabia*.

'Judeo-Christian values', as well as Islamophile Europeans who indict the Bible because they hate Israel ('Christian Judeophobia'), deny the Jewish-Christian relationship (the Judaic roots of Christianity), apologize for Islam by making the case for the historical legitimacy of Islam in Europe, and bestow Muslims with a 'privileged status as sources of immigration', are merely dhimmi 'Eurabians' who have opened the door to the Islamization of Christianity (and Europe). These dhimmis also promote the utopian myth of Andalusia (Al-Andalus) as the model of European integration, an idyllic 'coexistence' that has led to a 'multicultural Eurabia', although Andalusia was in fact characterized by 'cruelty, war, and slavery' against Jews, Christians and religious minorities. They also identify any opposition to mass immigration in general as 'racism, Arabophobia … Islamophobia' or 'Nazi antisemitism', thus preventing '[a] sober, comprehensive, and regular assessment of the impact of Muslim/Arab immigration into Europe'.[28]

Most reasonable people recognize the fallacious nature of the arguments about Islam being the fount of both Judaism and Christianity, Islam being integral and vital to the history of Europe, or Andalusia as a model to be emulated. Yet, Islamophiles, dhimmis, and apologists do indeed exist among the bureaucrats and leftists (and so-called 'moderate Muslims') of Europe. However, denying the importance of Judaism as foundational to Christian Europe does not necessarily open Europe up to Islamization or render the speaker a dhimmi. Neither Judaism nor Islamism are on equal par with Christianity regarding the foundation and development of European civilization. In fact, other non-Christian elemental factors have played much more integral roles to Europe than Judaism or Islamism, such as the aristocratic

28 Ibid, 115, 194, 206, 207, 223, 215, 163–167, 96. Andalusia was an area of the Iberian Peninsula that was under Muslim rule between 711 and 1492AD. It was also called La Convivencia. See: Fernandez-Morera, *The Myth of the Andalusian Paradise: Muslims, Christians, and Jews under Islamic Rule in Medieval Spain.* Intercollegiate Studies Institute. 2016.

culture of Indo-Europeans, Greco-Roman traditions, Catholicism, the Enlightenment, and the development of the sciences.[29]

What is important in this context is Ye'or's complete disregard of the highly influential contribution of the cultural Marxism of the Frankfurt School towards the negation of the Christian religion and the ethnic identity of Europeans. This ideology, among others, has created a hyper-individualist secular and materialistic Europe that has a demoralized ethnic identity, no traditional codes of morality, and a lack of defining judgment of the Other. The secularism and cultural Marxism in Europe and the negation of Biblical creeds and dogma directly challenge Israel's claim upon Jerusalem and the territory of Israel according to 'Biblical identity'. If people no longer believe in Christianity or even know the stories of the Bible or Biblical history, how can they support the Jews' claim over Israel and Jerusalem?

Ye'or suggests that Europe embrace its religious identity, its Christianity, and, in particular, its Judeo-Christian roots. Yet, unlike for the Jewish people, she neglects to mention the identity of Europeans beyond the religious dimension: their cultural and racial descent. European nations have traditionally stood for more than just religious identity; European ethnic groups have been homogeneous for millennia and ethnic unity has been an essential feature of the nation and the nation-state. To be a nation, in part, is to be a distinct people, with an identity based in history, culture, race, and a set of values and standards which are hinged upon a particular set of principles that have developed with that nation's intellectual culture and heritage.[30] Yet, throughout her book, Ye'or barely gives a glance to these or the fate of European ethnics — the radical and tragic displacement of Europeans and their traditions in the face of rapid immigration and demographic colonisation from the Third World (Muslim *and* non-Muslim). Her argument is not about the people, the ethnicity,

29 See: Kevin MacDonald, 'Going Against the Tide: Ricardo Duchesne's Intellectual Defense of the West'.

30 See: Anthony D. Smith, *National Identity*.

the homelands, or the roots of Europeans. Instead, she presents an ideological argument—religious and geopolitical—that is critical of Muslim immigration and their retention and promotion of their political and cultural customs but allows for large-scale immigration from the Third World if it is based on the successful *assimilation* of immigrants (Muslims and non-Muslims) into the liberal democratic structure of European nations.

14.2.5 European Eurabian Elites

Ye'or accuses the European elites (whom she calls Eurocrats or Eurabians) of being responsible for the 'mutation' of Europe into an anti-Zionist Eurabia via the Euro-Arab Dialogue, large-scale Muslim immigration, and multicultural policies. She claims these elites have harboured Islamists and have allowed jihadist anti-Semitism to enter Europe, which has 'rekindled latent Nazi and fascist vitriol in concoction of Eurabian culture'. In fact, she claims that the Euro-Arab alliance involves Muslims, European leftists, Third Worldists, Communists, and neo-Nazis, all of whom are aligned in that they are 'Arabophiles' and have a 'deeply ingrained' anti-Americanism and anti-semitism. She further argues that Eurabians have denied the reality of Islamic terrorism by 'brush[ing]...aside' the religious justifications given by Islamic terrorists and by placing blame on 'scapegoats' instead (Israel and America). For Ye'or, the constant airing of European anti-American and pro-Muslim propaganda is because Europe needs 'the Arab bloc in order to establish itself as a strategic rival to America' and because Europe has a false 'sense of moral superiority', i.e. Europeans prefer peace and dialogue over conflict and war. She also accuses these Eurabian elites of paying dhimmi 'tribute' to Muslims for their spending of 'billions...to purchase immunity' from Muslim terrorist attacks.

According to Ye'or, Israel is not to blame for Jihadi terrorism. She makes the case that the existence of Israel does not play a role in conflicts in other parts of the world that involve Muslims and local populations, such as 'the Chechen, Kosovo, Macedonian, Kurdish, Iraqi, Sudanese, Nigerian, Algerian, Kashmir, Indonesian, Philippines, and Thai conflicts'; rather, it is the concepts of jihad and Sharia and the drive toward world conquest contained within Islam that are the cause of Muslim terrorism. She thinks the European denial of Islamist terrorism and the deflection of blame onto Israel and America reveal a 'subordinate collaboration, if not surrender' to Islam. It is 'collaboration' in the sense of 'appeasement and collusion with international terrorism' so as to become a geopolitical bloc to challenge America, although it also involves 'abetting a worldwide subversion of Western values and freedoms'.[31]

The actions of the Eurabians, undertaken in an effort to also secure 'peace' and 'dialogue' with the Muslim world and encompassed by the Proximity Policy,[32] are, according to Ye'or, rather 'cowardly' and 'impotent' acts that reveal the European status of dhimmitude.[33] She thinks attempts at peace, dialogue, and historical revisionism, such as by British Foreign Secretary Robin Cook, who claimed in 1998 that 'Islam laid the intellectual foundations for large portions of Western civilization',[34] as well as the principle 'land for peace' concerning conflict resolution between Palestine and Israel, is 'crawling behaviour'. For Ye'or, such behaviour is a sign that Europe is in 'fear of conflict' and has surrendered to the 'political agenda' of Islam.[35]

---

31 Ye'or, *Eurabia*, 102, 129, 205, 75, 157, 227, 111, 77, 227, 159, 185, 184, 77, 158, 111, 227, 77, 109.

32 Proximity Policy was defined by Romano Prodi (President of the European Commission, 1999–2004) on October 13, 2003: 'To build security with our neighbours — not by building walls or installing missile shields, but through trade, exchange and dialogue'. This 'creates the conditions for cooperation and understanding. This is what we call "soft security"'. As cited in Ye'or, *Eurabia*, 230–231.

33 Ye'or, *Eurabia*, 242.

34 Cook as cited in ibid, 172.

35 Ye'or, *Eurabia*, 173, 242, 77. Ye'or mentions that in 1995 the European Institute for Research on Mediterranean and Euro-Arab Cooperation (MEDEA) supported

It begs the question whether it is logical for Nazis, who adhere to a national socialism based on ethno-nationalism, to align with leftist socialists, who are internationalists and cosmopolitans, and together promote Muslim communities, immigrants, and immigration, and then collaborate with Muslims in a collectively hostile way towards Israel (with the aim of essentially destroying it) and together create a geopolitical rivalry against America. It is more logical to say that neo-conservatives are aligned with leftists to ethnically transform Europe, a project that is based on socialistic idealizations of a future world federation of states and humanity, a global system based on perpetual peace and regulated by standardized economics, politics, and culture, and the creation of a new humankind, an abstract economic man that has no firm attachments to the roots of his particular ethnic, national, and traditional identity. Muslim (and non-Muslim) immigration into Europe from Africa, Asia, and the Arab world, besides being the product of the EAD and other Euro-Arab partnerships, is a tool used by the neoconservative and leftist alliance to diminish the strength of European ethnic identity in order to achieve steps towards World Federation. Eurabia is merely a single instance along the road towards perpetual peace.

It is true that many European elites have urged the withdrawal of Israel from 'occupied territories' and are critical of American neo-conservative foreign policy regarding the Middle East (war on terror, etc.), and leftists continue to provide a Marxist analysis of Muslim terrorism and whitewash the religious roots of militant Islamism. However, it is hardly 'scapegoating' to claim that Israel and America are in some way responsible for Islamic terrorism against the West. Islamists themselves have claimed that the military interventionist

---

'the principle land for peace' regarding lasting resolutions in the Arab-Israeli conflict. This principle, according to Ye'or, is 'the foundation of the Islamic *jihad*-dhimmitude system', and that through jihad Islam expanded into non-Muslim lands and Islamic protection (*dhimma*) was given to the subjugated by way of their surrender of land. See *Eurabia*, 104–105.

acts taken by America (and certain European countries) in support of Israel in the Arab-Israeli conflict, including Israel's claim over Jerusalem — 'the eternal city of the Jews' — are central factors to their cause. Just as Ye'or criticizes the Eurocratic whitewashing of the roots of Islamic terrorism (Islamists utilize the Quran to justify their terror and Eurocrats claim terrorism cannot be linked with Islam), she herself must be criticized for dismissing certain factors that do indeed contribute to Islamist hostility against the West, such as the war on terror and 'occupied territories'. In addition, Islamists are not just against America and Israel, but against Westernisation in general, which is called, by some, 'Westoxification'.[36]

While it is accurate to argue that Israel is not responsible for the conflicts between Muslims and local populations in the non-Western and non-Middle Eastern world (the geopolitical goals and totalitarian character of Islamism are indeed contributing to these conflicts, as well as to the conflicts in the Middle East and in the West), this does not, however, exempt Israel from its participation and contribution to Middle Eastern conflicts or alter the fact that Israel remains an issue for Muslims not just on a regional level, but most importantly, on a global level. The Ummah, the collective and international Muslim identity, unites Muslims together towards important and defining issues, such as Israel, so that Muslims from Asia, for example, may support their fellow brethren in Palestine.

Although one can make the argument that Europeans have indeed lost their will to survive as a people due to their pacification and are vulnerable to a complete takeover by Muslims due to their idealism, as stated in above points and in this work generally, peace has been a central element in European integration models since at least the eighteenth century and has become somewhat manifest post WWII.

36 Westoxification is defined as 'the fascination with and dependence upon the West to the detriment of traditional, historical, and cultural ties to Islam and Islamic world'. See Oxford Reference, 'Westoxification'. https://www.oxfordreference.com/view/10.1093/oi/authority.20110803121918757.

Peace has been a long-term choice of European elites in an effort to create a new type of man based on an abstract deracinated identity, a new type of society based on disarmament, and a new type of world order based on world federation. European pacification is a choice that has been made by the elites that to some is in fact 'morally superior' to war mongering, but, more importantly, it is a choice that has been made in regards to a greater, overall plan.

Striving for peace and preferring dialogue as a method of settling disputes rather than armed conflict is not synonymous with 'fear of conflict', 'dhimmitude', or 'submission to Islam'. Rather, it is a strategy in an effort to achieve a larger goal: Euro-Mediterranean integration and, at some point in the future, the World Federation of States. This goal requires the creation of a geopolitical bloc that unites the Mediterranean countries, not necessarily as a 'rival to America', but as a force to maintain the balance of powers at the World Federation level. Besides, despite accusations that Europe is anti-American, anti-Israel, and pro-Islamist because of its insistence on peace rather than warfare strategies towards the Middle East, back in 2003 senior advisor for homeland security and counter-terrorism, Thomas E. McNamara, stressed that 'Europe and the United States are fighting terrorism together' and that both, together, have 'built and sustained many institutions that now play special roles in this struggle', including the European Union (EU), the North Atlantic Treaty Organization (NATO), the Organization for Security and Co-operation in Europe (OSCE), the Organisation for Economic Co-operation and Development (OECD), the United Nations (UN), the International Monetary Fund (IMF), and so on. In addition, both have been working to fulfill UN Security Council Resolution 1373, adopted in 2001, which established the Counter-Terrorism Committee (CTC) and provided 'the legal, political, and moral foundations for the international community to organize and act against terror'.[37]

---

37 McNamara, 'Despite Divisions, Europe and the United States Are Fighting Terrorism Together'. Also see: United Nations Security Council Resolutions,

14.2.6 Holocaust Guilt Complex Exploited

Ye'or claims that the EAD exploited the European holocaust guilt complex by: conflating it with anti-immigration sentiments against Muslims (calling the opposition Nazis and racists); by equating Zionism with Hitler's National Socialism and deflecting Muslim terrorism onto Israel and America (in effect casting victims as aggressors and Jews as the new Nazis); and by engaging in historical and theological revisionism regarding the notion of *jihad* (i.e. jihad is recast as a defensive rather than offensive war in terms of resistance to conquest, or the liberation of Muslim lands governed by non-Muslims).

Ye'or makes the case that in the 1970s, Norman Daniel and Edward Said, among others, initiated the Arab holocaust exploitation trend in Europe by writing about a 'European guilt complex towards Muslims', describing European anti-Muslim racism based on an 'us and them' divide as the product of White ethnocentrism, while offering neither an analysis for the us-them divide created by the Muslim concepts of Dar al-Islam (Muslim lands) and Dar al-harb (non-Muslim lands of the enemies) nor the notions of *jihad* and *dhimmitude*. The EAD has emphasized the *dhimmi* mentality, the 'self-accusing complex', in university teaching and through the resolutions of Strasbourg and others, and, with its allusion to the erasure of 'hostile oriental stereotypes' regarding Islam, the Parliamentary Association of the Council of Europe (PACE) is committed to historical revisionism. These exploitative and revisionist elements, plus the political myth of an idyllic Andalusia, have, according to Ye'or, led to a 'growing Judeophobic culture' in universities and mainstream media and have prevented not just an open discussion on immigration, but also the rise of anti-immigration sentiments and movements and an accurate understanding of the geopolitical intentions of Islamism.[38]

Resolution 1373. Threats to international peace and security caused by terrorist acts. S/RES/1373. December 28 2001. http://unscr.com/en/resolutions/1373.

38 Ye'or, *Eurabia*, 186–189, 176, 112, 194, 196, 241, 166.

There is no doubt that Eurocrats and their kin want to rid the world of ethno-national identities, and this would include the ethnic identities of Europeans as well as the Zionists of Israel. Yet, in contradiction, leftist bureaucrats and cosmopolitan intellectuals also strive to defend the national identity of the Palestinians and their rights as a 'people' against the Israeli occupation of Arab territories that go beyond the 1949 armistice lines. They also protect and promote the ethnic identities of non-European immigrants in Europe through multicultural policies and immigrant rights, while deconstructing European identities. Islamists themselves employ the leftist cultural and political discourse of White privilege, White racism, affirmative action, human rights, and collective multicultural rights, so as to gain further ground on all spheres of life in their attempt to counter Western hegemony inside and outside the West and establish a world-wide Caliphate. Yet, although Islamists utilize leftism for their cause, they ultimately consider leftists as decadent infidels who produce spiritually and morally vacuous societies and thus, in the end, reject them.

It is very unfortunate that Ye'or does not provide much information on how European natives are actually affected by the imposed White guilt complex or the holocaust exploitation trend other than a few comments here and there about the loss of ethnic identity, the prevention of criticism about immigration, the prevalence of the guilt complex in universities and mainstream media, and dhimmitude. The consequences of such pernicious developments for European natives requires much more research and must be addressed fully, but Ye'or is more concerned about how these developments affect Israelis and the Jewish population in Europe and emphasizes these consequences throughout her book while neglecting the much larger populations of European natives. The Eurabia thesis, for all its insights, does not serve the long-term interests of ethnic Europeans since, ultimately, the driving preoccupation behind this thesis is the survival of Israel.

14.3 Melanie Phillips

Melanie Phillips is a British journalist and prominent neoconservative opponent of Islamism and leftism. She has written several books, including *Londonistan* (2006) and *The World Turned Upside Down: The Global Battle over God, Truth, and Power* (2010). In her work, Phillips delivers a relentless critique of leftism and Islamism and their pernicious roles in the destruction of European values. She accuses the British Left of developing an 'axis with militant, fundamentalist Islamism' because they have the same goal: 'the destruction of Western society and its foundation values'. In this view, Islamists and victim groups (homosexuals, feminists, etc.), ushered on by the Left, perceive normative or majority values as hierarchical and discriminatory, demand that majority values become subordinate to minority values, and employ various 'weapons' to get what they want — 'public vilification, moral blackmail, and threats to people's livelihoods'. This is all part of the movement of the radical left intelligentsia of the UK and Europe who have replaced Christianity with a new religion of human rights, and British national identity with multiculturalism.[39]

Phillips asserts that the British government has 'redefined' the 'principal responsibilities of a citizen' to mean 'responsibilities to an ideology' — multiculturalism. But, argues Phillips, British identity is not based on 'doctrines of secular human rights, multiculturalism and antidiscrimination', it instead is rooted in liberal individualism, 'Christianity, the common law and the history of an island people'. Similarly, she explains that traditional values and 'the three pillars of national identity — family, education and church' have been overturned because of a 'culture war' involving radical egalitarianism, individualism, mass-immigration and Third Worldism, secular humanism, and moral and cultural relativism, replacing national identity and objective standards of morality with 'self-actualization', minority beliefs and identities, a 'victim culture' and 'subjective opinions and

39 Phillips, *Londonistan*, xxiii.

feelings'. Morality is 'privatized', individual conscience is 'universalized', national values are 'despised', and moral legitimacy is found in multiculturalism, minority rights, universal progressivism, human rights law, and supranational institutions such as the EU, UN, and the International Criminal Court (ICC).[40]

Although Phillips provides many details that explain the rise of Islamic extremism in Britain and Europe and delivers a credible critique of leftism, multiculturalism, mass-immigration, and the human rights victim culture, you would think from the title of her book *Londonistan* that you would be reading details of the radical transformation of Britain into a Muslim enclave by mass-immigration and how the indigenous Brits are suffering as a result. But no. Although she does address the pernicious effects of leftism, the ineptitude of the British intelligentsia on dealing with homegrown Islamic terrorism, and the complicity of politicians in the tragedy by seeking the Muslim vote, Phillips does not elaborate on the interests of or the tragedy that looms over the indigenous Europeans who want to retain their ethnic identity and homelands in the face of multiculturalism, Islamism, and non-European mass-immigration. Instead, Phillips devotes most of her book (as well as *The World Turned Upside Down*) to the plight of Israel and threats that Jewish people face from European and Muslim anti-semitism and Islamist terrorism. Her primary aims are, in general, steering the critical discourse about Islamism in general and eliciting Western support for Israel in its conflict with Palestine and the Muslim-Arab world in particular.

The following is a critical examination and refutation of some of the main arguments Phillips puts forward in *Londonistan* and *The World Turned Upside Down*.

---

40 Ibid, xxxiii, 64, 69–72.

14.3.1 Islamist Aggression against the West and Israel: Metaphysics, Nationhood, History, and Land

Phillips gives several reasons as to why Islamists aim their aggression against the West and Israel: the degeneracy of Western culture, the decadence and spiritual vacuity of progressive leftism, the 1400-year war waged by Muslims against Christians and Jews, as well as overall Muslim anti-semitism and anti-Westernism. Yet, she dismisses the 'Arab view' (what Ye'or has called Palestinianism) which holds that the behaviour of Israel ('oppression' of Palestinians) and America (neo-conservative foreign policy in the Middle East) is a reason for Muslim aggression against Israel and the West. She claims that the real reason why the West and Israel are targets of Islamists is that Muslims have a religious hatred for the Jews and 'this hatred lies at the core of the war against the West'. In other words, because the West and Israel share religious roots — Judeo-Christian roots — they face the same religious enemy: Islam. She writes:

> It is not that *Israel's behaviour* has inflamed the jihad against the West.... It is rather that the jihad, which views the West as a threat to Islam, sees Israel's existence as living, breathing proof of the Western and Jewish intention to rule the planet. The battle with Israel is thus conceived as *a metaphysical struggle* between good — the Islamic world — and evil — the Jewish-backed Western world. Israel's struggle to defend itself against this monstrosity is therefore the West's struggle to defend itself against the same monstrosity. Israel's struggle is simply being played out in a unique place where metaphysics and geopolitics have become fused.[41]

Phillips also dismisses the connection between the geographical fact of land and ideological identity as a reason behind Islamist aggression, i.e. Israel and Zionism versus Palestine and Islamism. She writes, 'It is not a national or territorial conflict but a historical, religious, cultural and existential conflict between truth and falsehood, believers and infidels, prosecuted through jihad until victory or martyrdom'.

41 Phillips, *Londonistan*, 104, 102–103 (my emphasis).

While she claims that land is not the issue, in *The World Turned Upside Down*, Phillips argues that Israel is the ancient historic homeland of the Jews, as found in the Old Testament, and thus Jewish claims over Israel are determined by Biblical and racial ancestry. Phillips defends this claim on land as determined by ethno-religious ancestral factors, writing that

> [t]he Jews' aspiration for their homeland… derives from Judaism itself, which comprises the inseparable elements of the religion, the people and the land [….] The unique Jewish entitlement to Israel is not just a Biblical story but historical fact. The Jews are the only people for whom the land of Israel was ever their national homeland.

She further defends this racial-religious factor in the creation of the state of Israel in 1948 as the rightful homeland of the Jewish people by emphasizing the legal construction of Israeli territory, upheld by the British and bound by international law:

> The legitimacy of Israel rests not on the United Nations vote of 1947, which finally established it as a state, but on the setting up of the Palestine Mandate in 1922 by the precursor to the UN, the League of Nations, which paid recognition to "the historical connection of the Jewish people with Palestine and to the grounds for reconstituting their national home in that country".

In contrast, and despite UN Resolution 242 and other resolutions,[42] Phillips asserts that the territory of Palestine is an arbitrary

42 UN *Resolution 242*, adopted in 1967, acknowledges 'the sovereignty, territorial integrity and political independence of every State in the area [Middle East] and their right to live in peace within secure and recognized boundaries free from threats or acts of force.' See: United Nations Security Council, *Resolution 242*. In addition, in 2012, 138 members of the United Nations agreed to recognise Palestine as a 'non-member observer state' in the United Nations, with Israel, Canada, and the United States as three of nine that voted no. This resolution reaffirmed prior resolutions, namely those that recognised 'the inalienable rights of the Palestinian people, primarily the right to self-determination and the right to their independent State.' See: United Nations, 'Status of Palestine

invention—'The original land of Israel had simply been renamed "Palestine" by the Romans'. And, because the Palestinians are a mixture of different ethnicities—'Arabs...Greeks, Syrians, Latins, Egyptians, Turks, Armenians, Italians' and many others, they are not really Palestinians as a legitimate racial ethnicity with a long heritage that could defend the legal claim to the land as a 'people'. Further, she thinks the Palestinians had plenty of opportunities in the past to form a new, independent state of their own away from Israel, as it 'was on offer in 1936, 1948 and 2000, and could have been established at any time between 1948 and 1967 by Jordan and Egypt'.[43]

Phillips' emphasis on the metaphysical conflict between Islam, Christianity (the West), and Judaism (Israel), and her insistence that Islamist terrorism is just a struggle about values and metaphysical principles, dismisses some of the reasons given by Islamists themselves for their aggression,[44] namely: their rejection of Israeli foreign policy towards Palestine; American and British neoconservative Middle Eastern foreign policy and military support of Israel; and the effects of Western global hegemony in the Middle East (Westoxification). While religious factors do indeed play a central role for Islamists—a moral imperative and geopolitical striving—dismissing the legitimacy of the reasons given by Islamists themselves, as well as disregarding the relationship between land and ideology, in effect denies vital information necessary for a clear and objective understanding of what essentially lies behind Muslim aggression against Israel and the West. In addition, denying that these factors are indeed destabilising elements that

---

in the United Nations'. General Assembly. Sixty-seventh session. Agenda item 37. Question of Palestine. A/67/L.28, 26 November 2012. https://unispal.un.org/unispal.nsf/0080ef30efce525585256c38006eacae/181c72112f4d0e0685257ac500515c6c?OpenDocument.

43 Phillips, *Londonistan*, 109 (my emphasis); *The World Turned Upside Down*, 58, 55–56, 58; *Londonistan*, 104.

44 Such as accounts from their biographies. See: Christmann, *Preventing Religious Radicalisation*, 42.

contribute to the Islamist rationale against the West is to overlook the aggravation they elicit from Muslim communities across the world (civil unrest, war, terrorism), which is being transported into Europe by mass-immigration.

Phillips claims that on the one hand the conflict is not about territory or nationality but a metaphysical struggle, thus separating the link between ideology and nationality, while on the other hand, she acknowledges the importance of the link between ideology and land for the Jews of Israel. Although she claims that Palestine is a recent arbitrary construction and Palestinians are a mix of distinct ethnicities and thus do not have historical legitimacy to claims of nationhood or territorial right to Palestine, during the time of the 1922 British Mandate, the census revealed that the majority of the demographic population in Palestine was Muslim.[45] For Arab Palestinians, according to Fred Gottheil writing in the *Middle East Quarterly*, 2003, 'the character of their demography is at the heart of their claim to territorial inheritance and national sovereignty' in Palestine and they have 'deep and timeless roots in that geography and that their own immigration into that geography has at no time been consequential'.[46] In other words, the difference between Israeli and Arab Palestinian claims to 'territorial inheritance and national sovereignty' is the difference between their histories and demographics. Although no conclusions can be drawn in this work, the point is that the dispute over who has the sovereign right to Palestine — over the land — is clearly one that continues to fuel warfare between two ethno-religious rivals.

Finally, Phillips' claim of the 'unique Jewish entitlement' to Israel as their true homeland by an appeal to the League of Nations, which is now a defunct international organisation, is puzzling considering that she repeatedly denounces supranational organisations such as 'the European Court of Human Rights, the European Union, the United

45 See: Barron, *Palestine,* Table I: Population of Palestine by Religions.

46 Gottheil, 'The Smoking Gun', 54.

Nations … [and] the European Court of Justice' for increasingly becoming the 'sole sources of legitimacy'.[47]

14.3.2 Ethno-Nationalism and Alliances between Leftists, Islamists, and White Nationalists

Not only is there a leftist-Islamist alliance against America and Western society, for Phillips there is also cooperation between the far-right, the White nationalists, Islamists, and leftists. She writes that '[s]entiments, images and tropes appearing in the literature of the left and of the Islamists are similar to — and sometimes even drawn from — the outpourings of neo-Nazis and white supremacists'. White nationalists, who attempt to maintain their distinct ethnicity in the face of various forces (e.g. leftism, Islamism, and neoconservative Americanism), such as the British National Party, the National Front, and the White Nationalist Party, are called far-right 'racists', 'white supremacists', 'neo-Nazis', or 'neofascists' by Phillips. Part of the reason she labels them this way is because some White nationalist groups have made an alliance with Islamists, like the leftists, due to their criticism of the perceived influence of Zionism on American and Western foreign and domestic affairs. She further writes that '[t]hese ultranationalist, racist and anti-Jewish groups saw in the Islamists something beyond their wildest dreams: a global force, armed and trained, committed to the destruction of both Jews and the Western political order'.[48]

First, it is not logical for any European right-leaning counter-hegemonic group to join forces with Islamists in order to combat American global hegemony and cultural Marxism, for Islamists merely aim to supplant one global hegemonic order with a utopian version of their own. The same is true regarding alliances with leftists. Second, in contrast to accusations that ethno-nationalism is racist and must be done away with (which is similar to what Kalergi said about European

47 Phillips, *Londonistan*, 26.

48 Phillips, *Londonistan*, 129; *The World Turned Upside Down*, 216–217.

ethnic identity back in the 1930s), it must be said that every ethnicity should have a homeland that is safe and secure, and therefore have the right to defend that territory, and every nation should have the right to self-determination, such as independent decision making in accordance with national ethnic interests. Without these ethno-national guidelines, Israel itself would not exist based on its racial-religious territorial claims.

Despite her protest against minority rights superseding the majority, and her profession of bringing back British values and historical identity, Phillips implies that the only nation that is legally (and religiously) allowed to be ethno-nationalist is Israel. Much like Ye'or, Phillips devotes most of her books to the defense of Israel as the homeland of the Jewish people, as well as to the plight of Israel and the Jewish people in the face of Arab and Muslim anti-semitism and terrorism in Europe.

However, not once does Phillips meaningfully mention the White working classes, the ethnic identity and interests of the British masses, or how Muslim (and Third-World) immigration is affecting them on a day-to-day level other than a passing comment or two about the demise of their traditions and culture in the face of Islamism and leftism. She provides no distinct coverage of everyday native Britons experiencing the radical transformation of British towns and cities into racially dissimilar anti-British immigrant enclaves. Like leftists who decry White pride and preservation, she considers ethnic Europeans who attempt to maintain and promote their distinct ethnicity and nationality in the face of what they perceive as various destructive forces in their countries (mass-immigration, cultural Marxism, and neoconservative Americanism) to be racists. In this way, Phillips is hypocritical, for Israel is based on blood kinship ties for citizenship, i.e. is ethno-nationalist, while claiming it is also a democracy. According to Phillips' logic, it seems that the only group that can legitimately defend European and British societies are not the leftists, nor the European ethno-nationalists, but only neoconservatives, like herself.

14.3.3 Western-Israeli Alliance to Counter Islamism and Leftism

Phillips promotes an inter-religious cooperation between Israel (Judaism) and the West (Christianity) to counter the threat posed by Islamism and leftism. She thinks it is necessary that the West forms an alliance with the neoconservative view of Israel in the fight against these pernicious ideologies. She frequently declares that the West has Judeo-Christian foundations based on the Mosaic Code (Ten Commandments) and thus, according to these shared values, Israel and the West are closely united: 'Jews were at the very heart of those Western values [and] [a]t the core of those Western majority values lay the Mosaic Code, which first gave the world the concept of morality, self-discipline and laws regulating behaviour.' She then uses this as a main premise to argue against leftism and promote a Western-Israeli alliance (the civilized 'free world') against a shared religious and historical threat, the barbarism of Islamism: 'As [the left] took aim at morality and self-restraint, it seized a golden opportunity to pulverize the very people [the Jews] who invented the rules in the first place [and] the far left and the Islamists have become a marriage made in hell.... [using] each other to fight the West.'[49]

Phillips' claim that the West is Judeo-Christian at heart is quite new (Vatican II, 1960s) and is simply not true. Europe and the West do not derive their core historical values from Judaism; they may share the Ten Commandments but many more foundational morals for Europeans come from the New Testament based on Christ, the Classical Greeks, the Renaissance, and the Enlightenment. Christianity may have initially arisen from Judaism, but it developed independently thereafter; Old Testament Judaism was merely one

49 Phillips, *Londonistan*, 118–119.

strain of historical influence on the rise of European civilization and not the co-founder, others included Greco-Roman religions, Hellenic philosophy, and European paganism. In addition, not only do Christianity and Judaism differ in fundamental ways, such as the rejection of Christ by Jews and their following of the Talmud, but before Europe was known as Europe it was known as Christendom not Judeo-Christendom. In fact, because Europe is majority White European by ethnicity and majority secular Christian by ethics, the West primarily ought to have an interest in preserving and protecting the European people's native homeland and the European character and history of the West, not Israel. In the face of Islamism and leftism (as well as large-scale non-European immigration), European interests, including the preservation of their cultures and ethnic identity, are what matter, but Phillips seems to want these interests to become subsumed by the interests of Israel and its conflict with Islam. In this process, she conflates two separate issues regarding Islam: the problem facing Europe and the problem facing Israel.

14.3.4 Antonio Gramsci to Blame for the Destruction of the West

In her criticism of leftist practices such as mass-immigration, political correctness, and the human rights victim culture, Phillips suggests that these phenomena all stem from the writings of one person. She writes: 'During the 1960s, the decade in which so many of our current leaders remain firmly stuck, the most influential thinker was the Italian communist Antonio Gramsci [....] the philosopher who became the iconic thinker of the 1960s, [and] laid down the blueprint for exactly what has happened in Britain'. She writes that the Gramscian project

> promoted the idea that Western society could be overturned by capturing the citadels of the culture—the universities, schools, churches, media, civil service, professions—and subverting its values. Enacting Gramsci's

> precepts to the letter, the British intelligentsia have ensured that morality and culture have indeed been turned upside down.

Phillips adds that 'the intellectual elite' of these institutions were 'persuaded to sing from the same subversive hymn-sheet so that the moral beliefs of the majority would be replaced by the values of those on the margins of society'. And the new proletariat were the Palestinians. She writes that

> the left alighted upon the Palestinians as the new proletariat whose cause could be championed as a weapon against Western society. Since the left demonizes America and Western capitalism, and lionizes the third world and all liberation movements, the Palestinian Arabs were a natural cause to be championed—victims of American imperialist power through the actions of its proxy, Israel.[50]

While she is not wrong to claim that the Marxist and Lenin inspired Gramsci was responsible for outlining a pernicious plan to subvert Western civilization by infiltrating all of its institutions and utilising Third Worlders as the new proletariat, a plan that manifested first with the counter-culture movements of the 1960s, it is quite deceptive of Phillips to suggest that Gramsci is solely to blame. Many others contributed intellectually to this anti-Western subversive plan, especially cultural Marxists or Frankfurt School Critical Theorists, such as Theodor Adorno, Herbert Marcuse, Max Horkheimer, Erich Fromm, Friedrich Pollock, Leo Löwenthal, Otto Kirchheimer, and Franz Leopold Neumann, among many others. These theorists were significantly influenced by Sigmund Freud and György Lukács. And, rather than Gramsci being 'the iconic thinker of the 1960s', it was in fact Marcuse who was considered the 'guru' of the New Left.

Phillips may, without phrasing it as such, criticize the leftist 'long march through the institutions' and lament and vehemently critique the degeneration this has entailed, but she skips a major cultural force,

50 Phillips, *Londonistan*, 71, 118; *The World Turned Upside Down*, 343–344.

the Frankfurt School, out of which this strategy was developed, incorporated, and disseminated. Nor does she acknowledge the role of the socialist Pan-Europa movement of Kalergi and the plan of World Federation, the infiltration of institutions by Fabian socialists, and the striving for perpetual peace and denunciation of nationalism based on ethnicity by cosmopolitanists.[51] These ideologues have been the core contributors to the decadence, demoralisation, and downfall of the West. It seems that in her effort to rally support for Israel (and demonize any criticism of its dealing with the Palestinians), Phillips misrepresents the core causes of Western and European cultural demise.

14.3.5 Multiculturalism and Mass-Immigration

Phillips acknowledges that mass-immigration is rapidly changing the ethnic composition of Britain and that 'the strong majoritarian culture' has been undermined by multiculturalism. She states that the growth of the British population is now mostly from Third World immigration, from 'cultures [that are] foreign to the Judeo-Christian Western heritage'. In addition, she explains that Britain does not want to assimilate newcomers because it has adopted the 'revolutionary ideology of the left', including the view that 'Britain is now made up of many cultures that are all equal and therefore have to be treated in identical fashion, and that any attempt to impose the majority culture over those of minorities is by definition racist'. Despite all cultures and peoples being 'equal', they are, at the same time, also different. And, it is clear, the majority cultural identity of Britons is not considered as either equal or different, and their sovereignty over their country is merely something to radically deconstruct and even remove from existence. Phillips writes that '[m]ulticulturalism …[is] ruthlessly policed by a state-financed army of local and national bureaucrats

51 Please see Volume I for details on Fabianism, Cosmopolitanism, and cultural Marxism.

enforcing a doctrine of state-mandated virtue to promote racial, ethnic and cultural difference and stamp out majority rule'. Further, she writes that multiculturalism has 'unwittingly fomented Islamist radicalism' in Britain, and, with the help of the human rights victim culture, legitimate criticisms of Islamism are shut down by the weapon of 'Islamophobia'.[52]

To mitigate these pernicious developments, Phillips suggests several steps for Britain to take. Britain needs to recognize 'that Islamist ideology is a conveyor belt to terror' and needs to 'expel foreign radicals' by 'abolishing human rights legislation' and replacing it with British common law. Islamist institutions or organisations in Britain promoting the subversion of the West should be shut down and prosecuted. Britain must also reaffirm 'the primacy of British culture and citizenship' and disaffirm 'mass immigration, multiculturalism and the onslaught of secular nihilists'. According to Phillips, only through 'tough controls on immigration' can Britain assimilate 'the people it has already got', only through 'reaffirming the primacy of British values' can multiculturalism be 'abolished', and only through the restoration of 'British political history' and Christianity in schools, along with the end of the human rights victim culture, can the assault on British values, identity, and moral norms be stopped.[53]

In her two books, Phillips is plain in her support for American-led and British foreign policy in the Middle East (war on terror) and extremely critical of multiculturalism, which clearly pits her against leftists and Islamists, but she does not go far enough in terms of preserving European ethnicity and culture. She lambasts Islamism and leftism for destroying the traditions of the West, which is not wrong, but they are only two destructive mounts. Neoconservative globalism is another destructive mount. While neoconservatives maintain their warfare policies in the Middle East and press on for global markets

52 Phillips, *Londonistan*, 58–62, 69.

53 Ibid, 186–188.

and cultural standardization against traditional organic life, Islamists sustain their pernicious creed of non-violent infiltration, demographic conquest, and violent death jihad against the West, and leftists remain committed to furthering the spiritual nihilism and historical famine of European culture and ethnicity. These three groups are separate but interlinked anti-European ideologies. On the one hand, we have neoconservatives fighting European ethno-nationalism, Islamism, and leftism, on the other hand, we have Islamists and leftists fighting American militarism, corporate globalization, and traditional European institutions and identities.

All three ideologies also support non-European immigration into Europe. Neoconservatives promote immigration for economic ends; by spreading abstract man[54] — Homo economicus — they thus indirectly fund the utopian dream of leftists that strip European people of their ethno-national identity to establish a new global order. Although leftists are supposed to be in opposition to American-led hegemony, they contribute to the corporate agenda by supporting mass-immigration, miscegenation, and the end of Whiteness — immigration for ethnic ends. In addition, although leftists are supposedly against capitalism, they make alliances with capitalists; many prominent socialist writers and institutes have and are funded by millionaires, such as the Soros Institute, the Frankfurt School, and the Fabian Society. Leftists also use Islamism (though not necessarily the violent Islamism of ISIS and al-Qaeda affiliated groups) to counter European national institutions and identities and neoconservative global hegemony, and, in turn, Islamists utilize the leftist cultural and political discourse to gain ground in their attempt to counter Western hegemony and employ immigration for political and demographic ends. These three ideological groups are ultimately totalitarian and vying for global hegemony; they systematize all people into a homogeneous 'humanity' and

54 In the sense of propagating abstract human rights as a replacement for what has traditionally defined man in society — ancestral ties, traditions, history, ethnic and political identity, homelands etc.

demonize and attempt to forcibly change or eradicate any opposition whether through direct destruction by war and genocide, or indirect annihilation through cultural, economic, political, and demographic engineering.

Phillips' support for American corporate capitalism, Western global hegemony, and neoconservative foreign policy in the Middle East pits her against European ethno-nationalist groups. Although these groups are also (or mostly) anti-Islamist, anti-leftist, and against mass-immigration from the Third World, they also reject American foreign-policy, the spread of Western values around the world, and economic globalization. These groups often suggest ethno-nationalism as a solution to the cultural and ethnic transformations of their nations and the preservation of real diversity in the world. As Phillips is clearly anti-ethno-nationalist for European peoples — she supports preserving the cultural rather than the ethnic identity of European nations and labels Europeans who are ethno-nationalist 'racist' — and supports non-European immigration if it involves minorities assimilating into the majority culture and adopting liberal individual rights rather than multicultural rights, she might be considered anti-European. It seems she has no problem with Britain and other European countries becoming increasingly non-European in their national identities, as long as newcomers don't demand any kind of religious or cultural accommodations at the expense of the majority culture. This approach to immigrant integration will not lead to indigenous Europeans remaining the majority ethnic group of their own nations. Even if multiculturalism is overturned and assimilation is required, European natives will still become political and ethnic minorities in their own nations because of continued non-European immigration.

14.4 Bruce Bawer

Bruce Bawer is an American neoconservative and a peer amongst a very influential cadre of authors focused on the 'clash' between fundamentalist Islam and Western civilization, such as Bat Ye'or, Robert Spencer, Andrew Bostom, Claire Berlinski, Oriania Fallaci, Melanie Phillips, and Mark Steyn. Bawer, like the others, thinks Europe has a problem with Islam, and he's not wrong. The political and social reality of Europe today is characterized by the inundation of a foreign religion into the public sphere. Islam in Europe represents the re-insertion of an ultra-conservative patriarchal religion into European politics and public life after a long process of separating the traditionalist Christian religion from Western foundations, law, social relations, and public order in manageable ways conducive to individual rights and rule of law. But Islamism, with its literal reading of the Quran, its emphasis on collective religious identity, its insistence on the unity of public and private realms, and its anti-Westernism, is now pushing its way into mainstream secular Europe.

How did Islam arrive in the public sphere in Europe? Why are Europeans the recipients of the physically damaging aspects of Islamism and the destructive processes of Islamization? In his best-selling book, *While Europe Slept: How Radical Islam is Destroying the West from Within* (2006), Bawer explains that European establishment elites—'journalists, politicians, bureaucrats, and professors'—are 1968-era PC leftists who are responsible for initiating massive immigration from the Muslim world into Europe. They are also responsible for introducing segregating multicultural policies based on immigrant ethnic minority group rights, which have enabled distinct Sharia-abiding communities to arise all over Europe. As these separate Muslim communities grew and radical Islam developed, the elites looked the other way while the establishment media glossed over any problems. Borrowing terms from Bat Ye'or, Bawer asserts that European elites have taken no action against Islamism in Europe because they practice Palestinianism and are dhimmis. Ye'or asserts that Palestinianism is a 'modern European Judeophobia', 'a hate cult against Israel' based on a Third World ideology. Palestinians are portrayed as victims of Israeli oppression by 'the church institutions, the media, and Eurabian networks' and have become the new Marxist force of revolution. Similarly, Melanie Phillips explains that 'the left alighted upon the Palestinians as the new proletariat whose cause could be championed as a weapon against Western society'. Bawer agrees with Ye'or and Phillips, stating that the 'new anti-Semitism' in Europe is captured by the term 'Islamophobia'—'Muslims are now the victims, Jews the Nazis'.[55]

The championing of the Palestinians and the demonization of Israel and America have brought leftists and Islamists close together. The leftist elites have aligned themselves with Muslims in general against the Western establishment in what is called the 'Black-Red alliance'. Bawer writes that this 68er-Islamist alliance is evident in such people as the Danish journalist Jacob Holdt, who said the Hizb ut-Tahrir[56] radicals were 'the same bewildered, fanatical, idealistic, justice-seeking, sympathetic, angry, and, especially, dreaming young people we ourselves once were'; they share similar Marxist 'analyses and criticisms of capitalism and Western democracy' as well as opposition to American military intervention abroad.[57] Bawer further explains that as they entered the European establishment in the 1970s, the 68ers began their overall capitulation to Islam (dhimmitude) with the advent of the post-OPEC crisis Euro-Arab Dialogue (EAD). This project has been a 'political, economic, and academic collaboration between the European establishment and Arab governments' that has favoured massive Muslim immigration, and the promotion of Islamic culture in Europe.[58] The EAD project has led to an ever-increasing Islamic Europe: major and widespread construction of Islamic schools (*madrassas*) and mosques (some with loudspeaker calls to prayer),

---

55 Ye'or, *Eurabia,* 10, 181, 152, 176; Phillips, *Londonistan,* 118; Bawer, *While Europe Slept,* 50, 140.

56 The Hizb ut-Tahrir believe Islam and Sharia are the solution to all the problems of humankind and seek to establish a worldwide Caliphate. See Volume II.

57 Bawer, *While Europe* Slept, 101, 186.

58 Ibid, 103–104.

thousands of shrouded women in public, halal compliant school dinners and restaurants, mass Muslim prayers in the streets, segregation by gender in schools and university lectures, Muslim-only neighbourhoods, capital cities being referred to as 'Belgistan' or 'Londonistan'; Muslim political parties in Europe calling for the Islamic State and Sharia Law; and Mohammed becoming the number one baby name in several major European cities. Europe is being transformed into what Bat Ye'or calls 'Eurabia' and the leftist elites are responsible.

According to Bawer, European elites endorse Islamic norms and values, adhere to Muslim intimidation (cartoon riots, death *fatwas*, murders, claims of Islamophobia), and enforce politically correct speech codes upon critics of Islam and Muslim immigration at the expense of local European populations. European elites also appease Islamism by underplaying the politico-ideological element in Islam, which is a main element of Islamic ideology. They repeat PC claims that militant Islamism, such as al Qaeda, ISIS, and other Muslim terrorist groups, have nothing to do with Islam because Islam is a 'religion of peace'. They explain all problems exuding from Muslim communities in Europe in neo-Marxist terms and frame American-led military intervention in the Middle East (particularly the wars in Iraq and Afghanistan and the controversies surrounding Abu Ghraib and Guantánamo, but also the oil-hungry interests of the West), in terms of the Israel-Palestine conflict and side with the Palestinians (and other Muslims) on these matters. They also continually assert that the majority of Muslims in Europe are moderate and Muslim culture and religion enriches European nations. But Bawer disagrees. He claims there is no sizable moderate Muslim population in Europe, and if they do exist they are 'a silent majority' in the face of Islamic terrorism; they may fear speaking up, but unwittingly, with their silence, support death fatwas, Sharia law, the world Islamic State, and 'practically speaking, they're the radicals' allies'.[59]

---

59 Ibid, 227, 229. It is highly interesting to see that there is indeed a lack of significantly large Muslim protest movements in Europe against home-grown

Although one can agree with a great deal of Bawer's assessment of Islam in Europe and leftist complicity in this affair, *While Europe Slept* has key ideological faults. Let us now examine them.

14.4.1 American Superiority and Pro-War

Bawer writes that the PC 68ers were the European counterpart of the American new leftists or 'liberal elite' but, whereas the latter 'moderated their views and rhetoric and began to deal pragmatically with the real world's real problems', the 68ers remained stuck in their childish anti-authoritarianism when they entered positions of power. He writes, 'all too many of Europe's 68ers...continued to think, and behave, like protesting teenagers, savouring their reflexive, petulant opposition as a badge of honour'. Further, he writes that compared to the European 68ers who today 'make up the European establishment', the influence of the American elite 'is not monolithic'. Even though the 'liberal elite' in America are 'controlling some powerful institutions' such as universities, Hollywood, and various news outlets and political magazines, there are many 'conservative' and middle-of-the-road outlets (he mentions Fox News, *The Wall Street Journal*, *The Washington Times*, and *The New Republic*) that provide 'fiery polemic...or vigorous exchanges' that are influential in American politics too. These types of comparison of America to Europe are present throughout Bawer's book.[60] He thinks America has a superior economy, superior immigrant integration models, superior ideals, a superior nationhood, superior military prowess, a superior culture, superior rights, superior individuality, and superior self-awareness compared to Europe, and that Europe must emulate these supposed

---

and external Islamist terrorism on Western soil, a lack of public support from European Muslims and Muslim communities for victims of Muslim terrorism against Muslims and non-Muslims alike, and a lack of loud protests from European Muslims against ISIS. Please see Volume II.

60 Bawer, *While Europe* Slept, 47, 97–99, 50, 47.

magnificent qualities in order to combat Islamism, leftism, and fascism, and support and further American global supremacy.

A central character trait of America throughout its history is, according to Bawer, freedom through war — 'American history is largely an account of the advancement of freedom through armed conflict' and today America views the 'role of war' as the fight against the 'evil of tyranny' that must 'always be resisted'. This is something that Europe would do well to emulate. But because of WWII, Europe, according to Bawer, has unfortunately come to see the 'evil of war' and therefore thinks that war 'must be avoided at all costs'. He disparages Europe for this and its 'love of peace and dialogue' and is scathing of the overall European rejection of 'America's global supremacy' and American and Israeli foreign policies in the Muslim Middle East, which he says has 'seriously complicate[d] the effective prosecution of the war on terror'. Bawer continues this line of reasoning when he writes of American moral superiority: 'Americans…really do believe in fighting for liberty, even the liberty of strangers in faraway places with names they can't spell and languages they can't speak a word of and cultures they find ridiculous. In their view, to defend other people's freedom is to defend their own.' He is convinced that the American-led 'War on Terror' has been successful, worthy, and justifiable in its attempts to liberate the 'unfree' Islamic world. He truly thinks that US-led Western military force brings freedom and democracy to Muslim countries, and thus, when Muslim immigrants come to the West, they will integrate easily. In fact, he believes that both the war in Iraq (2003) and the war in Afghanistan (2001 — 2021) 'were predicated on the assumption that Islam is compatible with democracy'. Bawer, in other words, thinks crushing Islamist tyranny and spreading liberal democracy by military intervention in the Middle East will neutralize the Islamist threat both at home and abroad. America, thus, is the guiding light for the world, the bringer of liberty, and, in its superiority, also the 'savior and protector' of Europe.[61]

Like other neoconservatives, such as Ye'or and Phillips, Bawer fails to identify the pivotal roles of Pan-European Union socialism, Fabianism, and Frankfurt School cultural Marxism on post-WWII developments or how they influenced 68er leftism, the Euro-Mediterranean partnerships, and the EU, and formed the ideological core of European leftism we see today. His assertion that American new leftists 'matured' and assimilated into the American establishment is plainly false because leftist subversives have *become* the American cultural establishment, as seen in American education, media, and PC governance. And the news outlets and political magazines he claims are 'conservative' are actually neoconservative or liberal Right; they are not true conservative or paleoconservative outlets as they uphold many liberal ideals.[62] For example, Fox News and *The Wall Street Journal* are owned by neoconservative Rupert Murdoch.[63] *The Washington Times*, and many of its columnists, has historically been pro-war and neoconservative[64] and *The New Republic*, owned by Facebook co-founder Chris Hughes, publishes many articles that

61 Ibid, 82, 231, 86, 93, 234, 230.

62 See Volume I for differences between conservatism and neoconservatism.

63 See: Paul Gottfried, 'Murdoch is Daddy Warbucks to The Neocons'. *The American Conservative*. July 27, 2011. https://www.theamericanconservative.com/murdoch-is-daddy-warbucks-to-the-neocons/; Wikipedia, 'Fox Corporation'; and Wikipedia, 'News Corp.' Wikipedia. 'Fox Corporation.' https://en.wikipedia.org/wiki/Fox_Corporation; Wikipedia, 'News Corp' https://en.wikipedia.org/wiki/News_Corp.

64 See: New World Encyclopedia contributors, 'The Washington Post' and David Ignatius, 'Tension of the Times'. *New World Encyclopedia*. 28 December 2021 https://www.newworldencyclopedia.org/entry/Washington_Times#cite_ref-25; David Ignatius. 'Tension of the Times.' *Washington Times*. Page A29. June 18 2004. https://www.washingtonpost.com/wp-dyn/articles/A50909-2004Jun17.html.

are favourable to neoconservatism.[65] In addition, the so-called 'liberal' newspapers that Bawer mentions are more accurately called liberal Right, or neoconservative too. For example, *The Washington Post*, owned by Jeff Bezos, the founder and executive chairman of Amazon, supports neoconservative war policies, with many of its prestigious writers being neoconservative, such as Fred Hiatt, Max Boot, Robert Kagan, Paul Wolfowitz, David Ignatius, and Charles Krauthammer.[66]

Bawer's claim that Europe needs to be more like America in its bellicose character and to forgo its emphasis on peace and dialogue is simply dismissing the reasoning behind the European 'peace' after WWII, as detailed in this work — namely, the elitist vision of European unification, the changing relations of Europe with the Mediterranean countries that aimed at creating prosperity 'for all', and the vision of a World Federation based on the ideal of perpetual peace. Regardless, as mentioned in the section on Bat Ye'or, since 2001 the EU has been working to fulfill the UN Security Council Resolution 1373 to combat terrorism and in 2003 Thomas E. McNamara, senior advisor for homeland security and counter-terrorism, stated that Europe and the US 'are fighting terrorism together'. What is more, prior to 2013 the EU collaborated with the US in their anti-terror war efforts against

65 See: Anthony Elghossain, 'The Enduring Power of Neoconservatism'. *New Republic*. April 3, 2019 https://newrepublic.com/article/153450/enduring-power-neoconservatism; John B. Judis, 'A Kind Word About Neoconservatism'. *New Republic*, August 2, 2013. https://newrepublic.com/article/114142/danger-neoconservatism; and Jacob Heilbrunn, 'The Neocons Strike Back'. *New Republic*. January 23, 2020. https://newrepublic.com/article/156266/neocons-strike-back.

66 See: Stephanie Denning, 'Why Jeff Bezos Bought The Washington Post'. *Forbes*. September 19, 2018. https://www.forbes.com/sites/stephaniedenning/2018/09/19/why-jeff-bezos-bought-the-washington-post/?sh=3ca270603aab; Alan Macleod, 'With Bezos at the Helm, Democracy Dies at the Washington Post Editorial Board'. *Mint Press News*. June 18 2021. https://stage.mintpressnews.com/jeff-bezos-at-helm-democracy-dies-at-washington-post-editorial-board/277738/; and Eric Zeusse, 'Jeff Bezos's Politics'. Strategic Culture Foundation. August 24 2019. https://www.strategic-culture.org/news/2019/08/24/jeff-bezoss-politics/.

al-Qaeda and the Taliban in terms of 'providing intelligence that was used to identify targets'.[67] They may have not directly participated in airstrikes or had troops on the ground, but they were indirectly involved.

While Bawer may find it surprising, the definition of freedom for Westerners (and even within Western countries themselves) is distinct from definitions by other cultures and civilizations, such as Islam. The Cairo Declaration of Human Rights in Islam defines freedom in terms of Sharia law, which contrasts with the definition of freedom according to the Universal Declaration of Human Rights, which is based on human law.[68] Requiring local populations and immigrants to abide by the UDHR when in Europe and the West is not the same as attempting to impose this particular civilizational definition of rights and freedoms over another civilization, which is akin to prejudicial Western-centrism. By claiming that military intervention is necessary to establish Western-style freedom and 'democracy' (by force) in Islamic countries, values which are supposed to be compatible with

---

67 See: Anthony Dworkin, 'Europe's New Counter-Terror Wars'. European Council on Foreign Relations. October 21, 2016. https://ecfr.eu/publication/europes_new_counter_terror_wars7155/. In the years after the publication of Bawer's book, there have been changes to European approaches to the war on terror. Since at least 2013, EU member states have converged with the US regarding military counter-terrorism in the Middle East and North Africa. In 2016, Anthony Dworkin, senior policy fellow at the European Council on Foreign Relations, wrote that, 'In the face of new terrorist groups that have emerged in Europe's wider periphery, EU member states have launched a wave of counter-terror wars [... they have] undertaken military action against terrorists in Iraq, Syria, the Sahel, and elsewhere.' Further, he writes that 'European forces are simultaneously conducting relatively conventional counter-insurgency campaigns against non-state groups, as well as direct military counter-terrorism of the sort that the United States has pioneered over the last decade and a half.' See: Anthony Dworkin, 'Europe's New Counter-Terror Wars' and Dworkin, 'Europe's War on Terror'. European Council on Foreign Relations. June 23, 2017. https://ecfr.eu/article/essay_europes_war_on_terror/.

68 Organisation of Islamic Cooperation, 'Cairo Declaration of Human Rights in Islam', article 24; United Nations, 'Universal Declaration of Human Rights'.

Islam, is to dismiss the possibility that Islam is not harmonious with or does not want to embrace these Western values. In any case, what kind of democracy is Bawer talking about? There are various forms of democratic arrangements, such as liberal democracy, social democracy, participatory democracy, and deliberative democracy, among others, and who decides which is best for whom? How exactly has military intervention in the Middle East led by the Americans who are supposedly primarily focused on the 'freedom' of foreigners they do not even know (let alone understand), brought so-called democracy and liberty to the local populations there, when it is evident that such operations have not been successful? We can see this from the violent and rapid spread of ISIS within the destabilized countries of Iraq, Syria, Libya, and elsewhere,[69] the oppressive Taliban in Afghanistan,[70] and the continued functioning of al-Qaeda and its terror attacks against the West.[71] How can Bawer defend the democratic aims of American global supremacy through warfare when America acts more like an oligarchy than a democracy?[72] Rather than being humanitarian and rights based, is American military intervention in the Middle East not more to do with American interests of protecting its unipolar position of number one superpower in the world, what Bawer himself calls American 'global supremacy'?

Certain scholars, such as political scientist Bassam Tibi, may argue that Islam can be attuned with Western values or become 'Europeanized' thereby creating a Euro-Islam[73], an argument especially prevalent in Western immigrant-loving countries. But they are also faced with numerous other scholars who make the case that the political culture of Islam can never be reconciled with Western values and

69 See *Global News*, 'ISIS'; *SITE Intelligence Group: Jihadist Threat*.

70 Laub, 'The Taliban in Afghanistan'.

71 Shoichet and Levs, 'Al Qaeda Branch'; Chengu, 'America Created Al-Qaeda'; Dilanian, 'Taliban Control'.

72 *BBC News*, 'Study: US is an Oligarchy, Not a Democracy'.

73 Tibi, 'Europeanisation, Not Islamisation'.

rights. Even if Islamic countries and Muslim diasporic communities in the West adopt democracy, it will probably be based in accordance with Sharia rather than rule of law. Yet, some prominent Muslim leaders, such as the Turkish President Recep Erdogan, have gone further, saying that being a Muslim and being secular is impossible, and that they will use democracy for their own ends (Islamic aims) and then, when they are done with it, cast it off: 'Democracy is like a train: when you reach your destination, you get off'.[74] For secularists, the main foundation stone of democracy is secularism because democracy and religion do not mix. According to Secular Connexion Séculière (SCS), a Canadian-based humanist organization, 'A true democracy, one that treats all of its citizens as equals and respects fundamental individual freedoms such as freedom of conscience and religion, can not exist when there is a top-down imposition of any ideology'.[75] Likewise, Azmi Bishara, general director of the Arab Center for Research and Policy Studies, thinks that 'if freedom of thought and expression is an essential constituent of democracy, it follows that secularism…is an essential constituent of democracy', and, according to Raja Bahlul, professor of philosophy at the Doha Institute of Graduate Studies, 'freedom of thought cannot be ensured in a non-secular society'.[76] In 2003, the European Court of Human Rights declared that the rules of Sharia were incompatible with democracy and the European Convention of Human Rights.[77]

14.4.2 World War II Guilt and Leftist PC Brainwashing

Among the darlings of the European liberal Right, which include Pim Fortuyn, Theo van Gogh, and Ayaan Hirsi Ali, it is Lars Hedegaard,

74 Dias, 'Erdogan the Tyrant and his EU Accomplices'.

75 Murray Web Works, 'Open Secularism — Required for Democracy'.

76 Bisharah cited by Bahlul in 'Democracy Without Secularism?' 102.

77 Judgements on the merits delivered by the Grand Chamber, *Case of Refah Partisi (The Welfare Party) and Others v. Turkey*, 9; European Court of Human Rights, *Annual Report 2003*, 5–6.

a Danish historian, journalist, critic of Islam, and co-author of *In the House of War: Islam's Colonization of the West* (2003), who aptly explains for Bawer why ordinary Europeans and the elites are seemingly oblivious to the threat of Islamism. According to Hedegaard, Europeans now have an attitude like 'a repentant criminal' and are 'simply too willing to compromise their freedom'. Hedegaard thinks that Islamic extremism has been ignored by the European elites not because of 'snobbism or hippie nostalgia', but because of the 'psychic devastation of the First World War' which paved the way for Communism and National Socialism and produced atrocities that 'placed upon Europeans an unbearable burden of guilt'. But, ultimately, it was the Nazis that 'made Europe think it is doomed and sinful… and deserves what it has coming', a psychic state which was then furthered by the leftists who 're-educated' Europeans with pro-Muslim, anti-American, and anti-Semitic propaganda and reared complacent Europeans ignorant to their dhimmi fate.[78]

Overall, Bawer agrees with Hedegaard. He suggests that the contemporary psychological and national identity of Europeans is profoundly weak due to the guilt complex that arose out of European complicity in the twentieth century mass murder of Jews. The 68er leftists then exploited this vulnerable psychological state, indoctrinating Europeans with anti-war, anti-American, anti-Israeli, and pro-Muslim leftist PC propaganda, so that ordinary Europeans became spineless puppets who mindlessly believe whatever the establishment tells them about Muslims, Israelis, and Americans. He claims Europeans have been programmed to perceive America 'as a heartless, bloodthirsty imperial power, barely indistinguishable from Nazi Germany and certainly worse than the Soviet Union' and have been 'repeatedly…told that America had asked for 9/11—that the atrocity had been payback for American militarism, neocolonialism, capitalist exploitation, and support of Israel'. Whereas Europeans have been

78 Bawer, *While Europe Slept*, 186–188, emphasis in original.

brainwashed to think that Western Europe is different from America: Europe is 'more tolerant, more peaceful, more respectful of its fellow nations, more sensitive to the problem of poverty in the Islamic world, [and] more supportive of the Palestinian cause', and therefore not the target of Islamic extremism.[79]

Out of all of this, Bawer thinks that the psychological effects of guilt, political correctness, and the leftist explanation for militant Islamic attacks on the West (Palestinianism and thus anti-semitism), have resulted in the refusal of Europeans to engage in any form of conflict that may insult, offend, oppress, or discriminate against the Muslim 'Other', even if that means losing everything, including their freedom, identity, and heritage. He writes, the 68ers 'have sought to make [Europeans] feel ashamed of their heritage, contemptuous of their freedom, and willing and eager to settle for any kind of "peace" at any cost'. Furthermore, Bawer laments that Europeans have opened the door to a return of a Europe-wide anti-semitism and will remain on their path to Eurabia, a situation that thwarts America's striving for global hegemony. He writes, 'the strongest potential ally' of America in its fight against the 'tyranny of Islamism' is Europe, but '[t]he advent of fundamentalist Islam in Europe — and the eagerness of many Europeans to placate it — is a threat to American democracy and global supremacy'.[80]

Bawer is not wrong in his assessment of how world war guilt and PC leftism contributed to the weakening of European national identities and their facilitation of Islamism in Europe. However, while he rails against the leftist omission/dismissal of the politico-religious element within Islam, he himself omits/denies the antagonistic effects of Western intervention in Muslim countries on militant Islamism at home and abroad (and how counter-terrorism wars in Muslim countries leads to large flows of Muslim migrants into the EU,

79 Ibid, 187, 220, 154–55.

80 Bawer, *While Europe Slept*, 231, 104.

supplemented by human-rights family reunification).[81] Although he critiques the guilt complex that has arisen out of WWII and political correctness, and vilifies leftists for degrading European cultural identities, he omits the role of America in the creation of the EU and trashes European peoples, history, and ethnic nationalities while attempting to compel European action against Islamism and aid American global hegemony. And although he vehemently condemns PC leftism (accusations of Islamophobia) he himself imposes a neo-conservative style political correctness (accusations of anti-semitism and anti-Americanism) upon the European peoples while discussing Israel, America, Europe, and Islamism.

The possibility does not seem to occur to him that many ordinary Europeans are: not brainwashed but highly intelligent and capable of thinking for themselves; genuinely *do not* want to engage in war with foreign countries; actually *do* want to tackle Islamism in Europe but have no political representatives to serve these interests; honestly *do not* want to aid America in its quest for global supremacy; and are fed up with the eagerness of America's moral mission to spread democracy and liberty throughout the Muslim world by military force and the repercussions this has had for Europe due to its close proximity to Muslim-majority countries in the Middle East and North Africa, i.e. American-led wars have lead to massive flows of refugees and other migrants, mostly Muslim, into European nations.

Bawer is certainly aware that Eurabian elites collude in the Islamization of Europe, yet he doesn't seem to be aware of what ordinary Europeans actually think about immigration, Islam, and Muslims in Europe. Prior to the publication of Bawer's book in 2006, and as detailed in Volume II, the European Values Survey in 1999 showed that Muslims are the societal group that Europeans least-wanted as a neighbour.[82] Surveys in 2003 found that 66 percent of the population

81 See Volume II.

82 EVS, 'European Values Study 1999'.

in France, 73 percent in Germany, 78 percent in Great Britain, and 57 percent in Sweden wanted to reduce immigration and that there was 'an impression amongst the vast majority of people that things have "gone too far"'.[83] Two more surveys in 2003 showed that 62 percent of French thought that the values of Islam were incompatible with the French Republic and 56 percent of Italians thought that Muslims had 'cruel and barbaric laws'.[84] Many other polls and surveys prior to 2006 show the same trends among Europeans. After 2006, Europeans continued to reveal their concerns about Islam and Muslims in Europe. In 2010, only 20 percent of Germans and 30 percent of French thought Islam was suitable for the Western world and 42 percent of French and 40 percent of Germans thought Islam was a threat to their country.[85] In a 2011 poll it was revealed that 'scepticism about Muslim immigration is not limited to a "right-wing" political fringe, as proponents of multiculturalism often assert. Mainstream voters across the entire political spectrum are now expressing concerns about the role of Islam in Europe'.[86] In two other 2011 polls, the majority of respondents in Britain, France, Germany, Poland, and Spain were opposed to immigration from outside the EU and 56 percent of Europeans thought that there were 'too many immigrants in our country'.[87] In 2012 a poll found an overall rejection of political Islam in France, the UK, Germany, and the Netherlands and general agreement that Muslims had essentially failed to integrate.[88] In 2013 polls found that only 24

83 Hochschild and Mollenkopf, *The Complexities of Immigration,* 5; European Commission 2003 survey cited by Crawley, 'Evidence and Attitudes to Asylum and Immigration', 8.

84 Bures, *EU Counterterrorism Policy. A Paper Tiger?*, 25.

85 Pollack, *Wahrnehmung und Akzeptanz religiöser Vielfalt*, 4; Ifop, *Comparative survey France/Germany on Islam*, 4.

86 Kern, 'European Concerns Over Muslim Immigration Go Mainstream'.

87 *Guardian* (datablog), 'Guardian/ICM Europe poll'; Glover, 'Most Europeans see themselves as liberal'.; Ipsos, *Global Views on Immigration.*

88 Ifop, *Le regard des Européens sur l' I slam.*

percent of Britons thought Islam was compatible with the British way of life and 74 percent of French thought Islam was 'intolerant' and 'incompatible' with the values of French society.[89] In 2014 immigration from outside of the EU was viewed negatively by 57 percent of Europeans and a poll in 2015 revealed 52 percent of Europeans wanted lower immigration levels.[90]

In 2010, German President Christian Wulff declared that 'Islam has become a part of Germany identity'.[91] However, according to a poll by *Bild* newspaper, only 24 percent of Germans agreed with him.[92] Two polls in 2016 revealed that over 60 percent of Germans thought that there is 'no place for Islam in Germany', 51 percent said Muslims 'don't belong in Germany', and 46 percent were concerned about the Islamization of society.[93] In fact, a study by the University of Leipzig in June 2016 found that 40 percent of Germans think Muslims should be prohibited from immigrating to Germany and 50 percent felt like 'a stranger in their own country' because there are too many Muslims, a view that increased nearly 18 percent since 2009.[94] A 2017 poll found that 53 percent of German respondents agreed that Muslim immigration should stop.[95]

---

89 Oliver Wright, 'Baroness Warsi'; Gerard Courtois, 'Les crispations alarmantes de la société française'.

90 Esipova, Pugliese and Ray, 'Europeans Most Negative Toward Immigration'; European Commission, 'Public Opinion in the European Union, First Results', 13, 33.

91 Wulff, 'Valuing Diversity — Fostering Cohesion', 6.

92 *Der Spiegel*, 'The World from Berlin'.

93 *RT News*, 'Islam does not belong in Germany, 60% agree with AfD'; Bild, 'So denken die Deutschen wirklich über den Islam'. *Bild*. May 4 2016. https://www.bild.de/politik/inland/umfrage/so-denken-die-deutschen-ueber-den-islam-45606118,var=x.bild.html?jsRedirect

94 Decker, Kiess, and Brähler, *Die enthemmte Mitte*, 49, 50.

95 See Goodwin, Raines, and Cutts, 'What Do Europeans Think About Muslim Immigration?'

Bearing in mind the views of Europeans as shown in the above statistics, in 2015, Italian socialist Federica Mogherini, who held the position of high representative of the European Union for Foreign Affairs and Security Policy and vice-president of the European Commission in the Juncker Commission between 2014 and 2019, declared that 'Islam belongs in Europe'. She further stated that the religion of Islam is not only part of Europe, but 'political Islam should be part of the picture' as well.[96] However, results from a 2017 survey by Chatham House of over 10,000 Europeans from 10 European states revealed that 55 percent of respondents agreed that 'all further migration from mainly Muslim countries should be stopped'.[97] Finally, in a 2018/2019 poll by YouGov, 38 percent of British, 46 percent of French, and 47 percent of German respondents thought there was 'a clash between Islam and the values of society in their country'. In the same poll, 32 percent of British, 49 percent of French, and 53 percent of German respondents 'were unfavourable towards Islam' and 66 percent of British, 72 percent of French, and 72 percent of German respondents were 'concerned about the possible rise of extremism in Islam'.[98]

There are many groups throughout Europe that are attempting to address the Islamization of their nations and of Europe, but if they criticize Muslim immigration and promote the ethnic identity and culture of Europeans they are perceived with utter contempt from the establishment elites and accused of being racists or fascists. One example is the PEGIDA movement,[99] which originated in Germany in 2014 and stands for Patriotic Europeans against the Islamization of the West. PEGIDA has spread across Europe and the Western world,

---

96 European Union External Action, 'Federica Mogherini's remarks'.

97 See Goodwin, Raines, and Cutts, 'What Do Europeans Think About Muslim Immigration?'

98 Joel Rogers de Waal, 'Western/MENA attitudes to religion portray a lack of faith in common values'. YouGov. February 13 2019. https://yougov.co.uk/international/articles/22352-westernmena-attitudes-religion-portray-lack-faith-.

99 Noack, 'Anti-Islam Protestors March in Dresden, Germany'.

and stages marches which are attended by tens of thousands of people. Ten 'indispensable' proposals put forward by the German branch of PEGIDA include: calling upon 'those in power' to preserve and protect German identity; stopping 'political or religious fanaticism, radicalism, Islamization, genderization and early sexualization of children'; grounding German immigration law in 'a demographic, economic and cultural point of view'- '[q]ualitative immigration instead of unregulated mass immigration'; promoting 'a sustainable family policy... to achieve a halt or even the reversal of demographic change'; and the 'cessation of all warmongering'.[100] Despite these very reasonable calls for change, PEGIDA has been condemned by many European elites and labeled the 'pinstripe Nazis'.[101] Angela Merkel, former chancellor of Germany, has claimed that attendees of PEGIDA 'all too often ... have prejudice, coldness, even hatred in their hearts'.[102] And German intelligence services have declared PEGIDA to be an 'extremist' movement that propagates 'anti-constitutional ideologies'.[103]

14.4.3 American Melting Pot vs. European Multiculturalism

Bawer claims Muslim radicalism in Europe is an integration problem that has been facilitated by leftist policies of multiculturalism that afford special rights to immigrant minorities. These special rights have enabled Muslim immigrants to self-segregate into closed communities, preserve illiberal cultural practices, adhere to a parallel legal system, and affect change on many levels of society. Any criticism of

100 PEGIDA, 'Programm'. https://www.pegida.de.

101 Simon Jenkins, 'Germany's "Pinstripe Nazis" Show the Immigration Debate is Overheated'.

102 *Guardian*, 'Angela Merkel Issues New Year's Warning over Right-Wing Pegida Group'.

103 Deutsche Welle (DW), 'Germany: Intelligence agency labels Pegida "anti-constitutional"'. May 7, 2021. https://www.dw.com/en/germany-intelligence-agency-labels-pegida-anti-constitutional/a-57461336.

these developments is vehemently condemned and silenced by leftist dhimmi authorities. In comparison to European multiculturalism, Bawer thinks the American melting pot model of immigrant assimilation is a spectacular 'success'. According to him, America views immigrants with 'respect', sees them as 'individuals' and 'potential assets', and treats them as 'free, self-determining Americans', whereas Europe 'condescends' them, perceiving them as 'needy cases, wards of the state'—victims—and, as 'members of an ethnic and religious group', a collectivity with particular customs that need to be preserved.[104]

A dire result of European multiculturalism for Bawer is the trumping of individual rights by collective rights of minority groups; differences between cultures rather than between individuals are respected and preserved. What this means is that 'ethnic Europeans are viewed as individuals' but Muslims are not, as they are seen as members of the Muslim community, a 'common identity [that] is determined entirely by skin colour, ethnicity, and religious background'. The consequence of this, according to Bawer, is the view, held by the European establishment, that intolerance, self-segregation, and forced marriages within the immigrant community are 'aspects of cultural difference' that must be accepted in a multicultural society. However, Bawer also claims Europeans adopted multiculturalism not out of respect of ethnic differences, but because they have 'a profound discomfort with the idea of "them" becoming "us"'. In his view, European multiculturalism presents itself as an anti-racist method of preserving the diversity of distinct non-European cultural and ethnic identities, but it is actually an ethnocentric strategy to maintain the ethnic homogeneity of Europeans in the face of large-scale immigration from the Third World. As Europeans are aware of their ethnic differences, non-European immigrants are not treated as individual citizens but rather as 'guests'; they are seen as members of a particular ethnic immigrant group irreconcilable with the national identity of the host country

104 Bawer, *While Europe Slept*, 55, 58.

and, in consolation, are given special rights to remain separate and to promote and celebrate their collective ethnic identity.[105]

For Bawer, multicultural policies are merely segregating tools related to 'widespread' bigotry and xenophobia in Europe and have prevented immigrant minorities from assimilating into mainstream society and assuming a common national identity. These bigoted multicultural policies partly explain, according to Bawer, why Europe has a problem with radical Islamism: they have repelled many of the 'most liberal and easily integrated' Muslims from immigrating so that Europe is left with 'the more illiterate, reactionary ones' instead. Furthermore, rather than multiculturalism being 'an act of generosity', Bawer thinks it is really an 'act of cultural self-hatred and cultural suicide'. He perceives that this 'deep self-contempt' and xenophobic European multiculturalism and leftist PC dhimmitude have provided the conditions for Islamic radicals to flourish in Europe at the expense of liberal democracy.[106]

The solutions that Bawer suggests to counter leftist-enabled Islamism is for Europe to be more careful when selecting Muslim immigrants—'[a]uthorities must simply be more careful about whom they let in'—and to scrap multiculturalism in favour of the American way: assimilation into a non-ethnically defined national identity with liberal individual rights only. He writes: 'the answer to the narrow strictures of fundamentalist Islam lay...in democratic liberalism, pluralism, and tolerance—the liberty that had made America prosperous and powerful'. In this view, if all immigrants, especially Muslims, assimilate into a liberal democratic Europe which treats them as individuals and citizens rather than as guests with a separate collective religious identity, then Europe would have no problem with Islamism. Bawer believes that Islam can be compatible with democracy and liberalism, but the onus is on Muslims who 'must discover

105 Ibid, 66, 64, 56.

106 Bawer, *While Europe Slept*, 70, 72, 70, 219.

more liberal ways of understanding their faith'. Furthermore, Muslims in Europe 'can defeat extremism by disavowing and discrediting it as an expression of Islam', and their children must not 'be raised to see their religious affiliation as the be-all and end-all of their identity'.[107]

On the one hand, Bawer rightly states that European nations have had long and continuous ethnically contained histories prior to large-scale immigration from the Third World and are still 'ethnically very homogenous' compared to America; on the other hand, he dismisses this when comparing American and European integration models. He writes that Europeans 'don't understand the radical process that is true integration — a process that's been a part of American life for generations' because Europeans are too aware of their ethnicity and too wary of allowing outsiders to take part in their centuries-old traditions. He goes on, saying that across Europe there is a

> reflexive, inflexible clinging to native customs; the identification of nationality with ethnic identity; and the equation of membership in the society with an attachment to long-standing tribal traditions — all this is still part of the fabric of Europe, and it continues to make true, full, American-style integration next to impossible.[108]

Bawer claims that European multiculturalism has aimed at retaining ethnic distinctiveness and is ethnocentric, but, in reality, multiculturalism does not afford majority rights to ethnic Europeans (they only have liberal individual rights), and it is their ethnic identity that is in peril in comparison to immigrant minorities. Under the rubric of multiculturalism, unlike ethnic minority groups, when ethnic majority Europeans define themselves as distinct peoples by their race, heritage, and traditions they are called retrograde, racist, or White supremacist.

Contrary to Bawer's claim that multiculturalism was initiated due to self-centered ethnocentric considerations of Europeans, we shall

107 Ibid, 68, 218, 234, 230, 229.

108 Bawer, *While Europe Slept*, 50, 74.

take a quick look at the origin of British multiculturalism. In the 1960s, the conditions in Britain were ripe for an ideology to arise as some sort of companion-piece to the practice of immigration and a guideline for the settlement of non-Europeans in the UK. Roy Jenkins (1920–2003), an MP for the Labour party, Social Democratic Party, and Liberal Democrats, as well as a member of the Party for European Socialists and president of the European Commission between 1977 and 1981, first advocated multiculturalism in 1966. Jenkins was also a Fabian socialist, publishing his essay, 'Equality', in *New Fabian Essays* (1952). In December 1965 he was made Labour Home Secretary of the State, and in May 1966 he gave a speech in London to the National Committee for Commonwealth Immigrants, outlining his concept of multiculturalism:

> I do not regard [integration] as meaning the loss, by immigrants, of their own national characteristics and culture. I do not think that we need in this country a "melting pot", which will turn everybody out in a common mould, as one of a series of carbon copies of someone's misplaced vision of the stereotyped Englishman...I define integration, therefore, not as a flattening process of assimilation but as equal opportunity, accompanied by cultural diversity, in an atmosphere of mutual tolerance.[109]

This multicultural socialist egalitarianism wasn't nationalized in the UK until 1997 under the New Labour government.

But Bawer just wants to end multiculturalism. He assumes that assimilating European immigrants into a melting pot like America is necessary and good and that the ethnocentric identity of native Europeans (and ethnic minorities) must be replaced by American style values. What Bawer essentially wants is the casting off of collective ethnic, racial, and cultural identities by non-European immigrants and European natives alike so that all peoples will assimilate into a neutrally defined common national identity based on a set of secular liberal democratic values. This is paramount to him. He wants

109 Cited in Lester, 'Multiculturalism and Free Speech'.

people to be individuals — a diversity of characters — with their own lifestyle in tune with liberal rights but does not want people to identify with an ethnic collective displaying a distinct and unified way of life. The epitome of successful American-style immigrant integration, 'a true melting pot, an immigration triumph' is to him, the Chinese restaurant in a European town with Asian waitresses who speak several languages and the laughing mixed race couple eating Chinese food with their mixed-race child.[110] The notion of nationhood and identity based on an historic ethnoculturalism is anathematic to his dream of a world-wide American-style monoculturalism based on abstract liberal individual rights.

Like other neoconservatives, Bawer blames European leftists *and* European natives for the failures of Muslims to integrate into society and for the presence of Islamism in Europe. But there are other factors that have also contributed regardless of whether Europe practices multiculturalism *or* assimilation: many Muslim radicals in Europe are third generation immigrants, refugees, and illegal immigrants and many are radicalized over the internet and by satellite TV; many Muslims are indeed angry at the military endeavours of the West in the Middle East and at the antagonistic situation between Israel and Palestine; many may feel disillusioned from the impartial consumer society of liberal individualism and have a general disdain for Westernism; and some simply aim to conquer Europe and the West. Bawer does not seem to fathom that people also have strong attachments to their particular cultures and ethnic identities. Many Muslims have robust family and community traditions and transnationalism links them to the Middle East by strong physical, spiritual, and political connections (family, marriages, I.C.T., pilgrimages etc.). This matters, as Muslims will come to Europe and will stick together and keep their cultural particularities, practicing their way of life in private if necessary, and will push against and not conform to the universal idea

110 Bawer, *While Europe Slept*, 188.

of assimilation and American monoculturalism, no matter how much Bawer et al. want it.

Although Bawer deeply criticizes leftism and multiculturalism, not once does he mention the 'leading role' of Jews in the leftist transformation of Europe into a multi-ethnic and multicultural paradise, unlike Barbara Spectre (a Jewish activist and founder of Paideia, the European Institute for Jewish Studies in Sweden) who spilled the beans. A few years after his book was published, Spectre, in disregard of major European leaders who declared multiculturalism had 'failed' and was 'dead', said in an interview with Israeli IBA-News in 2010 that Europe must become multicultural in order to 'survive':

> I think there is a resurgence of anti-Semitism because at this point in time Europe has not yet learned how to be multicultural. And I think we are going to be part of the throes of that transformation, which must take place. Europe is not going to be the monolithic societies they once were in the last century. Jews are going to be at the centre of that. It's a huge transformation for Europe to make. They are now going into a multicultural mode and Jews will be resented because of our leading role. But without that leading role and without that transformation, Europe will not survive.[111]

Similarly, in an October 2015 European Commission speech, Frans Timmermans, first vice-president of the European Commission, stated, in reference to Jewish flight from European nations due in part to Muslim anti-Semitism and terrorist attacks, that '[w]ithout our Jewish community, Europe would cease to exist. Europe would simply cease to exist'.[112] Such claims of the importance of Jews in Europe for European survival are perplexing, considering the size of the Jewish community in Europe. According to Pew Research, there were around 1.4 million Jews in Europe in 2010, including Eastern Europe and the

---

111 'Barbara Lerner Spectre Calls for Destruction of Christian European Ethnic Societies', YouTube video (IBA News).

112 European Commission, 'Opening remarks of First Vice-President Frans Timmermans'.

former Soviet Union, constituting about 10 percent of the total world population of Jews.[113] In the EU, the Jewish population was estimated to be around 1.1 million in 2014 or about 8 percent of the total population of Jews in the world.[114] The total population of the EU is 508 million according to Europa, the official website for the EU.[115] This means that the Jewish population constitutes merely 0.23 percent of the EU population. How can such a small proportion of the population be so influential, not just for the political and ideological landscape of Europe but, more importantly, for its very existence?

In the end, Bawer doesn't grasp the tragedy (or does not care) that has unfolded for native Europeans. He doesn't perceive that Third World mass-immigration, cultural Marxism, and neoconservative universalism are assaulting European indigenous culture with results equally as destructive as Islamism. Although multiculturalism is better than assimilation, as it recognizes that ethnicity and cultural roots matter for people's identity, the problem with it is that it does not afford the White majorities of Europe the right to preserve their traditional societal culture, ethnic identity, and particular history. In the end, neither the current form of multiculturalism nor American assimilation is the answer to European problems of Islamism, as the fundamental problem facing Europe today is large-scale Third World immigration.

14.4.4 Large-Scale Third-World Immigration

Bawer is plainly pro-immigration, giving the typical well-worn reasons for it:

> Western Europe desperately needs immigrants. The native population is aging and its numbers are on the wane....more and more workers will be needed to keep national economies from shrinking and to help pay for

113 Lipka, 'The continuing decline of Europe's Jewish population'.

114 Dashefsky and Sheskin, *American Jewish Year Book 2014*, 351.

115 *Europa*, 'Living in the EU'.

> mounting retirement benefits and hospitalisation costs....there's no reason why the difficulties posed by fundamentalist Islam should prevent Western Europe from maintaining a steady flow of immigrants.

So, it is clear, Bawer considers massive immigration from the Third World into Europe as necessary. However, it's not just for demographic and economic reasons. He also thinks immigration from non-European countries is essentially culturally-enriching. He says: 'Time and again...I've encountered immigrants who've brought values and habits to Norway that the country needs more of [and immigrants tend to be] much friendlier... than Norwegians'.[116]

Bawer has no problem with mass-immigration from the Third World if it means immigrants assimilate into the contemporary Western way of life defined in terms of abstract individual liberal rights for all and contribute to its cultural progression to universalism. All immigrants as well as natives must assimilate into a liberal democratic culture and not demand special ethnic considerations. If Muslims in Europe assimilate into a liberal individual rights-based society, become secular, abandon their collective identity and their illiberal beliefs and practices, and stop their terror attacks on the West, then they can stay and more can come too.

Bawer seems to think that only Muslims pose an integration problem due to their strong collective identity and, for some, their militant radicalism, which are banes to American global supremacy in Europe and throughout the world. He believes no other ethnic minority groups in Europe are a problem because he thinks they have accepted their minority status and are integrating quite nicely; they do not demand special accommodations, do not bomb and commit terrorist acts against the West, and are not anti-capitalist or anti-democratic. Obviously, Bawer doesn't comprehend that immigration itself is a problem for the existence of European peoples themselves because he doesn't consider the erosion of the ethnic

---

116 Bawer, *While Europe Slept*, 68–69.

identities of Europe and the West as a problem. In these regards, he has, along with other neoconservatives, several elements in common with leftism: mass-immigration from the Third World into the West and miscegenation; outright rejection of distinct collective European ethnic identities; and complete opposition to the right of Europeans to maintain and preserve their identity at the national level in their own homelands. In the end, Bawer thinks ethnic identity, especially of Whites and Muslims, does not have a place in the American plan for global supremacy. Ethno-national identities and collective rights of distinct peoples must be replaced by individual rights and ethnically impartial identities.

Although Bawer opposes multiculturalism and favours assimilation, like leftists and other neocons, he supports the political ideal that all the races of the world should come to and settle in the West and that all races should mix together there. As such, neither leftism nor neoconservatism stress the importance of preserving real ethnic diversity in the world. Nor do they show concern for the demographic replacement of native Europeans in the work force, schools, government, national institutions, and homelands by non-European high birth rates and large-scale immigration. They have no qualms about European peoples being overwhelmed, stifled, and dispossessed by the practices of mass-immigration. Rather, they encourage and celebrate these destructive processes.

Bawer does not consider the diversity of ethnicities and cultures in the world, and their preservation, as goods in themselves. Despite being pro-Israel, he does not understand that geographical boundaries are integral to ethnic distinctiveness, or that ethnic distinctiveness is necessary for the brilliant diversity and vitality of the multitude of cultures and peoples of the world. Nor does he comprehend that ethnic particularity is a necessary feature of the psychological identity of social groups and that belonging and identifying with a distinct ethnic group with a collective identity and shared language, cultural heritage, norms, values, and traditions is an intrinsic feature of human psychology and of all human societies that have existed throughout human history. He wants to completely overhaul the historical traditions and character of Europe to suit the needs, wants, and aspirations of the American global supremacist engineering project, which aims towards the imposition of a universal monoculture on the whole world.

14.4.5 European Populism: Liberal Democracy or Fascism

For Bawer, the increasing popularity of populism in Europe could go two ways: liberal democracy or fascism. He hopes populism will lead to 'a more democratic polity that placed liberty above multiculturalism'. He sees this in liberal right-leaning types of people, who he calls 'the liberal resistance—a hodgepodge of writers, politicians, and activists', namely those who are pro-liberty, pro-America, pro-Israel, and against the Islamization of Europe, such as Pim Fortuyn, Theo van Gogh, Ayaan Hirsi Ali, and Lars Hedegaard. Although European leftists have branded this 'liberal resistance' fascist and racist for their stern policies regarding Islam and their pro-Israeli stance, these are labels that Bawer refutes with zeal. Liberal right wing populist groups are acceptable to Bawer due to their 'tolerance', which is 'familiar to Americans'. He admires them because they are not against immigration, are not for the repatriation of Muslims, and do not defend and promote the national ethnic identity of Europeans. Instead, they defend continued large-scale immigration and policies of 'education, emancipation, and integration', and have respect for democracy, secularity, freedom of expression, equality of women, sexual minority rights, and individual rights.[117]

In contrast, ethnic-minded Europeans responding to the Islamization of Europe and their homelands are a problem for Bawer. Although he observes that Europe has a history of ethnic and

117 Bawer, *While Europe Slept*, 222, 163, 45, 164–165.

cultural homogeneity, and is much more 'traditionalist and nativist' than America, he perceives non-liberal right wing populist groups that deal with issues of Islamism but want to also preserve aspects of the Old World order in Europe, such as the British National Party (BNP), Vlaams Belang (Belgium), National Front (France), the Freedom Party (Austria), and the National Party (Germany), are truly 'fascistic groups' because they are 'fixated on racial, ethnic, and cultural identity'. Bawer asserts, for example, that the ethno-nationalist BNP, which stands for the British working-class people, is 'an explicitly racist group that...also opposes mixed-race marriages, has had associations with neo-Nazi groups, and requires members to be of British (or "closely kindred") stock' and this is just '[n]ot a pretty picture'.[118]

The history of anti-semitism in Europe and the rise of so-called neo-Nazism makes Bawer worry that 'many Europeans ... [will] respond to the looming Islamist fascism in their midst with fascism of their own'. He writes, Europe has had a 'long history of anti-Semitism', and Nazi anti-Semitism 'was the culmination of centuries of Jew-hatred rooted in the European preoccupation with ethnic identity as the basis of cultural identity'. So, the 'resurgent right-wing nationalism' witnessed today in Europe is 'of a kind that had not been seen since the defeat of Hitler'. He fears that populist parties that are not already 'far-right, racist, or xenophobic' may 'easily move in that direction' as the crisis in Europe deepens.[119] For him, Europe must stop the leftist-enabled tide of Islamism by adopting the American strategies of assimilation, liberal individual rights, and neoconservative foreign policy and must prevent White nationalists rising in response to mass-immigration and Islamism, otherwise this will lead to a new era of anti-semitism in Europe.

While Bawer bemoans the weak identity of the sleeping brainwashed Europeans in the face of Islamism, he fears those Europeans

118 Ibid, 73, 44, 214.

119 Bawer, *While Europe Slept*, 222, 138, 159, 223.

who are awake and seek to preserve their distinct ethnic identity in the face not just of Islamism, but other pertinent issues too, such as rising non-European demographics and cultural demands of minority immigrant groups, PC leftism, and American hegemony. Quite simply, Bawer dreads indigenous Europeans promoting their ethnically distinct identities and collective belonging as a protective measure against encroaching enemies because he associates a strong European ethnic identity with anti-semitism. Bawer not only fears non-liberal right-leaning populist groups, but also fears European leftists and Islamists, all because of their purported anti-semitism. In fact, Bawer has a problem with any group or individual that is not pro-American, pro-Israel, pro-military intervention in the Middle East, pro-assimilation, or pro-immigration: if you do not ascribe to any of these descriptors you are labeled as either an anti-American, a brainwashed leftist, an Islamist, a racist, or an anti-semitic neo-Nazi fascist.

15. EUROPEAN DEMOGRAPHIC AND POLITICAL DECLINE: IS IT GENOCIDE?

'Fifth column [is a] clandestine group or faction of subversive agents [foreign or domestic] who attempt to undermine a nation's solidarity by any means at their disposal.... A cardinal technique of the fifth column is the infiltration of sympathizers into the entire fabric of the nation under attack and, particularly, into positions of policy decision and national defense. From such key posts, fifth-column activists exploit the fears of a people by spreading rumours and misinformation, as well as by employing the more standard techniques of espionage and sabotage.'[1]

WE HAVE seen in Volumes I and II, and so far in Volume III, the historical, geopolitical, international, demographic, and ideological influences on (and, where applicable, the consequences and critiques of) the development and current form of the European Union. In this final part, international laws and legal definitions of the aim and basis of the European Union, and of self-determination, discrimination, persecution, genocide, and indigenous rights are clarified. In the spirit of assessment, they are then applied to the EU cosmopolitan project, to demographic engineering that is motivated by economic and political interests, and to Islamism and leftist-Third Worldism, all of which directly influence the political and demographic decline of indigenous Europeans. Just

1 *Encyclopedia Britannica*, 'fifth column.'

to be clear, various census descriptions describe Europeans as 'White' and racial narratives designate Europeans as the 'White race'; as such, indigenous Europeans will interchangeably be referred to as either White, European, European peoples, ethnic European, or indigenous/native European.

15.1 International Laws and Definitions

This chapter will explore various laws that protect the well-being, security, and rights of European individuals and nations. It will examine the notions of the 'will of the people' and the right of peoples and nations to self-determination as legally explained by jurist Antonio Cassese, by international law and human rights professor Johan van der Vyver, and by lawyer Edward McWhinney, and upheld by the *Universal Declaration of Human Rights* (UDHR) and the *International Covenant on Civil and Political Rights* (ICCPR). It will provide definitions of discrimination and persecution, as well as definitions of race, nationality, social group, and political opinion, as enshrined by the UDHR, the ICCPR, the *Convention for the Protection of Human Rights and Fundamental Freedoms* (1953/2010), and the European Parliament and Council *Directive 2011/95/EU of 13 December 2011*. It will examine the definitions of genocide, ethnocide, and cultural genocide as put forward by the person who coined these terms, linguist and lawyer Raphael Lemkin, as well as the definitions of ethnocide and cultural genocide by the *United Nations Educational, Scientific and Cultural Organization* (UNESCO), and cultural and biological genocide according to the first draft (1947) of the Genocide Convention. It will also detail the definition of genocide in the finalized *Convention on the Prevention and Punishment of the Crime of Genocide* (1948) and examine the eight categories of the analysis framework provided by the Office of the UN Special Adviser on the Prevention of Genocide (OSAPG), a guide that helps to ascertain whether there is a 'risk of genocide in a given situation'. In the final section of the chapter, the definition of the term 'indigenous' is given according to the United Nations and the UN *Declaration on the Rights of Indigenous Peoples* (2007) and the rights of indigenous peoples are explained in terms of the 1994 draft version, the 2007 finalized version, and the 2008 annex of the *Declaration on the Rights of Indigenous Peoples.*

15.2 European Union Law and the Right to Self-Determination

According to article 3 of the *Consolidated Versions of the Treaty on European Union* (2012), the central aim of the EU is to 'promote peace, its values and the well-being of its peoples'. It aims to provide its citizens with 'an area of freedom, security and justice without internal frontiers' while taking 'appropriate measures' regarding its 'external border controls, asylum, immigration and the prevention and combating of crime'. It also seeks to 'respect' the 'rich cultural and linguistic diversity' of Europe and to 'ensure' that the 'cultural heritage' of Europe is 'safeguarded and enhanced'. In addition, according to article 4(2) of the treaty, 'the equality of Member States', their individual 'territorial integrity', 'national identities', and their 'safeguarding [of] national security' are all to be respected by the EU.

Article 10 of the treaty declares that the EU is to be based on 'representative democracy', with citizens being 'directly represented at Union level in the European Parliament'. European political parties are to 'contribute…to expressing the will of citizens of the Union'.[2] Article 10 reflects article 21(3) of the *Universal Declaration of Human Rights* (UDHR), which states that 'the basis of the authority of government' is the 'will of the people', a will that is 'expressed in periodic and genuine elections'.[3] In other words, based on democratic principles

2 EUR-Lex, *Consolidated Versions of the Treaty on European Union*, 17–18, 21.

3 United Nations, *Universal Declaration of Human Rights.*

and human rights, the will of European peoples determines the governance of European nation-states as well as the EU as a whole.[4]

The EU also abides by the *International Covenant on Civil and Political Rights* (ICCPR), which is a multilateral treaty that was adopted by the UN General Assembly in December 1966 and came into force in March 1976. According to article 1(1) of this covenant, 'All peoples have the right to self-determination' and, based on this right, 'freely determine their political status and freely pursue their economic, social and cultural development'. Member States are responsible, according to article 1(3), for promoting 'the realization' of this right of peoples to self-determination.[5] In his book *Self-Determination of Peoples: A Legal Reappraisal* (1995), the late Italian jurist Antonio Cassese writes that

> [i]nternal self-determination[6] means the right to authentic self-government, that is, the right for a people really and freely to choose its own political and economic regime — which is much more than choosing among what is on offer perhaps from one political or economic position only. It is an ongoing right.... the right to internal self-determination is neither

4 European nations are made up of European peoples, and European states are elected by European peoples and are meant to represent their will and interests. National institutions, including educational, media, and political, were created by Europeans for Europeans to reflect their ethnic and cultural identities and interests and have changed in a dramatic way since the end of WWII with the rapid rise of non-European populations in European nations (since the onset of non-European mass-immigration in the 1950s and 60s) and the development and expansion of the cosmopolitan EU integration project.

5 United Nations Human Rights Office of the High Commissioner (OHCHR), *International Covenant on Civil and Political Rights.*

6 Internal self-determination is 'a people's pursuit of its political, economic, social and cultural development within the framework of an existing state'. External self-determination is about secession and associated with decolonisation. See: Reference re Secession of Quebec [1998] 2 S.C.R. 217 at para. 126, 1998 SCC 25506. https://www.scc-csc.ca/cases-dossiers/search-recherche/25506/.

> destroyed nor diminished by its already once having been invoked and put into effect.[7]

In other words, just because a political and/or economic regime of a nation, and, by extension, a nation of nations such as the EU, has been established, does not mean that it is absolute; it remains continuously subject to being re-determined by the people.

The right of nations (based on self-determined peoples) to self-determination is an essential principle of international law and is linked to the right to self-determine the state (the coercive political apparatus) and to territorial integrity. In 2008, the UN General Assembly Security Council declared that the principle of self-determination 'may be interpreted as reinforcing the principle of respect for the territorial integrity of states since it constitutes a reaffirmation of the principle of sovereign equality'.[8] Ten years earlier, the Canadian Supreme Court declared that

> [t]here is no necessary incompatibility between the maintenance of the territorial integrity of existing states…and the right of a "people" to achieve a full measure of self-determination. A state whose government represents the whole of the people or peoples resident within its territory, on a basis of equality and without discrimination, and respects the principles of self-determination in its own internal arrangements, is entitled to the protection under international law of its territorial integrity.[9]

In 2003, Johan van der Vyver, I.T. Cohen professor of International Law and Human Rights at Emory University School of Law, wrote that 'the right to self-determination is almost always proclaimed in conjunction with the territorial integrity of states' and that self-determination had come to include 'the entitlement of national,

---

7 Cassese, *Self-Determination of Peoples*, 101.

8 United Nations General Assembly Security Council, *Protracted conflicts in the GUAM area*, 38.

9 Reference re Secession of Quebec [1998] 2 S.C.R. 217 at para. 130, 1998 SCC 25506. https://www.scc-csc.ca/cases-dossiers/search-recherche/25506/.

ethnic, religious, or linguistic societies within a political community to live according to the customs and traditions of their kind'.[10] Prior to WWII, self-determination was associated with nationalism and popular sovereignty and 'the constitution of ethno-culturally homogeneous nation-states'. It was only after WWII, according to the late Edward McWhinney, a Canadian lawyer, that self-determination became associated with 'peoples' rather than 'nations' per se, with its concentration on 'local, indigenous political movements in European colonial territories overseas' as well as national minorities and other minorities of nation-states.[11] Since this time, self-determination has scarcely applied to current ethnic majorities of EU Member States, although, according to various European and international law documents as discussed above and below, like all peoples, European ethnic majorities also have the right to self-determination.

15.3 Discrimination and Persecution

Article 12 of the UDHR and article 17 of the ICCPR declare that 'No one shall be subject to arbitrary or unlawful interference with his privacy, family, home or correspondence, nor to unlawful attacks on his honour and reputation' and that '[e]veryone has the right to the protection of the law against such interference or attacks'.[12] In article 20(2) of the ICCPR, it is stated that advocating 'national, racial or religious hatred' that incites 'discrimination, hostility or violence' is 'prohibited by law'.[13] In article 14 of the *Convention for the Protection of Human Rights and Fundamental Freedoms* (1953/2010) in Europe,

---

10 Van der Vyver, 'Self-determination of the Peoples of Quebec under International Law', 1–2.

11 McWhinney, *Self-Determination of Peoples and Plural-Ethnic States in Contemporary International Law*, 2.

12 UN, *Universal Declaration of Human Rights*; OHCHR, *International Covenant on Civil and Political Rights.*

13 OHCHR, *International Covenant on Civil and Political Rights.*

it is declared that 'discrimination on any ground such as sex, race, colour, language, religion, political or other opinion, national or social origin, association with a national minority, property, birth or other status' is prohibited,[14] a prohibition which is also found in article 26 of the ICCPR, which states 'the law shall prohibit any discrimination and guarantee to all persons equal and effective protection against discrimination on any ground'.[15] Similarly, in article 7 of the UDHR it is stated that all people 'are entitled to equal protection' against incitement to discrimination and the act of discrimination itself.[16]

According to article 6 of the *Directive 2011/95/EU of the European Parliament and of the Council* (on refugees and those qualifying for subsidiary protection), persecution can be undertaken by the State, by 'parties or organizations controlling the State or a substantial part of the territory of the State', and by 'non-State actors...including international organizations'. According to article 9(2) of this directive, acts of persecution can take various forms, such as 'physical or mental violence, including acts of sexual violence' and 'legal, administrative, police, and/or judicial measures which are themselves discriminatory or which are implemented in a discriminatory manner'. According to article 9(1a) acts of persecution must 'be sufficiently serious by [their] nature or repetition as to constitute a severe violation of basic human rights'.[17] According to article 2(d), persecution is based on 'reasons of race, religion, nationality, political opinion or membership of a particular social group'. In article 10, race is defined as including 'considerations of colour, descent, or membership of a particular ethnic group' and nationality is defined as *not* being

> confined to citizenship or lack thereof but shall, in particular, include membership of a group determined by its cultural, ethnic, or linguistic

---

14 European Court of Human Rights, *European Convention on Human Rights*, 12.

15 OHCHR, *International Covenant on Civil and Political Rights.*

16 UN, *Universal Declaration of Human Rights.*

17 EUR-Lex, *Directive 2011/95/EU of 13 December 2011*, 15–16.

> identity, common geographical or political origins or its relationship with the population of another State.[18]

As a brief supplementation to this definition of nationality, article 15 of the UDHR states that 'Everyone has the right to a nationality' and 'No one shall be arbitrarily deprived of his nationality nor denied the right to change his nationality'.[19] Carrying on with article 10 of *Directive 2011/95/EU of the European Parliament and of the Council,* we find that a particular social group is defined as a group where

> members of that group share an innate characteristic, or a common background that cannot be changed, or share a characteristic or belief that is so fundamental to identity or conscience that a person should not be forced to renounce it.

And political opinion is defined as 'the holding of an opinion, thought or belief on a matter related to the potential actors of persecution… and to their policies or methods, whether or not that opinion, thought or belief has been acted upon'.[20] In sum, persecuting and/or discriminating against individuals and peoples based on reasons that include race, religion, nationality, political opinion, or membership of a social group, is prohibited by law.

15.4 Genocide, Ethnocide, and Cultural Genocide

Raphael Lemkin, a Polish-Jewish linguist and lawyer who helped initiate the Genocide Convention (1948), coined the terms 'genocide', 'ethnocide', and 'cultural genocide' in the first half of the twentieth century. For Lemkin, the term genocide was a combination of the Greek word *genos* meaning race, tribe, or family, and the Latin word

18 Ibid, 13, 16.

19 See: UN, *Universal Declaration of Human Rights.*

20 EUR-Lex, *Directive 2011/95/EU of 13 December 2011*, 16.

cide or killing, i.e. race, tribe, or family killing. In his book *Axis Rule in Occupied Europe: Laws of Occupation, Analysis of Government, Proposals for Redress* (1944), Lemkin wrote that genocide

> does not necessarily mean the immediate destruction of a nation, except when accomplished by mass killings of all members of a nation. It is intended rather to signify a coordinated plan of different actions aiming at the destruction of essential foundations of the life of national groups, with the aim of annihilating the groups themselves. The objectives of such a plan would be disintegration of the political and social institutions, of culture, language, national feelings, religion, and the economic existence of national groups, and the destruction of the personal security, liberty, health, dignity, and even the lives of the individuals belonging to such groups. Genocide is directed against the national group as an entity, and the actions involved are directed against individuals, not in their individual capacity, but as members of the national group.[21]

According to this original definition of genocide, various actions aimed at the destruction of nations, the national group and its members, can occur immediately through physical/biological destruction or over time by deliberate actions aimed at destroying the 'essential foundations' necessary for the survival of national groups. Lemkin further wrote that

> [g]enocide has two phases: one, destruction of the national pattern of the oppressed group; the other, the imposition of the national pattern of the oppressor. This imposition, in turn, may be made upon the oppressed population which is allowed to remain, or upon the territory alone, after removal of the population and colonization of the area by the oppressor's own nationals.[22]

In other words, genocide does not necessarily involve the immediate biological destruction of a distinct peoples, but rather the destruction of their 'essential foundations', their distinct biological means and

21 Lemkin, *Axis Rule in Occupied Europe*, 79.

22 Ibid, 79.

'patterns' for survival at the national level that will lead to the eventual annihilation of a distinct racial grouping. The 'national pattern' is replaced by a foreign 'national pattern' that is imposed upon them by an oppressive or colonizing force. In this sense, this may be called American*ization*, Islam*ization*, African*ization*, Asian*ization*, Third World*ization*, and cosmopolitanin*ization*. Genocide involves denationalization but is more than this; it is aimed at depriving the racial group targeted of their actual existence as a distinct living group over the long-term.

Originally Lemkin intended the term ethnocide to be synonymous or alternative to the term genocide. The term ethnocide is a combination of the Greek word *ethnos* meaning nation and the Latin word *cide* meaning killing, i.e. nation killing. Lemkin also viewed cultural genocide, meaning the destruction of cultural heritage or cultural killing, as an aspect of genocide.[23] Similarly, in 1981 the *United Nations Educational, Scientific and Cultural Organization* (UNESCO) defined ethnocide as synonymous with cultural genocide, describing it in terms of

> an ethnic group [that] is denied the right to enjoy, develop and transmit its own culture and its own language, whether collectively or individually. This involves an extreme form of massive violation of human rights and, in particular, the right of ethnic groups to respect for their cultural identity.[24]

Likewise, in 2008 Spanish jurist and historian Bartolomé Clavero declared that 'Genocide kills people while ethnocide kills social cultures through the killing of individual souls.'[25] Yet, ethnocide goes beyond the destruction of cultural heritage; through various strategies it aims

---

23 Lemkin, *Axis Rule in Occupied Europe*, 79. In addition to cultural and biological aspects of genocide, Lemkin also viewed genocide as containing political, economic, social, physical, religious, and moral aspects as well. See: Lemkin, *Axis Rule in Occupied Europe*, 82–90.

24 As cited by Schabas, *Genocide in International Law*, 189.

25 Clavero, *Genocide or Ethnocide*, 100.

at killing the actual essence, the vitality or spiritual underpinnings of individuals who belong to an ethnic group. It can be understood as intentionally targeting a distinct ethno-national group for eventual destruction, in whole or in part, by attacking their collective attributes, such as their ethnic and national identity, language, institutions, and homelands, and their ancestral, social, and cultural heritage, ways of life, social bonds, and systems of thought.[26]

Cultural genocide as well as political genocide were included in the first draft version (1947) of the Genocide Convention, but the final Convention (1948) excluded cultural genocide as a separate form of genocide and limited protected groups to racial, national, linguistic, and religious groups.[27] According to the first draft (1947), cultural genocide involved

> [d]estroying the specific characteristics of the group by:
>
> Forcible transfer of children to another group; or
>
> Forced and systematic exile of individuals representing the culture of a group; or
>
> Prohibition of the use of the national language even in private intercourse; or
>
> Systematic destruction of books printed in the national language or of religious works or prohibition of new publications; or
>
> Systematic destruction of historical or religious monuments or their diversion to alien uses, destruction or dispersion of documents and objects of historical, artistic, or religious values and of objects used in religious worship.

And biological genocide involved

> [r]estricting births by:

26 See: Martin Shaw, *What is Genocide*, 65–67; Conversi, 'Genocide, Ethnic Cleansing and Nationalism', 320–333.

27 See: Gellately and Kiernan, *The Specter of Genocide*, 267; Staub, *The Roots of Evil*, 8.

(a) sterilization and/or compulsory abortion; or

(b) segregation of the sexes; or

(c) obstacles to marriage.[28]

In the finalized convention, called the *Convention on the Prevention and Punishment of the Crime of Genocide*, which was adopted by the General Assembly of the United Nations in December 1948, biological and cultural genocide are described as aspects of genocide as a whole, rather than separate acts. Article II defines genocide as

> acts committed with intent to destroy, in whole or in part, a national, ethnical, racial or religious group, as such:
>
> Killing members of the group;
>
> Causing seriously bodily or mental harm to members of the group;
>
> Deliberately inflicting on the group conditions of life calculated to bring about its physical destruction in whole or in part;
>
> Imposing measures intended to prevent births within the group
>
> Forcibly transferring children of the group to another group.

Those who commit and direct genocide, conspire to commit genocide, publicly incite genocide, attempt genocide, or are complicit in genocide, will be punished, 'whether they are constitutionally responsible rulers, public officials or private individuals', and will either be tried by the State where the act was committed or by an international tribunal.[29]

The Office of the UN Special Adviser on the Prevention of Genocide (OSAPG) provides an 'analysis framework' of eight categories to ascertain if there is a 'risk of genocide in a given situation'. In the first category, the relations of groups are analysed in terms of

---

28 *Convention on the Prevention and Punishment of the Crime of Genocide — the Secretariat and Ad Hoc Committee Drafts (1947 and 1948).*

29 *Convention on the Prevention and Punishment of the Crime of Genocide (1948).*

'tensions, power and economic relations, including perceptions about the targeted group' and 'existing and past conflicts over land, power, security and expressions of group identity, such as language, religion and culture'. Also involved is an investigation of '[p]ast and present patterns of discrimination against members of any group' and '[o]vert justification' for these practices, as well as other human rights violations including past genocidal acts. In sum, the first classification involves the identification and examination of present and historical conflicts between distinct groups of people over territory, resources, sovereignty, and their views of the Other, as well as an analysis of past and present records of discriminatory practices and human rights violations.

In the second category, '[c]ircumstances that affect the capacity to prevent [and deter] genocide', which include existing structures such as legislation, the judiciary, 'national human rights institutions', UN operations, and 'neutral security forces and independent media', are examined in terms of how effective they are and how accessible they are to 'vulnerable groups'. And in the third category, the 'capacity to perpetrate genocide—especially, but not exclusively, by killing' is investigated, including any involvement of state authorities in the formation and weaponizing of 'armed groups'. To clarify, category two focuses its investigation on national measures that are in place that effectively protect groups from acts of genocide and category three concentrates on access to and availability of resources that enable actors, including the state, to commit genocide.

The fourth category involves an examination of the 'underlying political, economic, military or other motivation' of state or regional actors that target a group and 'separate it from the rest of the population'. In addition, the motivation and the 'role, whether active or passive, of actors outside the country' is analysed. This category also investigates 'the use of exclusionary ideology and the construction of identities in terms of "us" and "them" to accentuate differences' as well as the use of 'propaganda campaigns and fabrications' that are 'used to justify acts against a targeted group by use of dominant, controlled media or "mirror politics."' In other words, the motivations of state or regional leaders, as well as non-state actors, as well as any acts they commit that justify and incite division between groups and isolate, exclude, and dehumanize a particular group, such as propaganda techniques, are examined.

The fifth category involves the examination of '[a]ny development of events, whether gradual or sudden, that suggest a trajectory towards the perpetration of genocidal violence, or the existence of a longer term plan or policy to commit genocide'. Such events include: preparing the 'local population' so 'to use them to perpetrate acts'; 'strengthening…the military or security apparatus' and creating or increasing 'support to militia groups'; introducing legislation that 'derogat[es] the rights of a targeted group'; and a 'sudden increase in inflammatory rhetoric or hate propaganda, especially by leaders, that sets a tone of impunity'. To be clear, the fifth category examines the 'gradual or sudden' onset of conditions that set the stage for the act of genocide to be committed, such as the strengthening of armed forces and the pitting of one indoctrinated group against the legally disparaged other.

The sixth category involves an analysis of 'obvious' genocidal acts, such as 'killings, abduction and disappearances, torture, rape and sexual violence; "ethnic cleansing" or pogroms' and 'less obvious methods of destruction', such as 'deprivation of resources needed for the group's physical survival' and the 'creation of [other] circumstances that could lead to a slow death'. The seventh category is about '[e]vidence of intent "to destroy in whole or in part …"'. It involves the investigation of 'hate speech', of 'widespread and/or systematic' discrimination, and other methods of exclusion that are 'designed to reach the foundations of the group', i.e. ethnic cleansing. It also involves investigating the deliberate 'destruction of or attacks on cultural and religious property and symbols of the targeted group' as well as the 'targeted elimination of community leaders' and of males and females 'of a particular age group (the "future generation" or a military-age group)'. And the eighth and final category involves analysis of 'triggering factors' for genocide, such as '[u]pcoming elections', military campaigns against civilians, and 'increases in opposition capacity... or rapidly declining opposition capacity'—the former may be seen as a threat, which triggers 'preemptive action', and the latter may lead to the erasure of 'problem groups'.[30]

In summary, the OSAPG 'analysis framework' assesses specific factors that help determine the risk of genocide in a given situation. This includes hard genocide, soft genocide, ethnic cleansing, and cultural genocide, as well as the 'gradual or sudden' onset of conditions and trigger factors that set the stage for the act of genocide to be committed. Some of the main issues that are examined include: past and present conflicts between distinct groups of people; motivations of state or regional leaders, as well as non-state actors, to commit genocide; access to and availability of resources that enable actors, including the state, to commit genocide; and acts that justify and incite division between groups by isolating, excluding, and dehumanising a particular group through propaganda techniques, abusive language, and discrimination.

15.5 Indigenous Rights

In article 7 of the 1994 draft version of the *United Nations Declaration on the Rights of Indigenous Peoples* both ethnocide and cultural genocide were included. This draft version is as follows:

> Indigenous peoples have the collective and individual right not to be subjected to ethnocide or cultural genocide, including prevention and redress for:
>
> Any action which has the aim or effect of depriving them of their integrity as distinct peoples, or of their cultural values or ethnic identities;

30 Office of the UN Special Adviser on the Prevention of Genocide (OSAPG), 'Analysis Framework'.

> Any action which has the aim or effect of dispossessing them of their lands, territories or resources;
>
> Any form of population transfer which has the aim or effect of violating or undermining any of their rights;
>
> Any form of assimilation or integration by other cultures or ways of life imposed on them by legislative, administrative or other measures;
>
> Any form of propaganda directed against them.[31]

The UN General Assembly adopted the *Declaration on the Rights of Indigenous Peoples* in September 2007, but, like the *Genocide Convention*, dropped both terms—ethnocide and cultural genocide—from the finalized version. Article 8, however, of the final document remains basically unchanged from the draft version above:

> 1. Indigenous peoples and individuals have the right not to be subjected to forced assimilation or
>
> destruction of their culture.
>
> 2. States shall provide effective mechanisms for prevention of, and redress for:
>
> (a) Any action which has the aim or effect of depriving them of their integrity as distinct peoples, or of their cultural values or ethnic identities;
>
> (b) Any action which has the aim or effect of dispossessing them of their lands, territories
>
> or resources;
>
> (c) Any form of forced population transfer which has the aim or effect of violating or undermining any of their rights;
>
> (d) Any form of forced assimilation or integration;
>
> (e) Any form of propaganda designed to promote or incite racial or ethnic discrimination directed against them.

---

31 *Draft United Nations declaration on the rights of indigenous peoples*, 1994/45.

In article 7(2), it is stated that 'Indigenous peoples have the collective right to live in freedom, peace, and security as distinct peoples and shall not be subjected to any act of genocide or any other act of violence'. This means that indigenous peoples are legally protected from both cultural and biological genocide according to international law.[32]

Although the UN does not have an official definition of 'indigenous', in a United Nations factsheet on indigenous peoples it is stated that indigenous peoples are

> the descendants…of those who inhabited a country or a geographical region at the time when people of different cultures or ethnic origins arrived. The new arrivals later became dominant through conquest, occupation, settlement or other means.[33]

Likewise, in the 2008 annex of the *Declaration on the Rights of Indigenous Peoples*, it states that

> indigenous peoples have suffered from historic injustices as a result of, inter alia, their colonization and dispossession of their lands, territories and resources, thus preventing them from exercising, in particular, their right to development in accordance with their own needs and interests.

In other words, being historically subject to colonisation and becoming a minority in one's own land are requisites to be considered an indigenous people by the UN. Also, in the annex it is stated that 'indigenous peoples are equal to all other peoples, while recognizing the right of all peoples to be different, to consider themselves different, and to be respected as such' and that 'all peoples contribute to the diversity and richness of civilizations and cultures'. So, various peoples give rise to human diversity in the world as they are distinct and different from each other, and these differences must be respected and are preserved under the law.[34]

32 UN, Declaration on the Rights of Indigenous Peoples, 10, 5.

33 United Nations Permanent Forum on Indigenous Issues, 'Who are Indigenous Peoples?'

34 UN, Declaration on the Rights of Indigenous Peoples, 1–2.

Returning to the 2007 *Declaration on the Rights of Indigenous Peoples*, we find that in addition to human rights, indigenous peoples 'possess collective rights which are indispensable for their existence, well-being and integral development as peoples'. These collective rights are similar to immigrant multicultural rights in that they recognize the importance of group rights and the need for collectivity for the well-being and development of the group, while, at the same time, possessors of group rights also have the possibility of full participation in liberal democratic societies. In other words, indigenous peoples have two sets of rights (collective and liberal democratic), and this creates two world spheres or ways of life and two identities based on particularity (ethnic) and universalism (national). Yet, in comparison to multicultural rights that do not allow autonomy and self-government for immigrant minorities, in article 4 of the declaration it is stated that indigenous peoples 'in exercising their right to self-determination, have the right to autonomy and self-government in matters relating to their internal and local affairs, as well as means and ways of enhancing their autonomous functions', and in article 9 it is declared that 'Indigenous peoples and individuals have the right to belong to an indigenous community or nation, in accordance with the traditions and customs of the community or nation concerned'. This means that indigenous peoples have the collective right to govern themselves according to their cultural norms and to form distinct ethnically closed communities or nations.[35]

Furthermore, according to article 11 (1) of the declaration, indigenous peoples have the right to 'maintain, protect and develop the past, present and future manifestations of their cultures', and in article 12(1) and 13 (1) they have the 'right to revitalize, use, develop and transmit to future generations their histories, languages, oral traditions, philosophies, writing systems and literatures' and to 'establish and control their educational systems and institutions…in a manner

35 Ibid, 4, 6.

appropriate to their cultural methods of teaching and learning'. This means that indigenous peoples have the right to control their cultural knowledge and its dissemination to next generations. In articles 18 and 19 it is stated that 'indigenous peoples have the right to participate in decision-making in matters which would affect their rights' and must give their 'free, prior and informed consent' before states adopt and implement 'legislative or administrative measures that may affect them'. In other words, actions taken by the State that have the possibility of affecting indigenous rights must be approved by indigenous peoples prior to their implementation.[36]

Article 26 states that 'indigenous peoples have the right to the lands, territories and resources which they have traditionally owned, occupied or otherwise used or acquired', and they have the right to 'control' these lands and resources due to their 'traditional ownership or other traditional occupation or use' of them. In addition, 'States shall give legal recognition and protection to these lands, territories and resources'. This means that claims and control over lands, territories, and resources by indigenous peoples is recognized and protected by the State because of indigenous peoples' ancestral or traditional ties to these goods. In article 32(3), it is declared that indigenous peoples must approve of any State projects that affect their lands, resources, and territories and States must provide 'appropriate measures…to mitigate adverse environmental, economic, social, cultural or spiritual impact' that has arisen as a result of these activities. In other words, actions taken by the State that may affect both the rights and the goods of indigenous peoples must be approved by them prior to their implementation and any negative impact on the rights and goods after implementation must be allayed by the State.[37]

In article 23, it is stated that 'indigenous peoples have the right to determine their own identity or membership in accordance with their

36 UN, Declaration on the Rights of Indigenous Peoples, 6–8.

37 Ibid, 10, 12.

customs and traditions', and in article 34 it is declared that 'indigenous peoples have the right to promote, develop and maintain their institutional structures and their distinctive customs, spirituality, traditions, procedures, practices and … juridical systems or customs'. This means that indigenous peoples have the right to self-identify and can decide what that identity represents, and can develop and maintain their own distinct institutions that reflect this identity, including their customs, traditions, ways of life, etc., without external interference. And, finally, in article 43, it is stated that '[t]he rights recognized herein constitute the minimum standards for the survival, dignity and well-being of the indigenous peoples of the world'. In other words, the aim of indigenous rights is the protection of the existence of indigenous peoples in a physically and mentally healthy way for the long-term and the acknowledgement that this requires recognizing them as distinct peoples who have the right to remain collectively different and to develop their own institutions and communities/nations without external interference. It also means that indigenous peoples have traditional claims to particular territory and resources, which they have full control over, including who can enter and access such land and resources.[38]

38 UN, Declaration on the Rights of Indigenous Peoples, 9, 12, 14.

16. POLITICAL AND DEMOGRAPHIC ENGINEERING IN EUROPE

> 'Ethnic groups are individuals who share a common trait such as language, race or religion, a belief in a common heritage and destiny, and an association with a given piece of territory. These shared ties are often intricately connected.'[1]

THE UN *Declaration on the Rights of Indigenous Peoples* implies that to be considered indigenous and to therefore have the rights of indigenous peoples, a people need to have been colonized and dispossessed of their land, resources, and territory in the past so that today they form a minority group within a dominant State. Even though current ethnic majorities of European nations have had a regional presence in Europe for tens of thousands of years, i.e. they are indigenous to Europe, and even though, due to immigration and settlement by foreigners, they are already minorities in some of their main cities and towns and are predicted to become minorities in their own homelands before the end of this century, they are still not considered to be indigenous by the UN and other international bodies. Only when they have become *proper* minorities within their own homelands can they be recognized as indigenous to Europe and be protected by rights and laws that may preserve their kind.

1 Toft, 'Indivisible Territory, Geographic Concentration, and Ethnic War', 87.

Similar to the UN, according to the popular online encyclopedia, *Wikipedia,* indigenous European peoples means those Europeans that

> have been *marginalized* by an immigrant population in recent times. The category is not for European peoples who remain the majority *in at least part of their historical homeland*, for these, just use Category: Ethnic groups in Europe.[2]

This is an astonishing definition. According to this logic, ethnic Europeans who are in the process of becoming minorities in their own homelands due to a combination of mass-immigration and low fertility rates, but remain a majority in *part of their homelands*, are not considered indigenous because they have not been completely 'marginalized' and thus do not have indigenous rights. Only *after* they become full minorities of the population *in their homelands* in Europe — estimated to occur between 2050 and the year 2100 — will they then be recognized as the indigenous peoples of Europe and be granted collective rights and protection by international law.

Currently, Europeans only have liberal individual rights.[3] In comparison, immigrants have both individual rights and multicultural group rights, and recognized indigenous groups have special group rights as well as individual rights. Multiculturalism, as a pluralistic political and social ideology and integration model, involves policies and goals that aim to preserve ethnic diversity (of minority groups) and prevent ethnic discriminations and 'cultural jealousies' between host and immigrant populations. To this extent it promotes, or protects, the particular traditions of each minority ethnic group — immigrants are allowed to adhere to their own cultural practices, values, institutions, laws, and ways of life in general. Yet, at the same time,

2 *Wikipedia*, s.v. 'Category:Indigenous peoples of Europe', accessed July 2016, https://en.wikipedia.org/wiki/ Category:Indigenous_peoples_of_Europe (my emphasis second sentence).

3 Duchesne, 'Will Kymlicka and the Disappearing Dominion'. Also see Volume I, chapter 4, and Volume III, Part I.

multiculturalism encourages immigrants to integrate into the society as a whole, i.e. according to certain universal principles we have come to associate with liberalism and rationalism, such as the equal rights of all individuals, economic competition, equality under the law, and democracy. So, on the one hand, differences and diversities are preserved such that every culture is considered as morally valid and no one culture is perceived to have the right to impose or force its values on the others or to have central ethnic, religious, or cultural community values that are representative of the entire country; but, on the other hand, the host (Western) culture is expected to function as a neutral promoter of universal values with no particular traditions of its own. Liberalism advocates universal values and adheres to a philosophy of relativism in relation to European culture while it simultaneously endorses the rights of non-Western cultures, as associated with multiculturalism. Both multiculturalism and liberal universalism fail to acknowledge the ethnic particularism of Europeans — majority rights and ethnic European identity are not included in either of these integration schemes. This amounts to the dissolution of the ethnic character of Europe into universalism while preserving the ethnic characteristics of the non-European 'Others' into particularism.

Neoconservative assimilation and critical cosmopolitanism are similar to multiculturalism, but they go further, advocating liberal individualism for all. They attempt to erase particularistic ethnic differences and standardize distinct ethnic groups according to an abstract notion of humanity devoid of any racial, ethnic, or ancestral identifications. They deny the particularistic ethnic identity of all the distinct peoples of the world, not just Europeans. Rather than organic bonds as a regulatory force of traditional societies (elevating the community over the individual), indigenous, immigrant, and minority populations must embrace racial diversity and deracination, and abstract universal rights and values (elevating the universal individual over the bounded community) as the moral standard for all.

The creation of a global world of universal people in perpetual peace is a dangerous utopian myth that was generated by Enlightenment thinkers who were still entrenched in the religious eschatological tradition. Versions of this myth have been carried into the twenty-first century by socialists, leftists, anti-nationalists, cosmopolitanists, progressives, liberals, humanitarians, universalists, neoconservatives, and Olympians (global corporate ideology). According to James Kurth, Claude Smith Professor of Political Science at Swarthmore College, the 'Enlightened' ones envision 'a universal empire — except that it will be called global "governance" — and a universal religion — except that it will be called universal human rights'.[4] During the twentieth century, utopia was about emancipation and was found on the far left. By the end of the twentieth century utopia was mainstream political ideology that sought to bring an 'American-style democratic capitalism — the final form of human government' to all the world.[5] The American Creed was born at this time, which holds to the 'ideas of liberty and individualism, institutionalized in liberal democracy, free markets, constitutionalism, and the rule of law' and has become the concept of Western Civilization as a whole. This creed was a 'combination of American energy and European legacy' known as 'the Allied scheme of history', also known as the 'NATO scheme of history'.[6] And it is this very scheme that is imposed the world over, often through force, which claims to speak for all races of humankind, and presents solutions to the human condition in the guise of humanitarian utopian universalism. This is what is known as Western universal imperialism or Westernization, or what some people call 'Westoxification', and is propounded by neoconservatives.[7]

---

4 Kurth, 'Western Civilization: Our Tradition', 11.

5 Gray, *Black Mass: How Religion Led the World into Crisis*, 29.

6 Kurth, 'Western Civilization: Our Tradition', 7.

7 Huntington, *The Clash of Civilizations*, 101.

Neocons have 'understood that free markets would not spread throughout the world in a peaceful process', so their implementation 'would have to be assisted by the intensive application of military force'.[8] The global democratic revolution as advocated by neocons sees itself as a creative-destructive force: 'Creative destruction is our middle name' says Michael Ledeen, neoconservative foreign policy analyst. He further writes:

> We tear down the old order every day, from business to science, literature, art, architecture, and cinema to politics and the law. Our enemies have always hated this whirlwind of energy and creativity, which menaces their traditions (whatever they may be) and shames them for their inability to keep pace. Seeing America undo traditional societies, they fear us, for they do not wish to be undone. They cannot feel secure so long as we are there, for our very existence — our existence, not our politics — threatens their legitimacy. They must attack us in order to survive, just as we must destroy them to advance our historic mission.[9]

In this way, the imposition of global corporate capitalism, and all it entails under the guise of humanitarian development and progress, requires the violent intervention of the American-led West into other countries that are considered 'backward' and 'unfree'. This intervention and the destruction of existing traditional cultures, which is mirrored by the cultural Marxist march through the institutions of the West and the use of liberal immigration by critical cosmopolitanists to radically alter European nations from within, is considered justified because it makes possible the construction of modern, democratic, capitalist, and standardized systems of American-style Western living based on an idealized notion of a future federation of humanity in perpetual peace. However, this socialist-capitalism, disguised as liberalism, seeks to create the kind of people that lack private property,

---

8 Gray, *Black Mass*, 32.

9 Leeden, *The War Against the Terror Masters: Why It Happened. Where We Are Now. How'll We Win*, 212–213.

that lack individual choice, that lack a sense of traditional community bonds—people who are atomized and alienated with no history, no ethnic identity, and no nation, at the beck and call of a heavily-taxed, materialist, consumer society run by multinational companies and supranational moral agencies.

Multiculturalism, liberalism, neoconservatism, cosmopolitanism, and universalism do not afford the indigenous majorities of European nations majority rights; they have individual rights only, which is premised on the assumption that they have replaced their societal culture and traditions with liberal individualism over the last few decades. Liberal individual rights are abstract laws that claim to exist outside of or before culture and race and view 'humanity' as if all people are equal, despite their distinct ethnicity, history, and heritage. But distinct peoples and societies are not blank slates; people are grounded in, belong to, and have loyalty to their race and social-cultural group (societal group), not to an overarching set of artificial neutral rights and rules created and imposed by elites. Culture and social norms create rules and laws (organic and grassroots), and laws reinforce these; rules and laws do not create culture. But it is assumed that European ethnic peoples are (or should be) 'enlightened' ethnically impartial cosmopolitans, liberal individuals with a universal identity and therefore they don't need collective rights to preserve, celebrate, enhance, and develop their distinct traditional cultures and ethnic identities. In fact, liberal individualism has been enforced upon European peoples through pressure tactics, indoctrination by media and education institutions, mandates of multiculturalism and racial diversity, and legal punishment of dissent. As such, no obvious legal protections (such as majority rights, collective rights) currently exist to prevent indigenous Europeans from becoming ethnic minorities within their own homelands.

However, the UN itself declares that the definition of indigenous peoples is not official. A simple definition of indigeneity can be found in the *Gage Canadian Dictionary*, which states that indigenous means 'originating or produced in a particular country; growing or living naturally in a certain region, soil, climate, etc.; native'.[10] Yet the indigeneity of Europeans in European homelands does not seem to matter to establishment elites. Take, for example, Britain, where a central narrative justifying non-European mass-immigration today suggests that Britain is an immigrant nation and British people are 'mongrels'. For instance, Sandy Walkington, former Liberal Democrat candidate for St. Albans, UK, stated 'We're all mongrels. I mean, this country is the most mongrel country in the world. In 200 years we'll all be coffee-coloured and I've no problem with that'.[11] Or Eddie Izzard, who, in an attempt to justify multi-racial immigration, declared in his 2003 Discovery Channel TV series *Mongrel Britain* that 'our country, after all, has been massively diverse for most of its history—a blend of Angles, Saxons, Romans, Vikings, Celts'.[12] This is absurd logic. Indigenous Britons have ancestral links in Britain that go back at least 11–12,000 years, just after the last ice age, and migration that occurred in history was sporadic, on a small scale over thousands of years, and from genetically similar peoples, i.e. European. In fact, according to a 20-year Oxford University study by geneticists and archaeologists, 'Romans, Vikings and Normans may have ruled or invaded the British for hundreds of years, but they left barely a trace on our DNA'. Around 30 percent of British DNA is Anglo-Saxon (German, around 1500 years ago), meaning around 70 percent of British DNA is from settlers that arrived just after the last ice age (around 11,000 years ago) when Britain was connected to continental Europe by a land bridge. Britons living in south and central England share about 40 percent of their DNA with the French, from a migration that occurred around 10,000

10 *Gage Canadian Dictionary* (1983), s.v. 'indigenous', 593.

11 Pierce, 'Nutters, Nick Clegg? They're closer than you think'.

12 *The Free Library*, s.v. 'Eddie Izzard' (retrieved Oct 18, 2016) https://www.thefreelibrary.com/Eddie+Izzard.-a0225478286.

years ago. The southern and central English also share about 11 percent of their DNA with the Danes and 9 percent with the Belgians.[13]

A genetic map of Britain also shows that tribes in 600 AD are almost identical to regional genetic variability now, which suggests that local communities have been living in the same areas for at least 1400 years. Other genetic and archaeological studies have found that the vast majority of British people have ancestors going back thousands of years.[14] One example is Cheddar Gorge Man. His bones were excavated in 1903 and they were found to be from 7150 BC, or just over 9,000 years ago. His DNA was analysed in 1993 and people from the nearby Cheddar village had exact matches, meaning that they were direct descendants and still lived in the same area.[15] In other words, British DNA is found to be rooted in thousands of years of history and regional identities, complemented by DNA from close European neighbours just across the Channel (with only subtle differences in genetic make-up) to the North, East, and South. This means that White Britons are indigenous to Britain; Britain is their ancestral homeland.

It is also clear, from archaeological and genetic evidence, that Europeans are native to Europe; Europe is their continental homeland. Strong genetic components of modern Europeans were already found in the Upper Paleolithic Stone Age, around 37,000 years ago, in the European continent. This was ascertained by the discovery of human skeletal remains that are between 38,700 and 36,200 years old. Eske Willerslev, the director of the Centre for GeoGenetics at the University of Copenhagen and co-author of the multiple-author

---

13 Hannah Devlin, 'Genetic study reveals 30% of white British DNA has German ancestry'; Leslie et al., 'The Fine-Scale Genetic Structure of the British Population'.

14 Kemp, *Four Flags: The Indigenous People of Great Britain;* De la Bédoyère, *Eagles Over Britannia: The Roman Army in Britain;* Alcock, *Arthur's Britain: History and Archaeology AD 367–634;* Laing and Laing, *Anglo-Saxon England;* Johnson, *Offshore Islanders: From Roman Occupation to European Entry.*

15 *Wikipedia*, s.v. 'Cheddar Man', retrieved June 2016, https://en.wikipedia.org/wiki/Cheddar_Man.

study *Genomic Structure in Europeans Dating Back at Least 36,200 Years* (2014) in the journal *Science*,[16] stated that the skeletal remains are from 'one of the oldest modern humans found in Europe' and 'all the major genetic components present in living-day Europeans were already present in Europeans 37,000 years ago'.[17] This means that, due to the stability of genes within European peoples over thousands of years on the European continent, there was very little in-migration.[18] The current situation is very different.

Today, Europeans (including Britons) have low fertility rates and are experiencing population decline. At the same time, this decline becomes relatively accelerated by the rapid emergence, concentrated urban settlement, and continuing growth of non-European minority ethnic groups and communities, particularly within Western European nation-states. These large minority ethnic groups and communities have arisen significantly in Europe only in the past 60 years as a direct result of their large-scale in-migration and high fertility rates. In addition to demographic decline, Europeans are also experiencing political decline. Establishment propaganda against European ethno-nationalism and alliances between leftists, liberals, Islamists, and non-European ethnic minority groups are rapidly altering the political culture, identities, and institutions of indigenous European nations and, as Europeans inch closer to becoming demographic minorities within their own homelands, their legitimacy for majority rule and political sovereignty weakens.

Such rapid changes to the ethnic compositions and political structures of European nations are directly related to the EU project. This leftist-liberal elite-imposed project is a deliberate plan to create

16 Seguin-Orlando et al., 'Genomic Structure in Europeans Dating Back at Least 36,200 years'.

17 '37 000-year-old European DNA Identical to Modern Day Europeans', YouTube video.

18 Law, 'The European Race Evolved in the European Continent — Relatively Recently'.

a cosmopolitan open society based on global economics, the ethnic/racial mixing of European populations through mass-immigration and settlement, multicultural immigrant rights and universal values, and an ethnically neutral European identity constructed around liberal individualism and universal rights. Such a project 'unbundles' and 'decouples' European ethnic groups from their national identity, dispossesses them of their right to sovereignty over their homeland territory, renders them minorities within their own homelands, neglects to afford them the rights to protect, preserve, celebrate, and enhance their traditional ways of life and their very existence in the long-term, and creates the conditions for civil war. As such, the current 'European project' is contrary to international laws, particularly those that protect against the destruction, 'in whole or in part', of national, ethnic, racial, or religious groups; thus, it can be understood as a form of genocide against indigenous Europeans.

There are three main consequences of the EU project and its affiliates that contribute to the genocide of European peoples: 1) the acceleration of European indigenous peoples becoming demographic minorities in their historic homelands; 2) the acceleration of native Europeans becoming political minorities in their nation-states; and 3) declining social cohesion and an increase in the likelihood of civil war. The following chapters provide a detailed discussion and critique of these consequences, guided by the international laws and legal definitions described in chapter 15 and the research and theories of several eminent scholars: Myron Weiner, Michael Teitelbaum, Monica Duffy Toft, Anthony M. Messina, James F. Hollifield, Dominic Johnson, Sharon Stanton Russell, and Kelly Greenhill.

16.1 Consequence One: European Demographic Decline

As discussed in Volumes I and II, prior to WWII, emigration rather than immigration characterized the history of most European countries, and

> when immigration did occur it was mainly intra-European. This changed in the post-WWII era of decolonisation and cheap labour power needs in Europe. In the late 1940s and during the 1950s various European nations granted citizenship to some of their former colonized subjects, and in the 1960s temporary work permits were granted to low skilled non-European peoples through 'guest worker' recruitment programs. Although both of these practices ended shortly after they began, many migrants decided to stay in European nations and immigration continued under family reunification and human rights laws.

A central reason given by European elites today to justify large-scale immigration into Europe is the low fertility rate and aging of Europeans, which have led to demographic decline, rising tax burdens, and decreases in both economic and political European power at the global level.[19] In order to remain a power hub on the world stage, it is argued that the number of people in Europe can be increased through demographic engineering, that is, the importation of a replacement population through large-scale immigration. At the turn of the twenty-first century, the United Nations (UN) released a report titled *Replacement Migration: Is It a Solution to Declining and Ageing Population?* According to this report, 'Replacement migration refers to the international migration that would be needed to offset declines in the size of population, the declines in the population of working age, as well as to offset the overall ageing of a population'.[20]

In one of its five scenarios, the UN report estimated the migration required 'to maintain the size of the working-age population (15 to 64 years) at the highest level it would reach in the absence of migration

---

19 Bershidsky, 'Europe Doesn't Have Enough Immigrants'; Citrin and Sides, 'European Immigration'; *Deutschland*, 'Germany needs more immigrants'; Merritt, 'The refugee crisis'; Piketty, 'For an open Europe'; Portes, 'Immigration Is Good for Economic Growth'; *RT News*, 'Germany needs 500,000 migrants a year until 2050'; University of California, 'Migration and Refugee'; Weiner and Teitelbaum, *Political Demography, Demographic Engineering*.

20 UN, *Replacement Migration: Is it a Solution to Declining and Ageing Population?* Executive Summary, 1.

after 1995'. In this scenario, the net number of migrants required for the EU between the years 2000 and 2050 would be around 80 million, or about 1.6 million per year. Another scenario 'to maintain the potential support ratio (PSR), i.e., the ratio of the working-age population (15 to 64 years) to the old-age population (65 years or older), at the highest level it would reach in the absence of migration after 1995', the net number of migrants required by the EU between 2000 and 2050 would be almost 700 million or around 13.5 million per year.[21] If the first UN scenario were implemented, then by 2050 roughly one-sixth of the EU population will be foreign-born (immigrants) with many more millions being second, third, fourth etc. non-European generations, possibly a quarter or more of the EU population. If the second scenario were implemented, then the entire EU population that exists today (Europeans and non-European post-war immigrants) will be completely overshadowed by a larger population of newer non-European immigrants, spelling the rapid and complete end of a European Europe.

A UN press release on the report[22] declared that for the EU to prevent total population decline it will need to continue with immigration levels of the 1990s. In the 1990s, gross immigration of non-EU migrants to the EU was around 1.7 million a year, which includes a conservative estimate of illegal migrants.[23] Therefore, according to the UN, the EU will 'roughly' follow the first scenario above of replacement population. Currently the EU has a net migration level of around 1.6 million people a year, which reflects this UN scenario, but it does not include the millions of irregular migrants that have entered Europe during the last few years of the 'migrant crisis'.[24]

---

21 Ibid, 2.

22 United Nations, 'New Report on Replacement Migration Issued by UN Population Division'.

23 Rossi, 'Managed Diversity', 121.

24 See chapter Volume II, chapter 7. Also see: Commission of the European Communities, 'Meeting social needs in an ageing society'; De Lima et al,

So where will the replacement migrants originate from to save Europe from demographic decline? According to political demographers and scholars of international migration and ethnic conflict, Myron Weiner and Michael S. Teitelbaum, 'high fertility in some countries and low fertility in others produce what might be termed the *demographic differential hypothesis*, in which it is the magnitude and longevity of differential fertility rates between countries that substantially determine international population movements'.[25] This means that because all European-based countries in the world have low fertility rates and are undergoing demographic decline, the source of foreign-worker immigration into Europe has to be from countries with high fertility rates and a young population. Typically, these countries are in the developing world, i.e. Africa, Asia, and the Middle East, and therefore are little different from the initial post-WWII source countries of immigration. In sum, mass-immigration into Europe of a cheap, young, and willing non-European labour force, a 'replacement population', is a deliberate engineering policy of European governments to offset demographic decline and to secure their power on the world stage.

In reality, mass-immigration into Europe is not really about demographic-economic decline. This is evident from the fact that since the mid-1970s the overwhelming majority of immigrants that have arrived in European nations have come for family not economic reasons.[26] Family reunification for immigrants and refugees[27] and marriage

---

'Migration and the EU'.

25 Weiner and Teitelbaum, *Political Demography, Demographic Engineering*, 87–88 (emphasis in the original).

26 Eurostat, 'All valid permits by reason on 31 December of each year'; International Organization for Migration, *Compendium of Migrant Integration Policies;* Messina, *The Logics of Politics of Post-WWII Migration to Western Europe.* Also see Volume II.

27 Brenner, 'A Family Reunification Dilemma for the EU'; European Union, Council Directive 2003/86/EC.

migration (often arranged marriages, not previous spouses) are based on human rights[28] and have resulted in perpetual chain migration.[29] Immigration in this form will not stop, as attempts to regulate such flows are limited by pro-immigration laws and lobbies, human rights laws, and an army of immigration attorneys.[30] In this sense, the main reason for immigration into Europe now becomes a matter of human rights, not economic or demographic decline. And, as most people are aware, immigrants in Europe are predominantly from Islamic countries in the Arab, African, and Asian regions of the world and Islam is now the fastest growing religion in Europe. Historian Philip Jenkins estimated that Muslims will constitute around 25 percent of the total European population by 2100. In contrast, historian Bernard Lewis projected that Europe would be Islamic by the end of the century.[31]

28 The Council Directive 2004/83/EC (EU, 2004) and the Directive 2011/95/EU (EU, 2011), EU Primary Law Articles 7, 9, and 33 of the Charter of Fundamental Rights of the European Union (EU, 2012), International Human Rights Law Articles 12 and 16 of the Universal Declaration of Human Rights (United Nations, 1948), Articles 17, 23, and 24 of the International Covenant on Civil and Political Rights (United Nations, 1966/1976), Articles 10, 16, and 22 of the Convention on the Rights of the Child (UN Human Rights Office of the High Commissioner (OHCHR), 1990), Article 8 of the European Convention on Human Rights (European Court of Human Rights, 2010), and the Family Reunification Directive (FRD) (EU, 2003), all state that third country nationals (TCNs, includes refugees) have the 'right to a family life', which is possible through family reunification.

29 According to political scientist James Hollifield, '[m]igration can quickly become self-perpetuating because of chain migration and social networks' and 'individual risks and costs associated with migration are reduced by these kinship networks, which can grow into transnational communities and constitute a form of social capital'. Hollifield, 'The Emerging Migration State', 889.

30 See: Teitelbaum, 'The Role of the State', 165; Hollifield, 'The Emerging Migration State', 897.

31 Jenkins, 'Demographics, Religion, and the Future of Europe'; *Die Welt*, 'Europa wird Islamisch' [Europe is becoming Islamic]; Kettani, 'Muslim Population in Europe: 1950–2020'. Also see Volume II.

Currently, EU population growth comes from net migration. On January 1st 2015, over 34 million (7%) of the EU-28 population (508 million) were born outside of the EU,[32] with millions more being second and third generation postwar non-European immigrants. Following the first UN scenario on replacement migration, by 2050 roughly 17 percent of the EU population will be foreign-born (first generation immigrants) with many more millions being second, third, and fourth generation, together constituting between 25 and 45 percent of the EU population, with even higher percentages in some European countries.

In light of the UN project of replacement migration, current EU net migration levels, and the unprecedented numbers of irregular migrants claiming asylum in Europe, it is clear what prolific French author Renaud Camus means by 'The Great Replacement'. Camus describes this phrase as meaning the replacement of native Europeans with different peoples, i.e. with non-European immigrants. In an interview with John Lambton of the think-tank *Right On*, Camus explained that

> [t]he Great Replacement is not a concept, it is not a notion, and it is not a theory: it is only the coining of a name for the most important phenomenon to affect Europe in the last fifteen centuries: namely, the replacement of its population and the changing of people.

He further said that 'The Great Replacement' is part of a larger process that aims in

> the industrial production of *l'homme remplaçable*: replaceable man; exchangeable man; decultivated, decivilised, denationalised, and unrooted, such as needed by and for generalised exchange: of man with man, of man with woman, of people with people, of animals with things, of man with machines, with prosthesis and with objects — the post-human condition.[33]

---

32 Eurostat, 'First Population Estimates'; Eurostat, 'Migration and Migration Population Statistics'.

33 Lambton, 'The Great Replacement — Part I'.

In other words, European peoples are seen as exchangeable by pro-immigrationists; Europeans can be replaced by non-co-ethnic peoples based on the view that European nations will remain the same, or be changed for the better, without a majority of ethnic Europeans. But of course, to supplement or even replace a nation's people with non-co-ethnic peoples means that the nation will no longer be defined in terms of its original and specific common features — shared ethnicity, language, culture, and history.

16.1.1 Seven Issues with Demographic and Economic Immigration Policies

Attempts to justify large-scale immigration into Europe by demographic and economic theories run into several issues. First, low demographic growth does not necessarily mean low economic growth or declining state political power at the global level. In fact, Europe had the highest period of economic growth in the nineteenth century, when it was undergoing high emigration flows.[34] In addition, although fertility rates of non-Europeans in Europe are higher than Europeans, it is often claimed that such fertility rates will level out over time and thus the non-European population will also age, recreating the situation of demographic decline and the need for more immigration.[35] However, the levelling of non-European fertility rates in Europe has not yet occurred and large-scale immigration continues.

In June 2016, German Financial Minister Wolfgang Schäuble claimed in an interview with *Die Zeit* that if Europe does not open its doors to mass-immigration then Europeans will have to inbreed, saying 'It is isolation that would destroy us, it would lead us towards degenerating in inbreeding'.[36] This is an odd statement for various reasons. Mass-immigration into Europe is predominantly from

34 Weiner and Teitelbaum, *Political Demography, Demographic Engineering*, 7.

35 Camarota and Zeigler, 'The Declining Fertility of Immigrants and Natives'.

36 *Zeit Online*, 'Afrika wird unser Problem sein'.

Muslim-majority nations. Marriage between first cousins is a common practice of Muslims and some Muslim populations have a disproportionate number of disabilities. For example, over half of British Pakistanis marry a first cousin and are 13 times more likely to bear children with genetic disorders than the general population.[37] In terms of the world-wide population of Muslims, it is estimated that around 50 percent are inbred. According to statistical research, up to 34 percent of marriages in Algeria are blood related, as are 46 percent in Bahrain, 33 percent in Egypt, 80 percent in Nubia, 60 percent in Iraq, 64 percent in Jordan, 64 percent in Kuwait, 42 percent in Lebanon, 48 percent in Libya, 47 percent in Mauritania, 28 percent in Morocco, 56 percent in Oman, 66 percent in Palestine, 54 percent in Qatar, 67 percent in Saudi Arabia, 63 percent in Sudan, 40 percent in Syria, 39 percent in Tunisia, 54 percent in the United Arab Emirates, and 45 percent in Yemen.[38] So Schäuble wants to import large volumes of inbred immigrants and then anticipates that these immigrants will breed with native Germans to prevent their inbreeding. Miscegenation is not a trend, however, because most ethnically distinct peoples prefer to marry their own kind.[39]

In any case, mass-immigration of peoples into Europe with high fertility rates has led to a rapid growth of non-European populations in Europe that challenge existing social and political orders. Oxford University demographer David A. Coleman writes that

> [a]lthough immigration can prevent population decline, it is already well-known that it can only prevent population ageing at unprecedented, unsustainable and increasing levels of inflow, which would generate rapid population growth and eventually displace the original population from its majority position.

---

37 Reid, 'It's time to confront this taboo'; Swinford, 'First cousin marriages'; Rowlatt, 'The risks'.

38 Tadmouri et al., 'Consanguinity and Reproductive Health Among Arabs', 3 of 9.

39 Simmons, *Immigration and Canada*, 219–220.

What this means is that mass-immigration, in terms of UN demographic replacement, clearly displaces European populations in favour of a foreign work-force and high-fertility migrants. Instead of relying on immigration, Coleman suggests that the effects of population decline can be managed by other means, such as by increasing labour productivity.[40] In a similar fashion, the prime minister of Hungary, Viktor Orbán, asks if 'Europe wants to take part in a demographic race', and states that it is neither desirable nor possible that 'our population grows at the same rate as other countries in the world'. He even thinks that a smaller population size would still allow Europe to be 'liveable, viable and sustainable'. Although he agrees that aging is a problem for Europe, he repudiates immigration as a solution and instead thinks that it can be solved by successful family policies.[41]

This is not the place to analyse why European fertility rates are so low but, to put it briefly, Weiner and Teitelbaum write that 'Fertility rates can be affected by economic conditions, changing opportunities for women, tax policies, public policies toward child care, housing costs, inflation rates, and changing cultural norms'.[42] Such affects involve women entering the labour force, deferment of child birth, and propaganda campaigns of the cultural Marxist type that promote abortion, planned parenthood, and derogate traditional norms and the family. Although writing about the situation in the former Soviet Union, what Turkmenian demographer Sh. Khadyrov says may also be applicable for Europe:

> In the first half of the 1980s, a whole group of demographers supported the thesis about the necessity to do away with the demographic exclusiveness (that is high fertility) of whole peoples with the help of widespread

---

40 David Coleman, '"Replacement Migration"', 583, 594.

41 Website of the Hungarian Government, 'Interview with Prime Minister Viktor Orbán on the Kossuth Rádió programme "180 Minutes"'.

42 Weiner and Teitelbaum, *Political Demography, Demographic Engineering*, 7.

> propaganda and proliferation of modern contraceptive methods and active involvement of women in economic activity.[43]

Surely, in regard to article 16.3 of the *Universal Declaration of Human Rights*, which states that 'The family is the natural and fundamental group unit of society and is entitled to protection by society and the State', there are reasons to bring European fertility rates back up to replacement levels, rather than rely on a foreign source of fertility and labour power (non-European migrants).

The second issue regarding attempts to justify large-scale immigration into Europe by demographic and economic theories is, as discussed in Volume II, the fact that the majority of immigrants that have arrived in European nations over the last fifty years or so are not economic migrants but family members making up a form of chain migration. These migrants are predominantly from non-European speaking, low education, rural, and religiously traditional areas in Africa and the Middle East. Since the 1970s, when labour recruitment programs were ended and restrictive immigration laws were implemented due to high unemployment, migrant unrest, and economic recessions, immigration continued anyway. The main reason was the 'right to family reunification' (which also includes marriage migration). Immigrants that resided in Europe as temporary 'guest workers' and refused to be repatriated despite various attempts by national governments, brought over their wives, children, and other family members, a process that has continued and become one of the main reasons for immigration into Europe today.[44] Such a form of immigration is not economic-based migration. In addition, as also discussed in Volume II, a significant portion of migration to European countries is in the form of asylum seekers. Refugees and those with subsidiary protection also have the right to family reunification, although there

43 As cited in ibid, 35.

44 *Europa*, 'Family Reunification'; EUR-Lex, Council Directive 2003/86/EC of 22 September 2003 on the Right to Family Reunification.

are various limitations to this practice.[45] Such a form of immigration exists due to international humanitarian laws and is not based on the economic needs of the host countries.

In other words, both family migration and asylum-seeking migration, two of the main sources of immigration into Europe, are non-economic in nature. Furthermore, statistics have consistently shown that foreign-born populations in Europe are generally low-skilled, low-educated, and low-qualified in comparison to native born populations. To be viable contributors to the European workforce they thus require European education, language, and other training courses, which are costly programs. Moreover, numerous studies have revealed that immigrants can take several years or even generations to gain employment or come close to the employment rate of natives. As such, many immigrants draw off social services and welfare without having contributed to society at all, and, as such, are a fiscal burden rather than a benefit.[46]

A third issue with justifying immigration by demographic and economic theories is that although immigrants may find employment as low-skilled cheap labourers, they often compete for such jobs with natives (particularly the poor and students) and may also monopolize low-income jobs. Such low-wage job competition inadvertently decreases already low wages.[47] Having a large low-skilled migrant population means there are more people willing to work for low wages and a continuously growing supply of cheap labour not only means there may be more demand for jobs than can be supplied, it also may lead employers to establish even lower wages, which affects both migrants and natives alike, who are both pushed out of jobs by newer arrivals willing to work for even less money. It is often said that

---

45 Brenner, 'A Family Reunification Dilemma for the EU'; also see Volume II, Part II.

46 See Volume II, chapters 9, 10 and 11.

47 Durch, 'Keepers of the Gates', 111.

'immigrants do jobs that natives won't do',[48] but this is misleading. It is more accurate to say that natives do not want to do particular jobs for a low wage or lowered wages after decades of activism for a fair wage, activism which is rapidly undermined by immigrants who will take an even lower wage for the same job. In sum, the mass-immigration of low-skilled cheap labourers increases unemployment levels, lowers wages, and puts more pressure on the welfare system.

To be clear, those that economically profit from immigration into Europe are not the mass of working-class Europeans. Those who do benefit fall under the category 'International Migration as a Business', which includes immigration attorneys, labor recruiters, non-profit religious and/or humanitarian organizations, foreign student recruiters, contractors (construction and services), multinational firms, and labor contractors. There are also unlawful people and organizations that financially profit from migration, such as human traffickers and smugglers, as well as unlawful 'immigration consultants' and farm labour contractors, as well as other employers that employ illegals for cheap labour.[49]

A fourth issue is the fact that mass-immigration from non-European countries in terms of 'population replacement' means also the importation of different cultures, identities, and behaviours that contrast with those of Europeans, and threaten to discredit and to replace the cultures, identities, and values of Europe. What is a nation if it is not defined in terms of its common features: ethnicity, language, culture, and history? Members of a nation are not interchangeable; you cannot replace a nation's people with people from other nations, for this would mean that the nation would no longer be defined in terms of its original common features or made up of its original members. In an interview with Red Ice Radio (2015), president of the European Centre

---

48 Legrain, *Immigrants: Your Country Needs Them*, 72; Citrin and Sides, 'European', 352.

49 Weiner and Teitelbaum, *Political Demography, Demographic Engineering*, 91–93.

for Information Policy and Security (ECIPS), Ricardo Baretzky, stated that the most pressing problem with mass-immigration is that

> Europe has its own background, its own history. You cannot replace a population by measures that is [sic] bound to fail. The biggest problem with this particular concept of population replacement or management is that of, well, we are mixing cultural backgrounds, we are mixing the change of cultural values. Then what is the point in the first place to develop and invest in our cultural values? What a lot of people forget, is that with different nations come different cultures, with different cultures come psychological behaviours and with psychological behaviours comes identity. And the danger is that when this identity is threatened by putting the force of the identities together, it is an absolute recipe for disaster. I cannot see that that would succeed, unless one stronger identity succeeds. And that's the threat to the values that we face.[50]

The continuous large-scale arrival of ethnically distinct peoples into European nations, whether through demographic engineering or chain-migration, significantly transforms the ethno-cultural compositions or identity-group ratios of European nation-state populations and brings ethno-politics into the mainstream. Many, if not most, foreign-born populations in Europe are Muslims who are ethnically and culturally distinct from Europeans and hold vastly different views of the world, views that are often mired in anti-Western and anti-European rhetoric. Backed by multicultural EU elites, Muslims in Europe tend to strongly retain and promote their own traditions, way of life, ethno-religious identity, and law, and tend not to integrate into liberal democratic Europe. In addition, as presented in other chapters, Muslims tend to have higher fertility rates than native Europeans, as well as higher crime and incarceration rates, lower educational and skill levels, and higher welfare dependency. All of these factors result in costly social, cultural, political, and racial problems to European nations in the short and long-term.

---

50 'Insight—Migrant Crisis: ISIS & The Security Threat to Europe', YouTube video (Red Ice Insight).

A fifth issue is population growth, particularly if it is from rapid mass-immigration, which contributes to environmental degradation and strains resources, such as housing, land, transportation, health-care and social services, sanitation and waste management, food, water, and education, and as such, produces resource scarcities and costly infrastructure programs and developments that damage the environment.[51] André Welti, secretary of ECOPOP, an environmentalist organization based in Switzerland, wrote that 'With the region already overpopulated, massive immigration cannot be a solution to these problems'. ECOPOP has estimated that the carrying capacity of Western and Central Europe is around 300 million people with modest consumption, far smaller than the current population of 445 million.[52]

A sixth issue is that many economic immigrants send a large portion of their wages in the form of remittances to their families in their homeland. These remittances help the economies of developing nations, but also tends to increase immigration from these countries as people seek higher paid jobs in wealthier First World nations. They also effect the service sectors of the host country as the consumption of migrants focuses on remittances rather than service goods.[53] Remittances also lower native wages. According to William W. Olney, associate professor of Economics at Williams College, 'a one percent increase in remittances depress the wages of native workers by 0.06%. Furthermore, remittances predominantly affect workers in non-traded industries that are more reliant on domestic consumption'. He explains that 'as remittances increase, the consumer base shrinks, and domestic wages decline. Furthermore, since non-traded industries are more dependent on local consumption, remittances will have a more

51 Krebs and Levy, 'Demographic Change and the Sources of International Conflict', 86.

52 Tarmann, 'The Flap Over Replacement Migration'.

53 Baas and Melzer, 'The Macroeconomic Impact of Remittances', 21–22.

negative impact on the wages of workers in these industries'.[54] Again, it is not the native Europeans that financially benefit from immigration, but employers, corporate elites, and other business interests.

Most important is the seventh issue, namely that indigenous Europeans are rapidly becoming minorities within their own historic homelands due to non-European mass-immigration (replacement population). This is already well known. On September 3rd, 2000, the British *Guardian* newspaper titled an article 'The Last Days of a White World' by Anthony Browne, the director of the UK think-tank *Policy Exchange*. In this article, Browne states that 'around the world, whites are falling as a proportion of population' and, citing an unnamed demographer, he writes that in Britain 'It's a matter of pure arithmetic that, if nothing else happens, non-Europeans will become a majority and whites a minority in the UK. That would probably be the first time an indigenous population has *voluntarily* become a minority in its historic homeland'. It is my view that, on the contrary, it is against natural inclinations, evolutionary theory, history, polls, and surveys to declare that native Brits and other indigenous Europeans are 'voluntarily' accepting the fact that they are becoming a minority within their own homelands due to large-scale non-European immigration. In fact, the program of mass-immigration has been publicly opposed by a significant number, if not majority, of indigenous Europeans since at least the 1980s, and public outcry has increased rapidly in recent decades.[55] Such opposition has been portrayed as racist, bigoted, neo-Nazi, and even criminalized. It is obvious that indigenous Europeans are not willfully becoming minorities in their own nations; they really don't have a choice in the matter.

The article by Browne further reports that the chairman of the British National Party, Nick Griffin, said 'I don't think there's any doubt that within this century, white people will be a minority in

54 Olney, 'Remittances and the Wage Impact of Immigration', 30.

55 See Volume II.

every country in the world' and that 'Every people under the sun have a right to their place under the sun, and the right to survive. If people predicted that Indians would be a minority in India in 2100, everyone would be calling it genocide'.[56] Lee Jasper, race relations adviser and non-White British citizen, disagrees with the concerns of Griffin, stating that 'There is no way that ethnicity of blood can be tied to a specific geographic place in a global world. You can no longer look at ethnic states, saying that Germany is Anglo-Saxon and so on'.[57] But this assertion by Lee not only ignores global trends towards re-indigenisation and anti-globalism (see chapter 8.3), it ignores the fundamental rights of European indigenous peoples and nations and the archaeological and genetic evidence described above. All European nations were overwhelmingly ethnically homogeneous before the program of non-European mass-immigration began in the 1950s and 1960s. It is only over the course of a few decades, in comparison to *thousands of years of history*, that European nations have swiftly become ethnically mixed and indigenous Europeans have become a rapidly decreasing demographic majority. This dramatic ethnic and demographic transformation of European homelands was not discussed with or approved by the European peoples themselves and has been opposed publicly since at least the 1980s.

16.1.2 Demographic Minorities through Immigration

Significant inflows of immigrants into European nations, both controlled and uncontrolled, demographically transforms and accelerates the rate of decline of indigenous European ethnic groups.[58] On the one hand, the ethnic compositions of European populations are radically changed by rapid and large-scale non-European mass-immigration.[59]

---

56 Browne, 'The last days of a white world' (my emphasis).

57 Ibid.

58 Weiner and Teitelbaum, *Political Demography, Demographic Engineering*, 36, 41, 65.

59 Ibid, 42.

On the other hand, low-fertility ethnic Europeans are increasingly becoming, relative to the swift growth of high-fertility immigrant populations, a declining demographic within their own nations. Demographic research shows that within a period of just 60 years native Europeans have already become minorities within a number of key cities and areas in their nations because of immigration and are expected to become full minorities within their homelands by the end of the twenty-first century. This means that in less than 150 years, from the onset of non-European immigration in the 1950s and 60s to the late twenty-first century, European nations will have transformed from being overwhelmingly homogeneous (i.e. ethnically European) to being majority non-European.

Writing in 2006, Coleman suggested that because of low fertility rates and mass-immigration, European countries are going through a 'third demographic transition' involving 'a radical transformation of the composition of their societies and the *cessation* of a specific [i.e. European] heritage'.[60] Indeed, replacement migration means more than European demographic decline to a minority ethnic group; it can also mean that immigrants are used 'to top up total numbers as the aboriginal population diminishes and eventually *disappears*'.[61] Not anticipating the 2015/2016 migrant crisis, in 2009 Coleman estimated that the population of first-generation immigrants and their children (second generation) in Germany will reach around 23 percent of the total population by 2050, and around 33 percent in Sweden.[62] However, the percentage of foreigners in Germany and Sweden is likely to be much higher as this estimate does not include post-war immigrants and their descendants who have been naturalized and are no longer counted in census statistics as immigrants. In 2010, Coleman predicted that White Britons, who are already a minority in

60 Coleman, 'Immigration and ethnic change in low fertility countries', 428–429, (my emphasis).

61 Ibid, 403 (my emphasis).

62 Coleman, 'Divergent Patterns in the Ethnic Transformation of Societies', 452.

various cities throughout Britain, will become a minority in Britain before 2070; he further stated that 'it would have occurred in younger age-groups and major urban areas rather earlier than that'.[63] This is because the majority of immigrants are young, have high fertility rates, and settle in urban rather than rural areas; the same applies to most European countries.

In 2011 Giampaolo Lanzieri, senior expert at the Statistical Office of the European Union (EUROSTAT), estimated that by 2061 Luxembourg, Austria, Spain, Belgium, Ireland, Germany, Greece, Portugal, and Italy could have foreign populations between 40 and 75 percent of their total populations; the UK, Sweden, Denmark, and the Netherlands could have foreign populations between 32 and 39 percent of their total populations; and France and Finland could have foreign populations between 20 and 22 percent. Lanzieri also estimated that by 2061 the percentage of the population of the EU with a foreign background could be around 35 percent.[64] These estimates, for both individual countries and the EU as a whole, are only based on data about migrant country of birth and their descendants beginning in 2008, and thus do not include immigrants and their descendants before this date. So, it can be assumed that the estimated foreign populations of individual countries in Europe and the EU overall will likely be much, much higher than Lanzieri predicted for 2061. Already in 2012, around two-thirds of the foreign population in the EU-27 were non-EU citizens.[65]

According to statistical information and estimates discussed in Volume II, in comparison to the predictions made by Coleman and Lanzieri above, around 20 to 30 percent of the populations of Belgium, Britain, France, Sweden, and Germany are of immigrant background already. For example, in Belgium around 25 percent or more of the

63 Coleman, *Immigration, Population, and Ethnicity: The UK in International Perspective*, 8.

64 Lanzieri, 'Fewer, older and multicultural?' 21, 31.

65 Vasileva, 'Nearly two-thirds of the foreigners living in EU Member States'.

population have an immigrant background, including second and third generations, and in 2021, around 30 percent of the population were not considered 'purely Belgian'. In 2012, 62 percent of the population of the capital city of Brussels, also the seat of the European Union, were of foreign origin and by 2021 'more than 80 percent' had 'a foreign background'. In 2010, Muslims made up between 10 and 49 percent of nineteen cities in Belgium, with Molenbeek set to become the first majority Muslim city by 2030. Currently, Muslims make up around 8 percent of the national population, and it is estimated they will constitute over 10 percent by 2030. In 2021, Mohamed was the number one baby name in Brussels and of the top ten names for boys in the capital city, '43 percent were...traditional Islamic names'.[66]

In Britain, White Britons are already a minority in various towns and cities, such as London, Leicester, Luton, and Slough, and many other major urban centers are quickly following suit, such as Birmingham and Manchester.[67] Immigrants are increasingly moving into rural areas, too, such that in 2011 only 800 wards out of 8850 were over 98 percent White; this is an extremely large decline since 2001, when there were 5000 such wards.[68] In 2008, less than two-thirds, or 63.6 percent, of new-born babies born in England and Wales were White British and by 2019 this had dropped to less than three-fifths, or 59.1 percent.[69] In 1991 Whites, including non-British Whites, made up 94.1 percent of the UK population and just 20 years later they had

66 Please see Volume II for more information about foreign-born, native-born, and other demographic statistics in the five countries mentioned. Also see: ReMix News staff, 'Mohamed races ahead as most common boy name in Brussels last year' and P. Magazine, '32,1 procent van de Belgen is geen "Belgische Belg"'.

67 Birmingham City Council, 'Census 2011'; Office for National Statistics, 'Table KS201EW: 2011 Census'.

68 Electronic Immigration Network, 'Demos'.

69 Hickley, 'Only two in three babies born in England and Wales are white British'; Office for National Statistics (ONS), 'Births and infant mortality by ethnicity, England and Wales (2007–2019).'

dropped to 87 percent. White Britons decreased from 87.1% of the population of England and Wales in 2001 to 80.5% in 2011 and to 78.4 percent in 2019.[70] In 2016 20 percent or more of the population in Britain was of immigrant background and by 2019, 9.5 million people were not British born; of these people 62 percent, or 5.9 million, were not born in the EU either. By 2021, the non-EU-born population had grown to 6.1 million.[71] And the Muslim population in Britain is growing also, estimated to reach around 10 percent by 2030. In 2018 around 3.4 million Muslims lived in Britain or 5.1 percent of the total population and by 2021 the estimated Muslim population was 4.13 million people or 6.3 percent of the total population.[72] Since 2009 the most popular name for new-born boys in Britain has been various spellings of Mohammed.[73]

In 2004, 85 percent of the population of France were of European origin, including the ethnic French. In 2008 around 20 percent of the total population were immigrants and their direct descendants (children, and not third or fourth generations), a percentage that is likely much higher today, possibly around 25 percent of the total population. An estimate of the ethnic minority population in France,

---

70 ONS, 'Table KS201EW: 2011 Census'; ONS, 'Population estimates by ethnic group and religion, England and Wales: 2019'; ONS, '2011 Census: Key statistics'; ONS, 'Ethnicity and national identity in England and Wales: 2011'; Somerville, Sriskandarajah, & Latorre, *United Kingdom: A Reluctant Country of Immigration*.

71 ONS, 'Population of the UK by country of birth and nationality: 2019'; ONS, 'Population of the UK by country of birth and nationality: year ending June 2021'.

72 ONS, 'Muslim population in the UK'; Statista Research Department, 'Islam in the UK — Statistics & Facts'.

73 In 2021, Muhammad continued to be the most popular baby name in Britain. See: Monica Greep, 'Revealed: The most popular baby names of 2021 so far'. Please also see Volume II for more information on the demographics of Britain.

going back three generations, for 2011 was 30 percent.[74] However, it was estimated that 27 percent of all new-borns in France in 2005 were non-White, rising to 31.5 percent in 2010, 34.4 percent in 2012, 35.7 percent in 2013, and is probably around 40 percent or higher today.[75] In the Paris region alone in 2013, 67.9 percent of newborns descended from non-Europeans, rising to 73 percent in 2015.[76] In 2020, the foreign-born population (which does not include their children who are born in France) was estimated to be 12.7 percent of the total population of France.[77] As for the Muslim population of France, it stands at around 10 percent. The city of Roubaix is over 50 percent Muslim, as is the county of Seine-Saint-Denis (part of the greater Paris region) and Marseilles is set to become majority Muslim in the very near future. In 2019, nearly 22 percent of newborns in France were given Islamic names, up from 18.5 percent in 2015.[78]

In Sweden, over 22 percent of the population in 2015 were of foreign origin, and it was predicted that by 2030 a third of the population will be foreign-born. In 2020, over 2 million of the total population of Sweden were foreign-born and almost 640,000 were Swedish-born with two foreign-born parents, together equalling 25.9 percent of the total population in Sweden.[79] In 2012, births to foreign-born mothers in Sweden amounted to 25.7 percent of all births, with this rising to 26.2 percent in 2013, 26.7 percent in 2014, 27.1 percent in 2015, and

74 Tribalat. 'Une estimation des populations d'origine étrangère en France en 2011'.

75 Martine, 'Drépanocytose: la carte du grand remplacement mise à jour + projection sur 35 ans (rediff)'.

76 Baumgartner, 'The Africanization of France…as of 2014' and Bilan D'activit, *Association Française pour le Dépistage et la Prévention des Handicaps de l'Enfant*, 63.

77 Eurostat, 'Foreign-born population by country of birth, 1 January 2020'.

78 Durocher, 'How Fast Is France's Muslim Population Growing?'

79 Statistics Sweden, 'Population in Sweden by Country/Region of Birth, Citizenship and Swedish/Foreign background, 31 December 2019 and 2020'.

30.4 percent in 2020.[80] If the births by non-ethnic Swedish-born are included, then it is likely that more than a third of all births in Sweden are foreign births. If trends continue, foreign-born births may reach around 50 percent or more of all births in Sweden before 2060, a percentage that will likely be higher if non-ethnic Swedish-born births were included. In 2020, the number of people with a foreign background[81] in Stockholm was 34 percent, in Malmo it was 47.2 percent, and in Gothenburg it was 37.5 percent.[82] The Muslim population of Sweden is between 10 and 15 percent with most living in the three largest cities, constituting over 30 percent of the population of Stockholm, over 15 percent of the population of Gothenburg, and around 25 percent of the population of Malmo. The size of the Muslim population in Sweden is likely larger today, due to high birth rates, family reunification programs, and large influxes of Muslim asylum seekers into Sweden in 2015/2016.[83]

In Germany, the foreign-born population reached 15 percent in 2011, and in 2014 it was estimated that over 12 percent were foreign born and 20 percent had a migrant background. In 2019, 21 million people had a migrant background in Germany, or 26 percent of the total population.[84] In 2020, almost 27 percent of the population had a migrant background and nearly one quarter (24.2 percent) of newborn babies had a foreign-born mother.[85] As for the Muslim popula-

80 Statistics Sweden, 'Demographic Reports: *The future population of Sweden 2012–2060*', 45; Statistics Sweden, 'Children per woman by country of birth 1970–2020 and projection 2021–2070'.

81 Foreign background means those that are foreign-born and those that are Swedish born with both parents born abroad; it does not include Swedish born with one foreign parent or their descendants, third generation etc.

82 Statistics Sweden, 'Sveriges befolkning 31 december 2020 Kommunala jämförelsetal'.

83 Please see Volume II.

84 Deutsch Welle, 'German population of migrant background rises to 21 million'.

85 Destatis, 'Births|Live births by citizenship of mother'; Statista, 'Distribution of the population* in Germany in 2020, by migration background'.

tion in Germany, they constituted around 5 percent in 2009 and 5.8 percent in 2010, and are most likely to be around 10 percent or more now due to mass-immigration, high fertility rates, and large influxes of Muslim asylum seekers and family reunification. Most Muslims in Germany reside in the main states, constituting up to 10 percent of the local populations.[86]

Since the 2015/2016 'migrant crisis', and as discussed in other chapters, Germany, more than any other country in Europe, has experienced extremely large influxes of irregular migrants claiming asylum. Professor Adorján F. Kovács of Goethe University in Frankfurt published 'Truths about the Refugee Crisis' (*Wahrheiten zur Flüchtlingskrise*) in *The European* magazine in late December 2015. In this work, he suggests that due to the unprecedented numbers of young male asylum seekers entering Germany on top of regular immigration, 'Of the 23 million people in this country who are between 20 and 35 years, approximately 11.5 million people [will] have a migration background within five years'. So half, 50 percent of all people in this age group, will not be native Germans by 2020.[87]

Native Germans, like other Europeans, will become a minority within their own homeland and this is celebrated by establishment elites. Speaking in November 2015 to Hamburg Parliament in Germany, Green politician Stefanie von Berg declared

> Our society will change. Our city [Hamburg] will change radically. I hold that in 20, 30 years there will no longer be [German] majorities in our city. That's also what (female and male) migration researchers say. We will live in a city that will thrive on having many different ethnicities. That we have plenty of people and will live in a supercultural society. This is what we will have in the future. And I want to make it very clear, especially towards those right wingers: This is a good thing![88]

---

86 Please see Volume II for more information on the demographics of Germany.

87 Kovács, 'Wahrheiten zur Flüchtlingskrise'.

88 'Green politician Dr. v. Berg: Good thing that Germans will be a minority in "supercultural" society', YouTube video.

Von Berg is right about one thing: Germans will become a minority, but in Germany as a whole rather than just Hamburg in the next few decades. Referring to statistics and experts, such as German integration expert Jens Schneider, in April 2016 an article in the *Augsburger Allgemeine* newspaper stated that one fifth of the people in Germany have 'foreign-roots' (immigrants since the 1950s and their descendants), but in urban areas this number rises dramatically. Augsburg, with a current foreign population of 43 percent and 50 percent of six-year-olds having a foreign background, will be one of the 'first major German cities where people with a migration background will form the majority population'. This is a trend that is becoming common across Germany. Two other cities, Stuttgart and Frankfurt, will join Augsburg as the first cities 'in which immigrants will become the majority'. This means that the 'country will change' irreversibly.[89]

As trends indicate, European cities will be populated by a majority of non-Europeans by 2060, with the majority of European natives living in the suburbs and rural areas. If European low fertility rates and simultaneous large-scale high-fertility non-European immigration continue, then by the end of the twenty-first century indigenous Europeans are likely to become minorities as a whole within their own homelands. Similar situations are found in most European-based countries in the world. Pew research estimates that White Americans will be a minority in the USA by 2042 and Statistics Canada estimates that almost 40 percent of the Canadian population will be visible minorities by 2036 and Whites will become a 'visible minority' by 2045.[90]

16.1.3 Majority Rule and the Homeland Principle

Ethnic transformations of European nations through large-scale and rapid mass-immigration, whereby ethnic Europeans become

89 Krogull and Stifter, 'Prognose: Zugewanderte sind in Augsburg bald in der Mehrheit'.

90 Passel, Livingston, and Cohn, 'Explaining Why Minority Births Now Outnumber White Births'; Rayne, 'Whites already "visible minorities"'.

increasing demographic minorities, can lead to what is called the 'tipping' phenomenon. Tipping is where the 'demographic situation' shifts the ethnic identity 'balance toward the settler community'.[91] Changes in the ethnic composition of nations through immigration most often lead to changes in power composition and distribution in favour of the immigrants, who become a majority. This is summed up by Coleman (2010), who said that the

> numerical reversal of [a European national] majority would symbolize transfer of power and underline a changed national identity: cultural, political, economic, and religious.... But the writing would have been on the wall long before, when the younger generation in school, college, workforce entrance, and upward had become majority ethnic.

Coleman surmised that this 'ethnic transformation... would be a major, unlooked-for, and irreversible change...unprecedented for at least a millennium'.[92] Such power transfer is aptly explained by Power Transition Theory (PTT). According to Monica Duffy Toft, professor of Government and Public Policy at the Blavatnik School of Government, PTT holds that in multiethnic or multinational states the population growth of distinct ethnic groups alter ethnic balances and challenge the control of the existing power structures.[93] Because 'ethnic groups are apt to vote as blocs' and because the basic principle of democracy is the 'notion of majority rule', demographic shifts in ethnic populations, whereby a minority becomes a majority, means that there is an exchange of power between ethnic groups based on democratic principles.[94] The democratic principle of majority rule means that if an ethnic and/or political group becomes 'quantifiable

91 Weiner and Teitelbaum, *Political Demography, Demographic Engineering*, 51.

92 David Coleman, 'Projections of the Ethnic Minority Populations of the United Kingdom', 473, 476.

93 Toft, 'Population Shifts and Civil War: A Test of Power Transition Theory', 245.

94 Ibid, 248.

and easily recognisable' as a majority group, it facilitates ethnic and/or political group mobilization and change.[95]

It is generally understood that power shifts between ethnic groups happen incrementally, but when a state suffers from low fertility rates, practices large-scale immigration from countries ethnically distinct from it, and is geographically proximate to such countries, power shifts may be more rapid and problematic.[96] Large inflows of migrants, particularly in the form of chain migration, who share common characteristics with each other in distinction to the receiving population[97] (could be African, Asian, or Arab, yet share a common religion [Islam], grievance [past colonialism, present wars, economic globalisation], and/or distaste for the host country and its inhabitants), have strong transnational identities and ties with their homelands[98] *and* high fertility rates, will rapidly expand already-settled minority populations in host nations, increase their social capital, and readily threaten to tip established ethnic-power relations.

One of the central problems embedded in European demographic decline and simultaneous non-European immigration and ethnic power tipping is the erasure of European control over their homelands. Toft explains that a territorial homeland is necessary for the

95 Toft, 'Indivisible Territory, Geographic Concentration, and Ethnic War', 91–92.

96 Weiner and Teitelbaum, *Political Demography, Demographic Engineering*, 21–22.

97 Distant in terms of ethnicity, race, and language for example. See Weiner and Teitelbaum, *Political Demography, Demographic Engineering*, 104.

98 Network theories of international migration argue that transnational social networks 'develop between migrants and their kin and neighbors in the origin country' and these 'connections reduce the risk and lower the costs (economic, psychological, and social) of subsequent migrations, thereby perpetuating and even increasing international migration flows long after the forces that began them have waned' (Weiner and Teitelbaum, *Political Demography, Demographic Engineering*, 90; see also Hollifield at footnote 11). Such was the case in the 1970s, when European nations stopped labour recruitment, yet immigration continued and increased in the form of family and marriage migration.

survival of distinct ethnic groups and is an 'indivisible attribute' of their collective identity.[99] Weiner and Teitelbaum describe a homeland as 'land [that] is not simply property with market value, but a place to which one is emotionally attached. It is not simply land, but a *home*land'.[100] In other words, distinct indigenous identities are deeply rooted and attached, culturally and historically, in their homelands, and homeland territory is foundational to the survival, development, and well-being of indigenous peoples.

Homeland territory is recognized in international law in the homeland principle, involving the right of self-determination and the right of indigenous peoples to sovereignty over their traditional lands, territories, and resources based on terms of investment (historical territorial contribution)[101] and tenure (indigeneity).[102] Loss of control over a homeland necessarily means the 'dilution of the national group, its loss of power, and consequent diminution of national identity'.[103] In the liberal-democratic multi-ethnic states of the EU, European sovereignty over their own national identities, institutions, traditions, and homelands is being increasingly challenged by non-European ethnic minorities. This is due to their increasing numbers and demands for political recognition (power tipping), as well as their desire to govern the territory in accordance with their own non-European identities and ways of life. In this situation, the size of ethnic groups really matters, as they determine who has legitimacy for national sovereignty.

According to Toft, concentrated indigenous majorities, which are 50 percent or more of the national population, have the highest form of legitimacy due to two principles: majority rule and the homeland

99 Toft, 'Territory and War', 190; Toft, 'Indivisible Territory, Geographic Concentration, and Ethnic War'.

100 Weiner and Teitelbaum, *Political Demography, Demographic Engineering*, 63.

101 This includes the development and sacrificial defense of the land.

102 Toft, 'Indivisible Territory, Geographic Concentration, and Ethnic War', 90–91.

103 Ibid, 90.

principle (indigeneity).[104] This means that because Western and Northern Europeans are still the majority ethnic group in their homelands and because they have indigeneity, they have the highest form of legitimacy for sovereignty. In terms of non-European immigrant minorities, the majority have settled and formed ethnic enclaves in urban areas in European nations and are already affecting local politics. As we have seen, numerous Muslim enclaves, for example, are under some form of self-appointed self-governance due to the logic of majority rule at the local level and are also forming and electing political parties that represent their particular non-European ethnic interests. However, at present, Muslims and other ethnic minority immigrant groups remain a demographic minority of the national populations in Western and Northern European countries, and thus lack majority rule at the national level.

16.1.4 Application of International Laws and Indigenous Rights

Currently, indigenous Europeans are not recognized by international law as indigenous to Europe and they are not afforded majority or collective rights; therefore, there are no laws in place to prevent ethnic Europeans from becoming minorities within their own homelands. If native Europeans were recognized as being indigenous to Europe and granted, in the words of international law, 'collective rights which are indispensable for their existence' as well as the right to control who enters and settles in their ancestral domains, they may not end up becoming full minorities in their own homelands in the near future. As such, an investigation needs to be conducted, according to the second category of the analysis framework of the UN Prevention of Genocide, of the specific circumstances and structures that exist that are affecting 'the capacity to prevent [the] genocide' of native Europeans. This includes the absence of collective group rights of European peoples

104 Ibid, 89, 92.

and the lack of international recognition of European peoples as being indigenous to Europe.

Demographic engineering, in terms of liberal economic interests of the EU, is defended on the grounds that rather than trying effective family policies and other strategic methods to offset population decline amongst ethnic European populations, decades of large-scale non-European immigration is necessary to top up the number of working age peoples that are required to provide the EU with the benefits of large supplies of cheap labour power, and by extension, geopolitical power. In this sense, Europeans are replaceable and non-Europeans are used for economic ends. As such, replacement migration requires investigation for violating numerous rights and for being genocidal in nature.

According to article 8 of the UN *Declaration on the Rights of Indigenous Peoples*, indigenous peoples have the right to not be deprived of their integrity as distinct ethnic peoples, to not be subject to any form of 'population transfer', and to not be subject 'to any form of forced assimilation or integration' to foreign cultures or ways of life or 'destruction of their culture'. Demographic engineering and the EU cosmopolitan project do just that. And according to the logic of the seventh category of the analysis framework of the UN Prevention of Genocide, mass-immigration into European nations based on demographic-economic goals targets a particular ethnic group (ethnic Europeans) and a particular age group (working age). It favours foreign sources of fertility, non-Europeans, that will come to outnumber and replace ethnic Europeans as working-age generations in the future. Therefore, because replacement migration reduces ethnic Europeans to demographic minorities in their own nations it threatens their long-term survival as the distinct indigenous peoples of Europe. As such, elite sanctioned demographic engineering is creating conditions that could lead to the 'physical destruction in whole or in part' of European peoples.

In fact, the very notion (and practice) of demographic engineering in the form of replacement population in Europe omits the possibility of increasing the fertility rates of indigenous Europeans. It therefore fails to protect European families, and by extension, their distinct cultures, while also deliberately ignoring the responsibility to provide for the security and well-being of European peoples in the long-term. This calls into question article 16.3 of the *Universal Declaration of Human Rights*, which states that 'The family is the natural and fundamental group unit of society and is entitled to protection by society and the State.' It also challenges articles 3 and 4(2) of the 2012 EU Treaty, which states that the central aims of the EU are to 'promote...the well-being of its peoples' and to 'ensure' that the 'cultural heritage' of Europe is 'safeguarded and enhanced.' In addition, as genocide 'does not necessarily mean the immediate destruction of a nation' (Lemkin), and as reliance on foreign sources of fertility without actively trying to increase European fertility rates can be understood as depriving Europeans of 'resources needed for the group's physical survival' and inducing power-tipping or transference of political power, replacement migration ought to be analysed according to the sixth category of the analysis framework on genocide, which involves 'less obvious methods of destruction,' such as deliberate actions aimed at destroying the 'essential foundations' necessary for the survival of national groups.

16.2 Consequence Two: European Political Decline

Ever since the onset of European integration projects in the twentieth century, ethnic European political institutions and traditional national identities have been undergoing a process of erosion. As detailed throughout this work, since at least the 1920s there have been major anti-ethnic-European movements and ideologues diligently designing and implementing their plans to alter and/or erase the borders and deconstruct the ethno-cultural identities of European peoples. In the first half of the twentieth century, there were people like the highly influential Richard von Coudenhove-Kalergi and his Pan-European Movement, the notion of Eurafrica and a future 'mixed race', and anti-nationalist campaigners; after the post-WWII era, there were abstract cosmopolitanists, 'anti-racist' critical theorists and new leftists, and Eurabian and Eurafrican advocates; and today, including the aforementioned, we have melting pot neoconservatives, global society neoliberals, pro-diversity and pro-immigration activists, and 'anti-fascist' no-border groups that declare Europe must be opened wide to global diversification and must silently submit to their forced 'mongrelisation'. The thrust and machinations of these socialist movements and political ideologies have been complemented by global economic corporations and organisations that promote and profit from mass-immigration and seek to create a new cosmopolitical world order based on global governance and economic capitalism, called the socialist-capitalist alliance. This situation reveals a convergence of economic, political, and cultural factors in the transformation of European nations into cosmopolitan multi-ethnic concoctions dedicated to human equality, corporate capitalism, and Eurabian and Eurafrican partnerships at the expense of European peoples.

16.2.1 The Relationship between Demographic and Political Decline

Although 'mongrelisation' may seem like a politically incorrect term, it is something that is advocated by numerous actors who seek to ethnically transform European nations. For instance, Roger Griffin, an illustrious and well-paid British professor of modern history and political theorist at Oxford Brookes University, stated in his 2008 book, *A Fascist Century*:

> Whatever the structural reasons for Britain's white racism and the counter-racism it breeds in its victims, such intolerance will not be rooted out until

> most Britons (of whatever background) not only tolerate the steady mongrelisation of British society, but celebrate it as the laboratory of exciting new forms of culture and human coexistence.[105]

A scientifically imposed experiment aimed at the forced 'mongrelisation' of a people, such as suggested by the likes of Griffin, Sutherland, and Habermas, is essentially a form of scientific racism. Enforced mongrelisation is the intentional act of destroying 'in whole or in part' a distinct people, which is genocide according to article II of the *Convention on the Prevention and Punishment of Genocide*. Enforced mongrelisation also deprives indigenous Britons (and Europeans) of their 'integrity as distinct peoples', deprives them of their 'ethnic identities', and imposes upon them 'legislative, administrative or other measures' that essentially forces upon them 'assimilation or integration by other cultures', which violates article 8(a) and article 8(d) of the UN *Declaration on the Rights of Indigenous Peoples*.[106]

Peter Sutherland is another influential figure who views migration as a central means to transform ethnically homogeneous European societies. He is an Irish international businessman, billionaire, founding father of the World Trade Organisation, chairman of Goldman Sachs between 1995 and June 2015,[107] the UN Special Representative for Migration, and head of the Global Forum on Migration and Development. In 2012, Sutherland stated that demographic decline due to low-fertility rates in European nation-states was the 'key argument...for the development of multicultural states' in Europe. He further declared that it was 'impossible' for European homogeneity to 'survive because states *have to become* more open states, in terms of the people who inhabit them'. But he didn't stop there. He also argued that 'the European Union...should be doing its best to *undermine*'

105 Feldman (ed.), *A Fascist Century: Essays by Roger Griffin*, 131.

106 See chapter 15.

107 Newenham, 'Peter Sutherland to retire as Goldman Sachs chairman'.

any 'sense of our homogeneity and difference from others'.[108] In other words, European demographic decline justifies the ethnic and cultural mixing of European populations by non-European immigration and justifies the weakening and eventual erosion of European ethno-cultural national homogeneity. But for Sutherland, like others, demographic decline is not the sole reason for non-European mass-immigration into Europe; immigration is an imperative humanitarian-political project to combat White 'racism' embodied by European national sovereignty, which he equates with Nazism.

Griffin, Sutherland, and other influential European elites seem to think that there is nothing wrong with imposing 'mongrelisation' on ethnic Europeans. Part of the reason why is that although the principle of majority rule is often based on an ethnic majority population, it has come to increasingly mean, via critical cosmopolitanism, a political rather than an ethnic demographic majority. Through a technique of critique and empirical sociology, critical cosmopolitanism has interpreted existing nations in a way that has progressively eroded traditional theories, social and political structures, and value beliefs (Kurasawa, 2011). By emphasising global processes such as mass culture, transnationalism, mass-migration, and other global issues, critical cosmopolitanism has undermined European ethno-national institutions and identities as well as homeland sovereignty.

A central figure of critical cosmopolitanism is German sociologist and philosopher Jürgen Habermas. As discussed in Volume I, chapter 4, Habermas is a second-generation Frankfurt Schooler who, like many others, envisions Europe becoming a universal nation *proper*, populated by peoples having cosmopolitan identities and world citizenship. He perceives ethno-nationalism, an ontological belonging and political destiny, as 'a kind of regressive credo'[109] and repudiates it

---

108 Brian Wheeler, 'EU should "undermine national homogeneity"' (my emphasis); Kent, 'UN Migration Envoy'; 'Peter Sutherland: Global agenda, nationalism & migration', YouTube video.

109 Mertens, 'Cosmopolitanism and citizenship', 335.

as a normative and valid form of national identity and as an organising principle of European political communities. Therefore, the majority or dominant native ethnic populations of European nations do not have the right to preserve or privilege their specific ethno-cultural and ethno-political life forms in their own nations.

Instead, Habermas argues that the national political culture of European nations should be universalist, procedural, and based on human rights, accommodating, as it were, a plurality of ethnic minority cultural identities. In other words, ethno-national patriotism needs to be replaced by a constitutional patriotism, a civic or enlightened post-national identity based on voluntary membership to a constitutional liberal democracy, a social contract (versus descent) bounded by legal rights. Constitutional patriotism means 'being loyal to the democratic procedures of the constitution',[110] not membership to a people as a political community bonded by historical, ancestral, ethnic, and cultural ties. In such a constitutional democracy, the ethno-national identities of indigenous Europeans are supplanted by a post-national cosmopolitan identity and the political culture of European nations is divorced from ethno-European characteristics.

In a strategic move to achieve this new universalist democracy in Europe, Habermas calls for a 'generous liberal immigration policy' as well as the 'right to migrate', which he claims is a basic liberty like religious freedom.[111] Essentially, he understands that immigration 'partially unbundle[s]' European nation-states.[112] He sees transnational migration (Third-World and intra-European) as mixing European populations so that they become constituted by individuals from disparate cultures and ethnicities. This ethnic mixing 'accelerates the decoupling of political culture from the pre-political identity

110 Ibid, 336.

111 Mertens, 'Cosmopolitanism and citizenship', 337.

112 Cheah, *Inhuman Conditions*, 56.

of the majority cultural group'.[113] What this means is that the ethno-political identities and institutions that have traditionally determined the political culture and identity of European nations and peoples are viewed as too European, although they were created and developed by and for Europeans. Accommodating and including the distinct ethno-cultural identities of immigrants into the national identity necessarily involves therefore, by the logic of Habermas, altering this identity in a way that reflects the new ethno-pluralism, i.e. a cosmopolitan constitutional identity, and not a 'privileged', i.e. indigenous European, ethnic group. As a result, European national institutions are pried open to all cultural and ethnic influences; they are undermined by large-scale inflows of ethnically distinct immigrants and the resultant ethnic mixing of European nations. Habermas thus sees immigration as a tool to increasingly dispossess European ethnic groups of their distinct foundations: their ethnic political cultures, identities, and institutions. This, by extension, also means that Europeans, as distinct ethnic peoples and indigenous majorities of their nations, are stripped of their legitimacy to national sovereignty and majority rule over their nations.

Through constitutional-cosmopolitan democracy and large-scale ethnically distinct immigration, the political culture, identity, and leadership of European nations becomes decidedly non-European in character. They become increasingly determined by a multi-ethnic political majority that is bound by abstract constitutional laws and cosmopolitan identities. In addition to these developments, immigration also accelerates the rate of decline of European majorities suffering from low fertility rates to demographic minorities within their own homelands. Hence, immigration is a force that contributes to both the demographic and political decline of indigenous Europeans and is therefore detrimental to their long-term interests. Any opposition by European ethnic majorities to the rapid changes wrought to their

113 Ibid, 56.

nations, identities, and homelands from ethno-political demographic engineering is, to Habermas, 'xenophobic' and, in the spirit of human rights, justifies further entrenchment of procedural cosmopolitanism.

On the one hand, we have elites who deliberately use non-co-ethnic immigration to ethnically mix European populations with the aim of undermining European national institutions and identities and creating a new type of society under global governance. On the other hand, we have a theory about the loss of government control over immigration because of the erosion of European political institutions. According to the chair of Political Science at Trinity College, Anthony M. Messina, the political institutional breakdown perspective sees immigration accelerating the 'long-term erosion' process that traditional political institutions, the 'policy making bodies and vehicles for popular representation', have been undergoing. This erosion can be understood as being directly related to the cultural Marxist 'long march through the institutions' (war of position), and has led, according to the theory, to 'the weakness of traditional domestic political institutions' and thus a loss of government and traditional political control over immigration and immigration policy, and by extension, border control. Messina explains that government immigration policy loses out to 'more credible and authoritative actors both within and outside of the state', such as 'the jurisdiction of national courts' and 'a predominantly liberal judiciary', as well as 'pro-immigrant welfare groups and activists' who are mostly leftists.[114]

In other words, because European political institutions are being eroded and reformed by various forces such as cultural Marxist and cosmopolitan attacks on the foundational structures of society, the power of government to control the entry of foreigners has become increasingly subservient to human rights lobbyists and left-liberal forces that are pro-immigrant and pro-open borders. This furthers the erosion of traditional political institutions because more immigration

114 Messina, *The Logics and Politics of Post-WWII Migration to Western Europe*, 8, 105.

accelerates the separation of European ethnic identity from the political culture and increasingly redefines political institutions as ethnically plural cosmopolitan entities. However, as the majority of European government elites, as well as EU elites, are pro-immigration, for the ethnic mixing of European populations, and promote human rights laws, it is hard to agree that governments have indeed lost control over immigration and immigration policy.[115] According to Teitelbaum (among others), it is 'commonplace…to find assertions that international migration is a "global flow" driven by overwhelming economic, social and political forces, and that governments can do little other than get out of the way'.[116] But he disagrees, concluding that such claims are 'greatly overstated'. He thinks that theories dealing with international migration are 'deficient in dealing with the role of states in initiating, selecting, restraining, and ending international migration movements' and that 'there is far less international migration occurring than would be the case if states were not regulating entry'. In other words, States do indeed exact various controls over cross-border migration flows into their sovereign territories, and it is only when there is a purposeful lack of regulation (and/or the handing over of immigration control to non-governmental pro-immigration bodies) that 'migrant crises' will arise. Teitelbaum further declares that 'the political implications of international migrations depend not only upon empirical facts but also on the ways these are perceived by political elites and publics', i.e. on how they are portrayed by intellectuals, political leaders, and other public figures and organizations (i.e. media) to their citizenry.[117] According to Weiner and Teitelbaum, social theorists tend to neglect to mention state intervention in their immigration theories because they

115 See: Teitelbaum, 'The Role of the State', 165; Hollifield, 'The Emerging Migration State', 897.

116 Teitelbaum, 'The Role of the State in International Migration', 157.

117 Ibid, 166, 157–158.

> prefer to describe international migration as an inexorable process, driven by hugely powerful economic, demographic, and social forces that overwhelm any efforts by governments to affect them — a kind of human tectonics.[118]

If international migration into Europe is described to the public as an 'inexorable' or necessary process, then the hope is that the European peoples will just go about their business and readily embrace the historically unprecedented importation and arrival of millions of non-Europeans into Europe every year. So much for the idea that European governments have lost control over immigration policies. It is clear the erosion of the traditional political institutions and national identities of Europeans through liberal immigration policies is part of the elite plan for the transformation of Europe into a multiethnic cosmopolitan society.

In addition to Griffin, Sutherland, and Habermas, numerous other pro-immigration elites in Europe lift the notion of diversity up to a teleological imperative, an inevitable and uncontrollable force that is bathed in political righteousness. As mentioned in chapter 4.3, Barbara Spectre called for the end of ethnically and culturally homogeneous nations in Europe, declaring that European nations will 'not survive' if they do not cease to be 'monolithic societies' and do not undergo a 'huge transformation', led by the Jews, into 'multicultural mode'.[119] This obviously begs the question: where is the concrete evidence that 'Europe will not survive' without multiculturalism and, by extension, mass-immigration into Europe? In an October 2015 speech, Frans Timmermans, vice-president of the European Commission, avowed that

> Europe will be diverse, like all other parts of the world will be diverse [... because] diversity is humanity's destiny. There is not going to be, even in

118 Weiner and Teitelbaum, *Political Demography, Demographic Engineering*, 94.

119 'Barbara Lerner Spectre Calls for Destruction of Christian European Ethnic Societies', YouTube video (IBA News).

> the remotest places of this planet, a nation that will not see diversity in its future. That's where humanity is heading.[120]

So apparently Timmermans has the psychic power to see into the future and the ability to understand the *telos* of human existence; for him, the future is predictable, history is lineal, and immigration is destiny. But his intentions are political, for, as one can observe, influential intellectuals who endorse government practices of demographic engineering intend to ethnically mix European populations despite indigenous opposition. This diversity is a preconceived plan that has been decades in the making and is really intended only for Europe and other European-based nations.

But what if you don't think mass-immigration, ethnic mixing, and the transformation of national institutions is necessary or good? You are demonized. Leaders, members, and supporters of European groups that are concerned about the unprecedented changes occurring in European nations from the process of elite-sanctioned demographic engineering, like PEGIDA and its offshoots, are called 'far right' and 'pinstripe Nazis' by lawmakers, politicians, the media, and pro-immigration activists.[121] North Rhine-Westphalia Interior Minister Ralf Jäger stated that the leaders of PEGIDA are 'Nazis in pinstripes', as did Thomas Oppermann of the Social Democratic Party (SPD) of Germany, and Bavaria's Interior Minister Joachim Hermann called them 'right-wing extremist Pied Pipers'.[122] During the height of the 'migrant crisis' in 2015, which saw over a million irregular migrants enter Germany, leftist German politician Gregor Gysi implied all indigenous Germans are 'Nazis' and, with a smirk on his face, called

120 European Commission, 'Opening remarks of First Vice-President Frans Timmermans at the First Annual Colloquium on Fundamental Rights'; 'Europe will be diverse, or war! — Frans Timmermans', YouTube video.

121 Oliver Harvey, 'March of the Pinstripe Right'; Simon Jenkins, 'Germany's "Pinstripe Nazis"'.

122 *The Local*, 'Government in a twist over "pinstriped Nazis"'; Withnall, 'Dresden march'.

their demographic decline and replacement through immigration 'fortunate'. Imploring people to attend a protest in Germany called 'Live better without Nazis — diversity is our future', Gysi claimed that

> [w]e have to take a stand against the Nazis. Because of our history between 1933–1945 we are obliged to treat refugees properly. We also have to save their lives in the Mediterranean....Oh, and by the way: Every year more native Germans die than there are born. That is very fortunate. It's because Nazis are not very good at having offspring. This is why they are so dependent on immigration from foreign countries.[123]

Gysi essentially suggests that the reason why native Germans have such low birth rates is because they are Nazis, and therefore it is great that they are disappearing and being replaced as a distinct ethnic group indigenous to Germany!

Another example of establishment elites demonising opposition was a divisive leftist propaganda video on Germany's public broadcaster *ZDF*'s NEO MAGAZIN ROYALE television programme, which is paid for by German taxpayers. Critics of mass-immigration who support politicians such as Geert Wilders, Donald Trump, Viktor Orban, and Frauke Petry, were called 'xenophobics' and 'authoritarian nationalist dorks' linked to Nazism. The video implied those who are welcoming of mass-immigration and the cultural and demographic changes it incurs were 'true Germans', but those who were not were 'murderous vandals'. According to ZDF, 'true Germans' are 'nice', 'liberal', 'compassionate', 'considerate', 'reasonable', 'social', 'temperate', 'peaceful', and they are 'proud of not being proud'. And Germany has 'freedom of speech', is characterized by 'unity' and 'diversity', and is 'open', 'multicultural' (despite Merkel herself calling multiculturalism a failure), 'modest', 'tolerant', 'enlightened', 'responsible', 'selfless', and 'forgiving'. It further declared that Germans who are critical of immigration and its transformative effects on Germany do not represent Germany at all by stating that 'You are not the people, you are the

123 'Germanistan — Diversity is our future!', YouTube video.

past'.[124] In other words, indigenous Germans who are critical of a government-mandated program of immigration and racial and cultural mixing that undermines their ethnic identities, radically transforms their nations and institutions, and relegates them to an ethnic minority within their own homeland are Nazis and don't deserve to exist.

A similar statement was made by Mona Sahlin, former leader of the Swedish Social Democrats party, who patronizingly stated that '[t] he White majority [in Sweden]... are the problem' that need to change and adapt to a new Sweden.[125] Obviously then, the only people who have the right to be called the people of Germany, Sweden, and Europe in general must be pro-immigration and tolerant or even celebrative of their own demographic and political decline and replacement as distinct peoples in their own homelands. European indigenes who are critics of immigration have no right to self-determination, national sovereignty, or European identity.

The Nazism/extreme Right narrative against Europeans (along with the Whites are racist narrative) is a dog-eared strategy, a propaganda technique, to condemn, alienate, and thus delegitimize any and all ethnic Europeans who exhibit their democratic right to criticize and oppose the calculated prying open of their societies to mongrelisation, cosmopolitanism, Islamization, and the associated destruction of the essential foundations of their ethnic identities. The monolithic generalisations of indigenous Europeans as guilty racists and Nazis, and other such dishonourable name-calling, is part of an effort to justify mass-immigration and the replacement of Europeans with non-Europeans. Anti-European narratives are part of the logic of governments and non-state actors who are hostile to indigenous Europeans and induce migration to politically engineer and ethnically transform European nations, and are acts of discrimination,

124 'BE DEUTSCH! [Achtung! Germans on the rise!] | NEO MAGAZIN ROYALE mit Jan Böhmermann — ZDFneo', YouTube video (Neo Magazin Royale).

125 'Sweden: Leading Social Democrat — "The White Majority is the Problem"', YouTube video (SSU).

persecution, and incitement to genocide. Those who are committing such acts should be tried to the fullest extent of the law.

The Nazi-racist narrative propaganda campaign against ethnic Europeans needs to be examined in terms of the analysis framework of the UN Special Adviser on the Prevention of Genocide. In the fourth, fifth and seventh categories of this analysis framework, we can see that the Europeans-are-Nazis or -racists narrative is an aspect of genocidal intent. This narrative is an 'exclusionary ideology', an alienating paradigm involving false 'constructions of identities in terms of "us" and "them" to accentuate differences'. It is 'inflammatory rhetoric or hate propaganda' used in dominant controlled media, in 'mirror politics', to justify acts against Europeans that are designed to reach the 'foundations of the group'.

The Nazi-racist narrative is an act of persecution according to articles 2(d) and 9(2) of the *2011 European Parliament and Council Directive*, and article 8(2e) of the *Declaration on the Rights of Indigenous Peoples*, as this form of propaganda targets the racial and national social groups of indigenous Europeans and their political opinions on government programs of mongrelisation through 'mental violence' and discriminatory legal, administrative, and judicial measures. Further, the Nazi-racist narrative violates article 12 of the UDHR and article 17 of the *International Covenant on Civil and Political Rights* (ICCPR), which state that attacks on the 'honour and reputation' of individuals are prohibited. It also violates article 20(2) and article 26 of the ICCPR, article 7 of the UDHR, and article 14 of the *Convention for the Protection of Human Rights and Fundamental Freedoms in Europe*, which state that any act of discrimination against a national or racial group or against the political opinion of an individual or group is prohibited. And the labelling of Europeans as racists and Nazis in an effort to justify political and demographic engineering and stamp out opposition violates the right of indigenous peoples 'to be different, to consider themselves different, and to be respected as such'.[126] Intentionally targeting a distinct ethno-national group in terms of attacking their collective attributes, such as their ethnic and national identity and institutions, and their ancestral, social, and cultural heritage, ways of life, and systems of thought, is considered ethnocide, i.e. nation killing.[127]

Using mass-immigration to purposefully mix European ethnic populations and actively transform and undermine their socio-political institutions and identities in order to create an open liberal democratic civil society bound by abstract constitutional laws and cosmopolitan identities while elites and migrants themselves claim it is inevitable or destiny is not only incredibly disingenuous, but also violates many international laws and rights. The EU demographic engineering project violates article II of the *Convention on the Prevention and Punishment of Genocide* on the right of ethnic Europeans as a national, racial, and ethnic group to not be destroyed 'in whole or in part'. Using non-European migrants to deliberately alter the ethnic, religious, cultural, and political compositions of European nations is a form of 'population transfer' that aims to undermine the rights of European peoples to their particular ethno-national identities and thus is in violation of article 8(2c) of the *UN Declaration of the Rights of Indigenous Peoples*. 'Decoupling' and 'unbundling' the national identity of Europeans from their ethnic identity by a program of demographic engineering that relies on non-European immigrants essentially deprives Europeans of their distinct ethnic identity. It dismisses the right of Europeans to preserve the foundations — political autonomy, self-governance, historic territory — that provide for their 'integrity' as 'distinct peoples', which violates article 15 of the UDHR and article 8(2a) of the *UN Declaration on the Rights of Indigenous Peoples*. It also violates article 4(2) of the Treaty on the EU, which states that the EU shall 'respect… national identities'. Using non-European

126 UN, Declaration on the Rights of Indigenous Peoples, 1–2.

127 Schabas, *Genocide in International Law*, 189; Martin Shaw, *What is Genocide*, 65–67; Conversi, 'Genocide, Ethnic Cleansing and Nationalism', 320–333.

migrants to alter and erase the political institutions of European nations and replace them with decidedly non-European institutions violates article 34 of the UN *Declaration of the Rights of Indigenous Peoples*, which states that 'indigenous peoples have the right to promote, develop and maintain their institutional structures'. It violates the right of European peoples to self-determination, which involves the right to live 'within a political community... according to the customs and traditions of their kind' (van der Vyver, and article 9 of the UN *Declaration of the Rights of Indigenous Peoples*). It is a form of genocide. Genocide involves denationalisation, the 'destruction of the national pattern' and the replacement of it by a foreign 'national pattern' that is imposed upon them by an oppressive or colonizing force (Lemkin). Depriving Europeans as a racial group of their particular 'national pattern', which is vital for survival at the national level, and subjecting them to American*ization*, Islam*ization*, African*ization*, Asian*ization*, Third World*ization*, and cosmopolitanin*ization*, essentially deprives Europeans of their actual existence as a distinct living group over the long-term.

All in all, the demographic and political decline of Europeans is not an organic result of foreign immigration, but a deliberate engineering process to structurally transform and 'open' European nations up to ethnic and cultural pluralism and a new type of society under some form of global governance. This engineering of a new civil society and population, an open liberal democratic society of mixed races and cultures bound by abstract constitutional laws and cosmopolitan identities and governed by a multi-ethnic political majority, destroys the ethno-political foundations of the ethnic majorities of European nations and discredits them from having the legitimate right (majority rule) to govern their own nations. As such, the cosmopolitan EU project creates the 'conditions of life' that will 'destroy, in whole or in part' European indigenous peoples and therefore is a form of slow genocide.

16.2.2 Leftism, Islamism, Third Worldism, and Demographic Engineering as a Weapon of War

Indigenous Europeans are still, for now, the ethnic majority and have the highest legitimacy to rule over their countries at the national level. However, as discussed above, majority rule has increasingly come to mean a political rather than an ethnic majority. This is partly the result of leftist elites and influential organisations (media, politicians, academics, NGOs), that, in contrast to economic and demographic arguments, systematically employ critical cosmopolitanism and Frankfurt School Critical Theory in an effort to justify mass-migration flows into European nations. With the aim of transforming European nations into ethnically diverse open cosmopolitan societies, they attempt to validate their project by continuous allusion to universal human rights and the so-called collective shame, privilege, thievery, guilt, and racism of Europeans. They use a range of arguments (Western wealth, imperialism, colonialism, exploitation, slavery, Nazism, global hegemony, and neoconservative foreign policies) that smear ethnic European peoples as a monolithic group, celebrate their political and demographic decline, actively encourage their replacement with different ethnic peoples, and silence opposition to these developments, while also claiming the survival and proper moral route of Europe must involve post-nationalism, universal values, and increasing ethnic diversification.[128]

This leftist-cosmopolitan narrative evidently appeals to non-European ethnic peoples in Europe who overwhelmingly vote for

128 See throughout this work and below, as well as: Alibhai-Brown, 'Don't blame migrants'; Browne, *The Retreat of Reason*; Buchanan, *The Death of the West*, 80; Coleman, 'Immigration and ethnic change in low fertility countries', 427–428; Hermanin, Guidetti, & de Kroon, 'Racism in Europe'; Liddle, 'Fabricant was WRONG'; Weiner and Teitelbaum, *Political Demography*, 47–48; and Vltchek, 'Refugee crisis'.

socialist-leftist political parties.[129] To this effect, ethnic immigrant minorities align with leftist political groups and socialist organisations over shared criticisms against the histories, identities, institutions, policies, traditions, behaviours, and practices of European nation-states, elites, and peoples, as well as in terms of promoting their own ethnic interests—including using the socialist Left to service their own counter-ideologies, movements, and agendas.[130] According to David Chandler, professor of International Relations, minority groups (ethnic and otherwise) are the 'universal people' or the 'multitude' who have cosmopolitan solidarity and global consciousness. They are the universalising political subjects, the cosmopolitan individuals involved in a normative political project that severs the connection between citizenship and state-based political community, challenges the power of state sovereignty, and ushers in a global civil society.[131] In other words, Chandler, like Habermas and others on the socialist left, views non-European immigrants as political tools to alter European nation-states from within. This is what is known, in terms of Critical Theory (cultural Marxism), as Third World oppositionism. To be clear, this oppositionism is a new proletariat (racial and minority groups) counter-hegemonic ideological position and

129 See: Bird, Saalfeld, & Wüst, *The Political Representation of Immigrants and Minorities;* Euro-Islam, 'Muslims in European politics'; *Fria Tider*, '*Muslimer mest vänstervridna*' and '*93% av franska muslimer röstade på Hollande*'; Laurence, 'Islam and Social Democrats'; Messina, *The Logic and Politics of Post-WWII Migration to Western Europe*, chapter 7; Ravnbak, '*Muslimerne i Danmark stemmer rødt*'; Sondage OpinionWay—Fiducial pour Le Figaro; Van der Brug, Hobolt, & de Vreese, 'Religion and Party choice in Europe'; Weiderud, '*Hjälp troende att rösta vänster*'.

130 Chandan, 'Taking Over the West'; Garbaye, 'Birmingham: Conventional Politics', 91; Gramsci, *Selections from the Prison Notebooks*; Howson, *Challenging Hegemonic Masculinity*; Kaufmann, 'A Comparative-Historical Perspective'; Kellner in Marcuse, *The New Left*, Introduction; Lavelle, 'Human Tidal Wave'; Whitehead, 'Illegal immigrants granted permanent residence by staying hidden'.

131 Chandler, 'Critiquing Liberal Cosmopolitanism?', 55–58.

movement opposed to Western and European (ethno)-political power and is led by the 'organic intellectuals'.[132] This is further confounded by European demographic decline and the lack of real political representation for native Europeans, i.e. mainstream pro-European political parties.[133] As a result, through the coalition of counter-hegemonic leftists and non-Europeans, ethnic minority immigrants can form a political majority prior to Europeans becoming a full demographic minority in their nation-states. In this situation, non-Europeans in Europe gain one principle of legitimacy to rule over European nations through political power.

According to demographers Weiner and Teitelbaum, demographic engineering involves 'the full range of government policies intended to affect the size, composition, distribution, and growth rate of a population'.[134] They explain that imperial regimes, such as the European Union, 'engage in demographic engineering by permitting or inducing settlers to enter'. European elites encourage and allow the entry into Europe of 'an immigration population that speaks another language, worships other gods, and competes for lands and jobs'.[135] According to American political scientist Kelly Greenhill, who is associate professor at Tufts University and a research fellow in the Belfer

---

132 This term was coined by Gramsci; they are the American New Left and the European 68ers, and currently include the leftist establishment elites. Kellner in Marcuse, *The New Left*, 17. Also see Volume I, especially chapters 2 and 4, and chapter 14 of this volume.

133 Mainstream political parties on both the so-called Left and Right that have conservative policies on mass-immigration are decidedly absent due to the dominant post-war ideology of liberalism, in its various forms, that pervades mainstream politics. As discussed in other chapters, mass-immigration and multicultural regulations are enforced government policies, whether Left or Right, that essentially impose a cosmopolitan and individualist rather than collective ethnic identity on Europeans and requires them to accommodate collective groups of non-European peoples, cultures, and ways of life.

134 Weiner and Teitelbaum, *Political Demography, Demographic Engineering*, 63, 54.

135 Ibid, 73.

Center's International Security Program, demographic engineering may be used as a political weapon of war.[136] Migration as a weapon of war can be used in several ways, but 'the coercive variant' is the most relevant here, which is 'the class of cross-border migrations designed to influence the political or economic behaviour of potential host states and other state-level actors farther afield'.[137] Such instrumental manipulation of in-migration can be used 'by both state and non-state actors' as a strategy to 'augment, reduce, or change the composition of the population residing within a particular territory, for political or military ends' and specifically aims to 'alter the ethno-religious-political balance within said territory'.[138] In this way, the promotion of liberal immigration policies by Habermas and his ilk to ethnically mix European populations, further unbundle indigenous European political cultures, institutions, and identities, and usher in new cosmopolitan civic societies (at the same time as employing propaganda campaigns [cosmopolitan-multicultural media and education and 'diversity is destiny'] and discrimination against Europeans [the Nazi-racist narrative]) can be understood as the employment of a political weapon against European peoples. Both the Left and liberal elites benefit from using immigration in such a way.

On the one hand, economic liberals can replace low-fertility populations and a shortage of labour power and maintain (and increase) multinational corporate-economic hegemony in the region and at the global level. On the other hand, leftists can gain an ever-increasing number of non-European votes and further de-couple and destroy the ethno-cultural and ethno-political foundations of European nations and peoples. Economic liberals benefit from this also.[139] Yet the use of immigration is not a one-way street. Politically and

---

136 Greenhill, 'Strategic Engineered Migration as a Weapon of War', 6.

137 Ibid, 7.

138 Greenhill, 'Strategic Engineered Migration as a Weapon of War', 6–8.

139 Other political benefits may include the generation of crises, a constructive chaos (Leo Strauss), or creative destruction (neo-conservativism, Michael

racially-motivated non-European immigrants in Europe (Identitarian immigrants) are mobilising as non-Europeans and some are using the Left, the liberal-democratic system, and immigration as tools to radically alter the political, ethnic, and cultural environments according to their own anti-European agendas, as mentioned above. Many of these anti-European immigrants consider themselves as Third World oppositionists with historical grievances against Western colonialism, slavery, and imperialism, or see themselves as oppressed present-day counter-hegemonics against Western globalism, racism, and military liberal-democratic interventionism in the non-Western world.

In this sense, migrants may take the form of settlers, such as those who desire demographic conquest, rather than benign immigrants looking for employment or genuine refuge. Weiner and Teitelbaum describe migrants as those people who most often respect and wish to integrate (into European societies), whereas settlers are usually a demographic minority characterized by the refusal to integrate 'into the native culture and social order' and 'regard themselves as superior to the natives'.[140] They also describe settlers in terms of demographic colonization, which is 'the movement into a territory of one's own people to settle the land, build or gain control of the urban settlements, and establish the political authority of the victors'.[141] Governments may send migrants to settle in another country and use settlement policies 'to establish control over [that] territory'.[142] Greenhill calls this form of strategic engineered migration 'exportive', which may be used by state and non-state actors to undermine, 'discomfit or destabilize foreign governments'.[143] For example, political dissidents may be expelled from a particular country but are provided asylum in another country,

Leeden) that are used to justify methods that change the foundational nature of European societies.

140 Weiner and Teitelbaum, *Political Demography, Demographic Engineering*, 62.

141 Ibid, 57.

142 Weiner and Teitelbaum, *Political Demography, Demographic Engineering*, 60.

143 Greenhill, 'Strategic Engineered Migration as a Weapon of War', 8–9.

where they may continue their dissidence and set up various networks that aim to alter both the domestic and foreign policies of their host country and the domestic policies of their homeland. As discussed in Volume II, chapter 8, numerous Muslim 'refugees' came to Europe in the 1980s and set up radical Muslim organizations and networks that funded and contributed to political efforts in their homelands and committed terrorist acts upon their host countries. ISIS has also employed exportive migration by the generation and use of refugee flows to infiltrate and destabilize Europe. They have used 'militarized' strategic engineering in that they displaced peoples in Syria and Iraq to gain military advantage against said governments and territory (establishing the Caliphate) and acquired both resources and manpower from doing so. Such displacement is an 'effective way to consolidate control over territory' and 'economically quite remunerative', such as in the form of asset appropriation (housing, banks, government documents, national resources such as oil) and 'departure taxes' of would-be-refugees (such as selling passports).[144]

Foreign governments may also use their exported populations or cross-border population movements and refugee flows as a method of coercion. Greenhill describes this strategy of coercion as

> the class of events in which (real and threatened) outflows are used, as a foreign policy tool, to induce (or prevent) changes in political behaviour and/or to extract side-payments from the target(s); coercive use includes the propagandistic use of outflows (which are generated by others) for their own benefit.[145]

Coercive engineered migration is often used by weak actors to generate migrant crises in more powerful states, after which they will then 'offer to make them disappear for financial or political pay-offs'.[146] For example, as mentioned elsewhere, Turkey repeatedly threatened to

144 Ibid, 17–18.

145 Ibid, 8.

146 Ibid, 14.

unleash millions of 'refugees' into Europe to extract various political deals and economic benefits from the EU, such as accession to the EU, visa-liberalisation, and billions of euros in aid, both repayable and non-repayable. In fact, during the 'migrant crisis' of 2015 and 2016 before the EU-Turkey deal (March 2016), Turkey did very little to stop the hundreds of thousands of irregular migrants crossing the Turkish border into Europe. It was only after a political and economic deal was reached that Turkey started patrolling its borders to reduce or prevent illegal migration. Another example is the refusal of developing countries of origin to accept back deportees from Europe, countries that have instead demanded more legal entryways for their people to enter Europe and more money (in the billions of euros) for them to accept back voluntary deportees.[147]

Very importantly, there are also non-state actors who create and use refugee/migrant out-flows to produce large in-flows into another region to ethnically mix, destabilize, and subvert existing populations and governments for economic and political ends.

Some of the clearest examples of the use of immigration as a weapon of war are Islamists who advocate the demographic conquest, colonisation, and Islamization of Europe. We already know that most immigrants in Europe come from Muslim countries in Asia, Africa, and the Middle East and are racially and ethnically distinct from indigenous Europeans. Even though there are various Islamic sects (Sunni, Shia, Sufi, Alevi, etc.) and various ethnicities that are Muslim, many self-identify as Muslims in general and come together over shared concerns, such as Palestine, the war on terror, neoconservative-led wars in Muslim countries, anti-Islamic sentiments, neoliberal Western hegemony, Sharia law, and so on. And what is known as the global Muslim community, the *Ummah*, provides Muslims in Europe with transnational social capital for political action in European nation-states, which has been aided by EAD elites since the 1970s. In

147 See Volume II, chapters 8.3 and 11.4.

addition, many Muslim groups in Europe are provided foreign funding, often from theocratic Muslim countries who have vested interests in the maintenance, growth, and political representation of Muslim populations in Europe, such as Saudi Arabia, Kuwait, and Turkey. All of these developments positively affect the organizational capabilities and capacity of Muslims in Europe to place demands on European states, which, in effect, alters local as well as national politics.

We also know that a significant portion of Muslims in Europe think their way of life is superior to Europeans' and refuse to integrate into secular European culture and adopt European values and laws. At the local level in many European nations there has already been a power shift between Muslim minorities and European majorities. Muslims have concentrated and settled in urban areas and key parts of major European cities, suburbs, and towns forming vast transnational ethnic networks and condensed self-governing parallel communities that are diametric to the national juridical system and mainstream way of life. Hundreds of these ethnic enclaves have disproportionate levels of crime, incarceration, and unemployment rates and are posing serious social, economic, and political issues for European societies. More importantly, the risk of radicalisation and political Islam, in both its violent and non-violent forms, is high in these neighbourhoods and has increased substantially over the years with continuous inflows of new Muslim migrants. As a result, European peoples have been subject to Islamist terrorism on European soil over the last few decades and peaceful 'rejectionists' have attempted to make European societies grant power to their politico-religious doctrine of Sharia.[148]

We also know about the Black-Red alliance, the alignment of Islamists and 1968ers (leftist establishment elites of the EU), as discussed in chapter 14, as well as the Euro-Arab Dialogue (EAD), which fosters Muslim immigration and the implementation of Islam in Europe. We also know, as detailed in Volume II, chapter 8, especially

148 See Volume II.

subsections 8.2 through 8.4, that Islamism is a counter-hegemonic global ideology; that there are three types of Islamists in Europe 'violent rejectionists, non-violent rejectionists and participationists' (Lorenzo Vidino); and that Islamist networks invest in three main types of activity: proselytism *(da'wa)* and indoctrination (*tarbiyah*), radicalisation, and infiltration (Alex Alexiev). Moreover, we know that numerous Muslim leaders have declared that Europe will be demographically colonized by high-fertility Muslim immigrants and turned into an Islamic state. Jihad today is often in terms of migration (associated with *hijrah*) or the spreading of Islam to where it is not, i.e. non-Muslim societies (the land of the *Kufr*).

In 2015, Cardinal Bechara Boutros al-Rahi stated that 'I have heard many times from Muslims that their goal is to conquer Europe with two weapons: faith and the birth rate', and in 2016 Cardinal Christoph Schönborn said 'Will there now be a third Islamic attempt to conquer Europe? Many Muslims think that and want that, and they say "Europe is at the end"'.[149] There is a long history, coming from the mouths of leading Islamists, behind what these cardinals have said. In 1974, Algerian President Houari Boumédiene stated that 'One day millions of men will leave the southern hemisphere to go to the northern hemisphere and they will not go there as friends. Because they will go there to conquer it. And they will conquer it with their sons. The wombs of our women will give us victory'. Then in 2006, former Libyan leader Mu'ammar al- Qadhafi stated on Arabic T.V. that 'We have 50 million Muslims in Europe. There are signs that Allah will grant Islam victory in Europe without swords, without guns, without conquests. The fifty million Muslims in Europe will turn it into a Muslim continent within a few decades'. Abu Imran, a.k.a Fouad Belkacem, an Islamic leader of Sharia4Belgium, stated in 2011 that the black flag of jihad will fly on top of 'all the...palaces of Europe'. Egyptian cleric Ali Abu al-Hasan stated in January 2012 that 'Europe will become a single Islamic

149 Tomlin, 'Cardinal: Islam's goal is to conquer Europe'; Schönborn as cited by the Archdiocese of Vienna, 'Schönborn'.

state, which will know nothing but "There is no god but Allah, and Muhammad is His Messenger". This will happen whether they like it or not. This is the decree of Allah. Islam is coming!'[150]

Imam Abu Baseer, a leading supporter of al-Qaeda, stated that 'One of the goals of immigration is the revival of the duty of Jihad and enforcement of power over the infidels. Immigration and Jihad go together. One is the consequence of the other and dependent upon it'. Syrian Islamist Omar Bakri, founder of the UK-based Salafi-Wahabbi organization *al-Muhajiroun* (the Emigrants), which was banned as a terrorist organization in 2010, said 'It is our duty to establish an Islamic State in every part of the world, even in Great Britain' and in 2015, in the context of the migrant crisis, Sheikh Muhammad Ayed from the Al-Aqsa Mosque in Jerusalem, urged Muslim asylum seekers to 'give [Europeans] fertility. We will breed children with them, because we shall conquer their countries'. In 2015, President Erdogan of Turkey, a candidate country for EU membership, stated he wanted to recreate the Ottoman Empire through conquest and, calling the Dutch and Germans Nazis and fascists, in 2017 he urged Turks in Europe to outbreed Europeans, saying to them 'Have not just three but five children' because 'you are the future of Europe'.[151]

Various experts describe how Islamists in Europe aim to create the socio-political conditions for the eventual replacement of the

---

150 Boumedienne as cited by Hashmi, *Global Jihad and America*, 22; Al-Qadhafi, 'Europe and the US Should Agree to Become Islamic'; and *The Middle East Media Research Institute (MEMRI)*, 'Belgian Islamist Sheik Abu Imran' and 'Egyptian cleric Ali Abu Al-Hasan'. Also see Volume II chapter 8.4.

151 Abu Baseer as cited by Paz, 'Middle East Islamism in the European Arena', 73; Omar Bakri as cited by Israeli, *Muslim Minorities in Modern States*, 15; Muhammad Ayed as cited by Pickles, 'Imam tells Muslim migrants to "breed children" with Europeans'; Turkiye Cumhuriyeti Cumhurbaskanligi, 'İstanbul'un Yüreğinde'; *Press TV*, 'Turkish diaspora in Europe'; Sanchez, 'Erdogan calls on Turkish families in Europe'.

European order with Islam.[152] Lorenzo Vidino, director of the Program on Extremism at George Washington University, makes the case that Islamists are 'modern-day Trojan horses, engaged in a sort of stealth subversion aimed at weakening European societies from within'.[153] Similarly, the American Foreign Policy Council stated in 2014 that

> [i]n an effort to establish Islamic governance, the [Muslim] Brotherhood seeks to manipulate and subvert local power structures by positioning themselves as the gatekeepers to the Muslim community, infiltrating civil society and state structures, and creating parallel ones. In practice, this involves establishing close contacts with editorial boards of newspapers; news producers; prominent journalists; government, law enforcement, defense, and intelligence officials; prominent academics; [and] civil society groups.[154]

The *Bundesamt für Verfassungsschutz* (BfV), the domestic intelligence service of Germany, stated that Salafism is 'the most dynamic Islamic movement in Germany and at the international level', and their aim is

> the complete reformation of the state, the legal system and society, according to a Salafist system of rules which they regard as the "divinely ordained order". Ultimately, they aim at establishing an Islamic theocracy, where essential basic rights and constitutional positions guaranteed in Germany will no longer apply.[155]

---

152 See Alexiev, *The Wages of Extremism*; Butko, 'Revelation or Revolution' and 'Terrorism Redefined'; Phares, Vidino, & Hamzawy, *Political Islam in Europe and the Mediterranean*; Tibi, 'Europeanisation, Not Islamisation', 'International Relations and the Study of Islam', and 'The Totalitarianism of Jihadist Islamism'. Also see Volume II, chapter 8.

153 Vidino, 'Islamism in Europe', 10. Also see Vidino 'A Dagger in the Soft Heart', 'Aims and Methods of Europe's Muslim Brotherhood', 'Political Islam in Europe', and 'The Tripartite Threat of Radical Islam to Europe'.

154 American Foreign Policy Council, *The World Almanac of Islamism*, 28.

155 BfV, 'Salafist efforts', para. 3. Also see Volume II, chapter 9.5.

Islamist groups also appeal to youth by advertising themselves as a counter-hegemonic movement. Susanne Schröter, head of the Frankfurt Research Center for Global Islam (FFGI), states that Salafist groups target non-Muslims and non-Salafist Muslims for recruitment and 'attract marginalized youths with and without migration background' by 'explicitly stag[ing] themselves as a protest movement and subculture' in distinction to European culture.[156] Gilles Kepel, a French political scientist, sociologist, and specialist on the Islamic and contemporary Arab world, thinks that numerous Muslims of the third generation in Europe are increasingly radicalised by Salafism into what he calls the 'Jihad Generation'. Kepel has argued that ISIS terrorism aims to generate fears of the 'enemy within' in order to increase anti-Muslim sentiments and Muslim radicalism, with the final aim of civil war between Muslims and Europeans. This war, which is thought will destroy Europe, will lay the groundwork for the creation of an Islamic society.[157]

One person who also seeks the demographic conquest of Europe and epitomizes the new proletariat Third World-leftist alliance against Europeans is the influential socialist blogger and activist Sukant Chandan, who is originally from North India but has British citizenship. In 2007, Chandan set up the 'Sons of Malcolm' website which he describes as being

> [i]nspired by the principles of Malcolm X/Malik El-Hajj Shabazz. A 'Third Worldist' perspective focusing on the increasing pace of south-south co-operation which is challenging and defeating neo-colonial hegemony, and the struggles of those oppressed by neo-colonialism and white supremacy (racism) who fight for their social, political and cultural freedom 'by any means necessary'.[158]

156 Schröter, 'Salafism and Jihadism', 2.

157 Erlanger, 'A Quandary for Europe'; Tomlinson, 'Islamic scholar'.

158 Sukant Chandan, 'What is Sons of Malcolm?' *Sons of Malcolm* (blog), n.d. http://sonsofmalcolm.blogspot. ca/p/what-is-sons-of-malcolm.html.

Malcolm X, although later assassinated by the Nation of Islam, was an African-American Muslim leader of the Black separatist organisation for many years. The previous leader of the Nation of Islam, Elijah Muhammad, taught his followers that: Whites were inferior to Blacks; that 'white people were a race of devils who were created by an evil scientist named Yakub'; that 'the demise of the white race was imminent'; and that all Black people were 'Muslim by nature'. Malcolm X also taught that White people were genetically inferior to Blacks and that all races, apart from Whites, were part of the Black nation.[159]

In the transcript of a video for the *Monthly Review* magazine, Chandan stated that non-Whites are 'strategically positioned in the metropolitan areas of the West, which are the most important areas'.[160] He stated further that

> [w]e have won, historically, the right to come here, in the 50s and the 60s and the 70s, when the West wanted, literally, us to do their dirty work here and they wanted us *out*. But we fought for our right to stay here, against the government and against the Far Right and racist organizations and movements. So, we've won our right to stay here. We're here to stay, permanently. That right has been won. Now, I think, the final challenge is for us to completely take over the West.[161]

Then, in early 2016 on a *Russia Today* episode of CrossTalk entitled 'Human Tidal Wave', Chandan advocated the complete replacement (or colonisation/demographic conquest/genocide) of Europeans with non-Europeans:

> I tell you one thing: Black and Asian people should come here in the hundreds of millions. It's not right that for 500 years, imperialism has looted our countries of all our wealth, has destroyed our countries. We will come

159 *Wikipedia*, s.v. 'Malcolm X', retrieved June 2016, https://en.wikipedia.org/wiki/Malcolm_X; Matthews, *World Religions*, 359; X & Hayley, 'The Playboy interview'.

160 Chandan, 'Taking Over the West'.

161 Chandan, 'Taking Over the West'.

> here, we have been coming here, and we will continue to come here in the hundreds of millions until, indeed, as Gaddafi said, Europe will turn Black![162]

In 2015, Chandan helped set up the Malcom X Movement (MXM) 'within the heart of whiteness', a.k.a. the United Kingdom, which he describes as 'a Black and Asian decolonial [sic] and anti-imperialist initiative…trying to develop unity between the peoples of the Global South' against 'white supremacy, misogyny, environmental destruction and the physical and mental genocide against those resisting and being oppressed by neo-colonialism'.[163] MXM is a revolutionary Islamic movement based on 'radical Black and Asian politics' and has provided a free course on 'white supremacy' at their Assata-Tupac Liberation School, which is in partnership with the Islamic Human Rights Association and aims towards the creation of 'revolutionaries'.[164] MXM has also hosted events on the Black Panthers and on Black Lives Matter.[165]

Black Lives Matter (BLM), which is funded by socialist and liberal donors including notorious regime meddler George Soros and his Open Society Foundation, emerged as a radical leftist/Marxist organisation in 2013 in the USA but has since travelled to Europe and elsewhere.[166] BLM states on its website 'The Movement for Black Lives' under the title 'Policy Demands for Black Power' that 'Black humanity and dignity requires black political will and power' and that 'We are a collective that centers and is rooted in Black communities, but we

162 Lavelle, 'Human Tidal Wave'.

163 Chandan, 'Introducing the Malcolm X Movement', paras. 16, 4.

164 Ibid, paras. 7, 6, 13; Islamic Human Rights Commission, 'Year long course: Counter-racism'.

165 Malcolm X Movement, 'In *Facebook* [BlackLivesMatter vs BlackLiberation]' and 'In *Facebook* [2016: Year of the Panther & the Black Panther research project]'.

166 Klein, 'Hacked Soros memo'; Richardson, 'Black Lives Matter cashes in with $100 million from liberal foundations'; Simpson, 'Reds exploiting Blacks'.

recognize we have a shared struggle with all oppressed people; collective liberation will be a product of all of our work'.[167] Many Islamist movements and organisations have expressed their solidarity with BLM, such as MXM, the Council on American-Islamic Relations (CAIR, the foremost Islamist lobby group in the USA), the Nation of Islam, the Muslim Brotherhood (MB),[168] and even ISIS, as well as other groups and individuals who work together against what they consider as the historical, contemporary, and monolithic oppression, racism, and xenophobia of the White West.[169] In other words, Black people, who consider themselves oppressed by White people and the White 'system', are racially mobilising as an ethno-political identity group and aligning with other non-Whites against the 'institutional racism' of Whites and White supremacy, as well as with left-wing Whites, but they themselves aim towards non-White power and supremacy.

There has been no international uproar around Chandan and like-minded groups who promote Black, Asian, and Muslim supremacy while denigrating the White race, and even encouraging the genocide of Europeans. Not for them, and not for German citizen Lamya Kaddor, of Syrian descent, either. Kaddor is an Islamic scholar, the head of the German Liberal-Muslim Union, researcher for Islam Studies, and expert for religious education. She publicly celebrates the demographic decline of ethnic Germans and their replacement

---

167 The Movement for Black Lives, 'Platform'.

168 In 2016, Nihad Awad, the Executive Director of (CAIR), declared that 'Black Lives Matter is our matter' and 'Black Lives Matter is our campaign'. CAIR has been associated with Islamic terrorism, and the Nation of Islam is listed as a hate organization. See: Svirsky, 'Cruz proposes bill to label Brotherhood, CAIR as terror orgs'; Southern Poverty Law Center, 'Nation of Islam'; Kilpatrick, 'Islam, Revolution, and Black Lives Matter'.

169 Be the Change Network; Hall, J., '"How is democracy treating you guys?"'; Kilpatrick, 'Islam, Revolution, and Black Lives Matter'; New Urban Collective; Raza, 'Why Muslims must support #BlackLivesMatter'; Simpson, 'Reds exploiting Blacks'; Winsor, 'Black Lives Matter protests go global'.

by non-Europeans and happily declares a radical change in German identity. On German state television she said that

> I think we have to be aware that we are a country of immigrants. "Being German" will mean having a migration background in the future. This is what being German will mean in the future! No more blue eyes, light hair and claiming "we're all German!". Being German also means wearing a Hijab (Muslim headscarf), having dark hair. This is what being German means today![170]

Deliberately focusing on and promoting the replacement of the historically racial and religious characteristics of Germany to fit in with an immigrant narrative is clearly a celebration of the disappearance of German ethnic identity. And there was no international uproar over Lee Sam-dol (Gunnar Tobias Hübinette) either. Hübinette, a Swedish citizen of Asian descent, is the co-founder of the Swedish far-Left, anti-racist organization Expo and lectures at the University of Karlstad. He incited European genocide, stating that

> [k]nowing or even thinking that the white race is inferior on every conceivable plane is natural considering its history and current actions. Let the white race in the west country perish in blood and suffering. Long live the multicultural, interracial and classless ecological society! Long live anarchy![171]

Viewing Europeans as 'inferior' and implying they are 'collectively guilty' and deserve to be punished by extermination, by 'blood and suffering', and by displacement and replacement by non-Europeans fits within the rubric of demographic conquest, rights violations, and incitement to genocide.

In summary, prior to the time when Europeans become demographic minorities, commonalities and alliances between leftists,

---

170 '"No more blue Eyes & blonde Hair!"—Islam Researcher who taught ISIS fighters applauded on German TV', YouTube video.

171 Tobias Hübinette, *Creol,* no. 1/1996.

ethnic minorities, and radical Third Worldists, as well as their funding by socialist elites and foreign countries, may mean that 'universal people' and their handlers can gain one principle of legitimacy in European nation-states: political majority rule at the national level. When ethnic tipping does occur, non-Europeans will then have a high legitimacy to claim the full transference of European territorial power and sovereignty to themselves. At this stage, native Europeans will still lack the homeland principle. But this does not seem to matter at the moment for four reasons: i) Indigenous Europeans are currently not recognized by international law as indigenous to Europe and are thus not afforded indigenous rights; ii) constitutional liberal-democracy does not recognize the distinct ethnic identities of Europeans or bestow them with majority or collective group rights; iii) left-liberal EU elites, the establishment, do nothing to stop ethnic Europeans from demographic and political decline, in fact they celebrate it; and iv) pro-ethno-European political parties that have conservative immigration policies are decidedly absent from the political mainstream.[172] Again, if native Europeans were recognized as indigenous to Europe and afforded collective rights as distinct ethnic peoples living in their ancestral homelands, these four issues that are central to their demographic and political decline could be assayed, mitigated, and resolved.

Demographic engineering, in terms of political interests, is used as a weapon of ambitious state and non-state liberals, leftists, Islamists, and Third Worldists to deliberately alter and even supplant ethnic European populations and institutions. They use immigration, defended on the grounds of universalism, destiny, existentialism, anti-racism, and anti-colonialism, as a way to undermine the national sovereignty, alter the political culture, transform the national institutions,

172 Conventional politics is dominated by the post-war ideology of pro-immigrant and cosmopolitan liberalism. However, alternative political parties that address the consequences of the liberal project for Europeans are becoming more popular.

and deconstruct the ethnic identities of native Europeans. Such demographic engineering raises serious questions as to the short- and long-term well-being, sovereignty, and survival of indigenous Europeans in their homelands. As such, the use of demographic engineering by these different agents needs to be analysed in terms of rights violations and genocide.

Socialist-leftist cosmopolitan elites in Europe not only undertake a 'long march through the institutions', but also deliberately use demographic engineering to further dismantle the basic foundations of the indigenous populations of Europe. They view non-European immigrants (the 'new proletariat' or the 'universal people') as political weapons that will alter the ethnic, religious, political, and cultural compositions of European host nations. As political tools, migrants provide ethnic votes and political influence that decouple European ethnic identity from state and national institutions. As such, migrants aid the socialist Left in their endeavour to form a multi-ethnic political majority and create a new type of society under cosmopolitical governance. At the same time as using migrants as political weapons to further the demographic and political decline of native Europeans, the socialist Left also openly celebrates this decline of Europeans, actively encourages their replacement, and silences any opposition by employing propaganda campaigns that smear Europeans as a monolithic group that are guilty of racism and White supremacy.

Non-European settlement immigration is the *principal* reason why European national majorities are quickly becoming demographic minorities within their own homelands. It is also a central reason behind European political decline. Elite sanctioned demographic engineering uses migrants as political weapons and tools to ethnically mix and 'mongrelize' European nations and to decouple ethnic Europeans from their political institutions and identities, which essentially deprives them of their ethno-political identity, and induces the transference of power from ethnic Europeans to a multi-ethnic political majority. These are acts that are 'designed to reach the foundations of the group' and are creating the conditions that could lead to the 'physical destruction in whole or in part' of European peoples. Depriving Europeans as a racial group of their particular 'national pattern', which is vital for survival at the national level, essentially deprives Europeans of their actual existence as a distinct living group over the long-term. It therefore needs to be analysed according to the analysis framework on genocide. It is also in violation of articles 8(a), 8(c), and article 34 of the UN *Declaration of the Rights of Indigenous Peoples*, article 15 of the UDHR, and article 4(2) of the Treaty on the EU.

Actors who use demographic engineering as a political weapon do so while conducting a propaganda campaign against Europeans involving 'exclusionary ideology', 'hate speech' and monolithic generalisations and concocted 'fabrications' about Europeans to silence their opposition, the Nazi-racist narrative, and justify their own agendas. As we discussed at the end of chapter 16.3.1, anti-European narratives are acts of discrimination (article 20[2] and article 26 of the ICCPR, article 7 of the UDHR, article 8[2e] of the *Declaration of the Rights of Indigenous Peoples*, and article 14 of the *Convention for the Protection of Human Rights and Fundamental Freedoms in Europe*) and persecution (articles 2[d] and 9[2] of the 2011 *European Parliament and Council Directive*). These anti-European narratives are also an attack on the 'honour and reputation' of Europeans, which is prohibited according to article 12 of the UDHR and article 17 of the *International Covenant on Civil and Political Rights* (ICCPR). In addition, according to the fourth, fifth, and seventh categories of the UN analysis framework on the Prevention of Genocide, the Nazi-racist narrative is an aspect of genocidal intent as it is designed to reach the 'foundations of the group'. As already seen in consequence one, indigenous peoples have the right to not be forced to assimilate or integrate to alien ways of life 'imposed on them by legislative, administrative or other measures'. Attacking the collective attributes of Europeans, such as their ethnic and national identity, institutions, and ways of life is considered ethnocide, i.e. nation killing.[173]

Despite the Black-Red alliance and the Euro-Arab Dialogue, Islamists and Third Worldists in Europe use the cosmopolitan EU project, anti-European narratives, and liberal immigration policies to service their own interests and agendas. They view themselves as counter hegemons that are oppressed by White supremacy, imperialism, and racism and want non-Whites to mobilize, to cooperate as an ethno-political identity group that counters European hegemony in Europe and European-based nations. To this end, they view non-European migration in terms of colonization and conquest. Like the socialist Left, they use migrants as political weapons to alter the political, ethnic, and cultural structures of European nations. But rather than integrate and conform to the cosmopolitan project, they aim to destabilize Europe from within by building, settling, and radicalising non-White parallel communities in strategic cities, towns, and suburbs, as well as by infiltrating and subverting European civil society and state institutions. Their aim, as payback for the supposed collective guilt of Europeans, is to establish control of European nations and subjugate the native inhabitants, with some actively calling for their genocide.

Similar to the socialist Left, Islamists and Third Worldists stereotype, discriminate, and persecute native Europeans to justify the non-White colonisation and conquest of Europe. They themselves, by using migrants as political weapons against European nation-states, violate the same rights that European elites infringe upon, as detailed above. But they are slightly different, as they clearly incite the genocide, in whole or in part, of European peoples by stating their aims to colonize, conquer, and destroy the ethnic fabric and the historical-territorial identity of European peoples and replace them with non-White people, power, and supremacy.

---

173 Schabas, *Genocide in International Law*, 189; Martin Shaw, *What is Genocide*, 65–67; Conversi, 'Genocide, Ethnic Cleansing and Nationalism', 320–333.

16.2.3 George Soros and the Open Society Foundations Network

The ethnic mixing and political transformation of European nations is inextricably tied in with the arrival of supranational political and economic institutions, such as the European Union, the United Nations, and other international 'humanitarian' NGOs that erode the legitimacy of the nation-state and its borders. One of the most influential NGOs that facilitates this transformative cosmopolitan project in Europe is the Open Society Foundation of George Soros.

Soros is a Hungarian-born American citizen, multi-billionaire business magnate, and a self-described philanthropist. He is the founder and chairman of the Open Society Foundations (OSF, formerly known as the Open Society Institute [OSI]), which was first established in Hungary and is now active in more than 120 countries in the world.[174] The OSF aims to create a global network of governments, international institutions, and NGOs, an 'Open society Network', to '*foster open society on a global level*'. According to the OSF, the Foundation is

> a *private* operating and grantmaking foundation based in New York City, [it] implements a range of initiatives that aim to promote *open society* by *shaping government policy* and supporting education, media, public health and human and women's rights, as well as social, legal and economic reform.[175]

Since 1984 Soros has donated more than $32 billion to the OSF and has also provided support to many 'independent organizations'.[176] And how does Soros imagine the open society? In his own words, Soros

---

174 Open Society Foundations, 'George Soros'. Soros' finances are managed by his Quantum Group of Funds. See: Bryne, 'Panama Papers reveal George Soros' deep money ties to secretive weapons, intel investment firm.'

175 Open Society Foundations, 'OSI Announces New Fund to Protect Immigrants' Rights' (my emphasis).

176 Open Society Foundations, 'George Soros'.

describes the open society as 'an abstract idea, a universal concept' that 'transcends all boundaries'. The open society is 'a society open to improvement', a society based on individual rights, 'freedom of expression and protecting dissent'; it is a society 'aware' of and coexisting of multiple religions and cultures, and a society that 'offers a vista of limitless progress'. In contrast to 'closed societies' that 'derive their cohesion from shared values' that are often 'absolute' as they are 'rooted in culture, religion, history, and tradition', an open society 'does not have [such] boundaries'. Shared values 'that hold [the open] society together' are to be found in 'the concept of the open society itself' and are 'a matter of debate and choice'.[177]

For Soros, the liberal-democratic EU was built on the principles of an open society: regional integration based on cultural and religious pluralism; critical thinking and freedom of thought; and humanitarianism, equality, political freedom, human rights, democracy, individualism, abstract or depersonalized social relations, and man-made law.[178] In fact, in 2013, Soros established the Open Society Initiative for Europe (OSIFE), which declares its aim is to 'build on three decades of the Open Society Foundations' work in Europe' and 'narrow the gulf between the promise of Europe as the *prototype* for an open society and reality'.[179] The ultimate goal of Soros is a global society without borders, as well as a global economy and global governance. And the global society will be the prop for the global economy and not the other way around: 'we need some global system of political decision-making. In short, we need a global society to support our global economy'.[180] In sum, his main goal is the creation of an ideal

177 Soros, 'The Capitalist Threat'.

178 Wikipedia, s.v. 'Open Society', retrieved June 2016, https://en.wikipedia.org/wiki/Open_society.

179 Open Society Foundations, 'Open Society Initiative for Europe' (my epmphasis).

180 Soros, *The Crisis of Global Capitalism*, xxix.

world order, an un-bounded and deracinated global society based on economic globalization and universal abstractions.

In his effort to promote and spread his 'open society' project to all corners of the globe, Soros elicits regime change by funding opposition parties and 'social justice' movements in various nations. For example, according to Neil Clark writing for the *New Statesman* magazine,

> [f]rom 1979, [Soros] distributed $3 million a year to dissidents including Poland's solidarity movement, Charter 77 in Czechoslovakia and Andrei Sakharov in the Soviet Union. In 1984, he founded his first Open Society Institute in Hungary and pumped millions of dollars into opposition movements and independent media. Ostensibly aimed at building up a "civil society", these initiatives were designed to weaken the existing political structures and pave the way for eastern Europe's eventual exploitation by global capital. Soros now claims with characteristic immodesty, that he was responsible for the "Americanization" of eastern Europe.[181]

In addition, Soros was also involved in the break-up of Yugoslavia. Clark writes that

> [f]rom 1991, his Open Society Institute channeled more than $100 million to the coffers of the anti-Milosevic opposition, funding political parties, publishing houses and "independent" media such as Radio B92, the plucky little student radio station of western mythology, which was in reality bankrolled by one of the world's richest men on behalf of the world's most powerful nation. With Slobo finally toppled in 2000 in a coup d'etat financed, planned and executed in Washington all that was left was to cart the ex Yugoslav leader to the Hague tribunal, co-financed by Soros along with other custodians of human rights, Time Warner Corporation and Disney. He faced charges of crimes against humanity, war crimes and genocide, based in the main on the largely anecdotal evidence of (you guessed it) Human Rights Watch [which is Soros funded].[182]

---

181 Clark, 'NS Profile — George Soros'.

182 Ibid.

For Soros, any nation that wants to remain 'closed' to globalism needs to be forcibly transformed. According to Leandra Bernstein, writing for the *Executive Intelligence Review* in 2008,

> Soros arms his philanthropic organizations with cash, buying up key sectors within the population who are then let loose to overthrow a government that tries to maintain a "closed society". If a nation wishes to control its own natural resources, it's a closed society. If a nation wants to develop its economy and power of labor through tariffs and regulations, it's a closed society. Any nation that rejects globalization…is a closed society and subject to attacks from Soros and his shadow government of national agents.[183]

Soros is also known as 'The Man Who Broke the Bank of England' in 1992 by short-selling $10 billion in British sterling, which led to the collapse of the pound and Black Wednesday; from this speculation he made a profit of $1 billion.[184] He has contributed and profited off the currency meltdown of many other national economies, including in Asia and Russia. In reference to his betting on national economies to make profits from their financial collapse (that he himself fuels because of his high-profile involvement), in a *60 Minutes* interview in 1998 he declared that 'I'm a player' of 'the system'. As a 'competitor' in 'the game' he said that: 'I am there to make money. I cannot and do not look at the social consequences of what I do'. At the same time as being a speculative capitalist that doesn't care how his actions affect society, Soros declares that he is a 'human being' who is 'concerned about the society in which I live'. He says that he is 'one person who at one time engages in amoral activity and the rest of the time tries to be moral'.[185] Journalist Victoria Friedman aptly writes 'The concept of "what is right" is fluid for the billionaire, depending on his financial

183 Leandra Bernstein, 'George Soros: The Forced-Open Society', 71. To make note, globalism is a more accurate term than 'globalization' to describe the implementation of the new world order.

184 Litterick, 'Billionaire who broke the Bank of England'.

185 'George Soros Interview 60 Minutes [FULL]', YouTube video.

stake' and 'he attempt[s] to rationalize his waves of destruction on sovereign nations through his speculating with his "philanthropy"'.[186]

In North America and Europe Soros' philanthropy involves funding numerous left-wing special interest groups and NGOs whose campaigns paint these White regions of the world as being rife with sexism, racism, and discrimination against minority groups, especially non-White minorities. In America he has funded the Malcolm X Grassroots Movement, the Feminist Majority Foundation, the Ella Baker Center for Human Rights, the Ms. Foundation for Women, the National Association for the Advancement of Colored People (NAACP), the Public Justice Center, the Southern Poverty Law Center, and so on.[187] Some of the other organizations he directly funds include those that support world government, liberal immigration, illegal immigrants, and open borders, such as: the Brookings Institute,[188] Human Rights Watch, the Immigrant Defense Project, the Massachusetts Immigrant and Refugee Advocacy Coalition, the National Immigration Law Center, the Immigrant Workers Citizenship Project, the Immigration Advocates Network, the Immigration Policy Center, the Mexican American Legal Defense and Education Fund, the Migration Policy Institute, the National Council of La Raza, and the National Immigration Forum, among many others.[189] Soros has also either directly funded or indirectly funded (through other organisations)[190] 'social justice' movements and ethnic groups behind some of the most violent riots and protests in America,

---

186 Friedman, 'Soros Pledges Renewed Fight Against "Dominant Ideology" of Nationalism'.

187 *Discover The Networks*, 'Organizations Funded Directly by George Soros and his Open Society Foundations'.

188 Brookings is involved with the Global Governance Initiative that seeks to establish a UN-dominated world government.

189 Ibid; *The Event Chronicle*, 'Organizations Funded Directly by George Soros and his Open Society Institute'.

190 Such as Democracy Alliance, Moveon.org, and Media Matters.

such as the Ferguson and Baltimore protests,[191] Black Lives Matter,[192] and violent anti-Trump protests.[193] These movements have contributed to a worsening of race relations across America. All-in-all, Soros gave over $92 million to 54 racial justice groups in America between 2016 and 2020.[194]

As in the USA, Soros foments racial politics and racial strife in Europe. The OSF funds numerous Muslim groups in Europe, many of which are associated with political Islam and the Muslim Brotherhood. For example, the Collective against Islamophobia in France (CCIF), which has been accused of having an Islamist agenda and ties with the Muslim Brotherhood,[195] received 35,000 euros from Soros in 2012, and nearly 50,000 US dollars in 2014 to influence European Parliament elections. CCIF was dissolved by the French government in 2020 for being 'an "enemy of the Republic"'.[196] In 2013, the Forum of European Muslim Youth and Student Organisations (FEMYSO) collaborated with the CCIF on an OSF-funded project.[197] On its website, FEMYSO writes that it 'is a pan-European network of 33 Member Organisations across 20 European countries, and is the voice of Muslim youth in Europe'.[198] But, according to the German Bundestag, FEMYSO is 'close

191 Riddell, 'George Soros funds Ferguson protests'; Corcoran, 'Billionaire George Soros spent $33MILLION'.

192 Vogel and Wheaton, 'Major donors consider funding Black Lives Matter'. Black Lives Matter, a radical-left Marxist organisation, also has the support of the Muslim Brotherhood.

193 Bremmer, 'Soros-funded group promises even more anti-Trump protests'.

194 Vazquez, 'George Soros is spending billions'.

195 Bastié, 'L'universitaire Gilles Kepel ravive la fracture à gauche sur l'islam'; R.K, 'Attentat de Christchurch'.

196 Harley, 'French "Islamist pharmacy" charity CCIF is forced to close'; Kovacs, 'Islamophobie: la campagne qui derange'; Open Society Initiative for Europe (OSIFE), 'List of European Elections 2014 Projects'.

197 FEMYSO, 'Islamophobia Monitoring & Action Network'.

198 FEMYSO, 'We are FEMYSO'.

to the Muslim Brotherhood'[199] and according to Lorenzo Vidino, FEMYSO has 'interconnectivity with fellow Islamist movements' and is governed by 'top Islamist players' that are tied to the 'Brotherhood milieu' in Europe.[200] FEMYSO receives funding not just from Soros, but also support from the Council of Europe, the European Union, the European Parliament, the European Commission, the Organisation for Security and Co-operation in Europe (OSCE), the United Nations, and many other European and international organisations.[201]

FEMYSO is a member of the European Network Against Racism (ENAR). The ENAR is an organisation that focuses on migrants and ethnic and religious minorities in Europe and promotes their voices in political debate. On its website it declares that its aim is 'to end structural racism in the European Union and to build structures, institutions and attitudes based on race equality and equal distribution of power, privileges and rights'.[202] Obviously ENAR is a central player in the weakening of existing political structures, the 'decoupling' process in European nations, with its focus on dismantling 'structural racism' and creating new institutions based on multi-ethnic politics. Even though ENAR targets specific types of racism in Europe — Islamophobia, Antigypsyism, Afrophobia, and Anti-semitism — there is no mention of projects to tackle the specific type of racism against Europeans: anti-White racism.[203] Some of the leading figures of ENAR have ties to the Muslim Brotherhood and

---

199 Deutscher Bundestag, *Islamische Organisationen in Deutschland*, 39.

200 Vidino and Altuna, *The Muslim Brotherhood's Pan-European Structure*, 76,78. The European Brotherhood network created the Federation of Islamic Organizations of Europe (FIOE; known as the Council of European Muslims [CEM] since 2020), which gave rise to many Muslim NGOs, such as the Forum of European Muslim Youth and Student Organisations (FEMYSO). See Vidino and Altuna, *The Muslim Brotherhood's Pan-European Structure*, 50, 72–84.

201 FEMYSO, 'FEMYSO — Annual Report 2014'.

202 ENAR, 'About Us. Our theory of change'.

203 ENAR, 'Annual Report 2019'.

terrorist organisations, such as the co-founder, Michael Privot, who was a member of the MB.[204] Tufyal Choudhury, who was senior policy advisor to the OSF between 2005 and 2015 and researches how Muslims are affected by counter-terrorism measures, has written and spoken about racism and racial justice for the ENAR and for the Open Society Initiative for Europe.[205] Between 2016 and 2018, ENAR received €706,015 from the OSF, and the EU gave a total of €5,422,678 to ENAR between 2014 and 2019.[206] In 2020, a French MEP, Mathilde Androuët, rightly questioned the European Parliament about EU funding of the ENAR partly due to its links with the OSF. She stated that the OSF was 'an NGO that funds a number of associations seeking to undermine the national unity of our Member States'. She then asked the following question:

> at a time when Europe is being threatened with submersion by a wave of migrants orchestrated by the Muslim Brotherhood working in close collaboration with the Turkish authorities, does the Commission regard continued funding and support for such organisations to be necessary and in line with its own values?[207]

Androuët also mentions that the Council of Black Associations in France is funded by the ENAR. This group is also funded by the OSF. The campaign of this Council involves the view that 'descendants or inhabitants of lands previously colonized and subjected to slavery should receive redress, including in the form of financial reparations'. It has received funding from the OSF via its Open Society Fund to

---

204 Abelson, 'Muslim Brotherhood Front Group'; Hoft. 'Massive Scandal'.

205 ENAR, 'ENAR Extraordinary General Assembly 2021'.

206 Abelson, 'Muslim Brotherhood Front Group'; Hoft. 'Massive Scandal'; Open Society Foundations. 'Contributions to JEKHUTNO'; Open Society Foundations, 'Awarded Grants: ENAR'. In fact, between 2014 and 2019, the EU paid over 36 million euros to groups associated with the Muslim Brotherhood. See: Hoft. 'Massive Scandal'.

207 Androuët, 'Subject: Is funding for the ENAR in line with EU values?'

Counter Xenophobia.[208] In 2013, Louis-Georges Tin, the president of the Council, launched a lawsuit against the French state-owned bank CDC (Caisse des dépôts et consignations/Deposits and Consignments Fund) demanding it pay ten million euros for its role in the slave trade.[209]

The OSF network supports and funds cadres of migrants, Muslims, racial and other minorities, and ultra-left-wing human rights activists and NGOs in Europe, perceiving them to be 'the activists and civil society organizations confronting Europe's many challenges'.[210] Such 'challenges' to the OSF agenda include non-leftist dominant narratives, national sovereignty (Soros wants 'the subordination of national sovereignty to a supranational, European order'[211]), the external borders of the EU, populism, and anti-immigration sentiments. In an effort to overcome these challenges the OSF engages in advocacy efforts, education campaigns,[212] media influence, and grant-funding that aim to affect electoral outcomes and defeat populist candidates and movements that are opposed to mass-immigration in Europe.

A 2013 OSF leaked document declared that 'national-populist xenophobia' dominated 'EU, national, and local debates' and these 'dominant narratives' must be transformed to conform with the goals of the OSF. This document goes on to say that the 'aim' of the OSF, the OSEPI (Open Society European Policy Institute), and the OSIFE (Open Society Initiative for Europe) is 'to affect the agendas and campaigns of the European parties in order to decrease the danger of a greater number far-right candidates being elected to the European

208 Guidetti & Grosset, 'Slavery and Reparation in France'.

209 Colonialism Reparation, 'France: reparation is possible'.

210 Open Society Foundations, 'Open Society Initiative for Europe'.

211 Soros and Schmitz, '"The EU Is on the Verge of Collapse" — An Interview'.

212 Especially through his Central European University in Europe and his Open Society University Network. See: Central European University, 'George Soros's Open Society University Network' and Vazquez, 'George Soros is spending billions'.

Parliament'. This will be partly achieved by '[a]mplifying the voices of ethnic minorities and migrants....in public policymaking'.[213] We can see the extent of the meddling of OSF in European political affairs through a 2014 'flagship project' of the OSIFE. This project granted over $6 million in funding for 90 different projects that aimed to influence the 2014 European Parliament elections, and included strategies to 'name and shame' populist politicians, to mobilize and 'amplify the voice and demands' of leftists, socialists, migrants, Muslims, and other minority groups, to change media coverage to align with the OSF globalist worldview, and to condemn nationalism, Euroscepticism, populism, the far-right, so-called Islamophobia, and anti-migration discourse.[214]

We can see that with his wealth, aspirations, and involvement in the creation of a global open society, Soros has (unelected) political influence over sovereign nations across the world. One could say he supports leftist causes but for liberal economic profits. His OSF also influences the European Court of Human Rights (ECHR). A six-month study by the European Centre for Law and Justice (ECLJ) involving background checks on ECHR judges found that there were serious concerns about 'the independence of the Court and the impartiality of the judges'. The study found

> seven NGOs that are both active at the Court, and have judges among their former staff. At least 22 of the 100 judges who have served since 2009 are former staff or leaders of these seven NGOs. Among these, the Open Society Network stands out for the number of judges linked to it (12) and for the fact that it actually funds the other six organisations identified in this report. The powerful presence of the Open Society and its affiliates is problematic in many ways. But even more serious is the fact that 18 of the

---

213 Open Society Foundations, 'Contributions to JEKHUTNO', 8, 35, 44, 34.

214 Open Society Initiative for Europe (OSIFE), 'List of European Elections 2014 Projects'; Hale, 'EU Elections'.

> 22 judges were found to have served on cases initiated or supported by the organization with which they were previously associated.[215]

Not only does Soros influence the sovereign nations of Europe and its Court of Human Rights, he also influences migratory movements into the EU based on open-border campaigns and migrant rights. The OSF has an International Migration Initiative that aims at preventing *deterrence* policies of *illegal* immigration. It states that

> [t]he assumption is that security-centered policies do not stop migration, and instead put migrants at risk. Policies that maximize options for movement through safe, legal channels will decrease both the human costs of migration and spending on migration control and border enforcement. The International Migration Initiative seeks to ensure that alternative migration channels extend protections to more people, that asylum systems and migration policies respond to the pressure of mixed flows, and that states detain migrants only as a last resort.[216]

This Initiative has a cross-border 'strategic corridor approach' that aims to 'facilitat[e] coordinated action in countries of origin, transit, and destination' and specifically focuses on three corridors: 'Asia/ Middle East, Central America/Mexico, and Eurasia'. It also has a 'targeted project' that seeks to 'reform' the EU Asylum system.[217] As an important note, Gerald Knaus, a senior fellow at the Open Society Foundation and founding member of the Soros-funded European Council on Foreign Relations (ECFR),[218] is also founding chairman of the Soros-funded European Stability Initiative (ESI), a think-tank in Berlin.[219] The ESI was responsible for the creation of the Merkel-

---

215 Puppinck, 'ECHR: Conflicts of Interest Between Judges and NGOs'.

216 Open Society Foundations, 'International Migration Initiative'.

217 Ibid.

218 The ECFR was initially funded by Soros. See: European Council on Foreign Relations (ECFR), ECFR Internship Rome, 2012.

219 Knaus, 'European Stability Initiative (ESI)' and 'European Stability Initiative (ESI)' (September 2, 2009). The OSF has been a 'core funder' of this initiative.

Samsom Plan (the EU-Turkey deal, March 2016) during the European migrant crisis.[220] So, is the Merkel Plan really the Soros Plan?

In terms of an African/Asia Minor corridor into Europe, Soros supports various left-wing activists that are involved in projects dedicated to the free movement of people. The notion of the free movement of people is perhaps best captured by Robert Barsky, who is professor and chair of the French and Italian Department at Vanderbilt University in Nashville. In his 'An essay on the free movement of peoples' in *Refuge*, Canada's Journal on Refugees, he states that

> [p]eople have the inalienable right to move around as they wish, for whatever reason they think appropriate. Period. Borders between states are an aberration, the idea of the nation is reprehensible in its consequences, and restrictions imposed upon people who wish to travel from one region of their world to another are absurd and hurtful.[221]

One free-movement-of-people project that Soros funds is Boats4People. This organisation was set up in 1989 to 'end deaths at maritime borders and to defend migrants' rights at sea', deaths which they attempt to use to pressure Europe to open its external borders to unlimited inflows of migrants.[222] Boats4People involves a coalition of fourteen organisations, which include Migreurop Euro-African Network, Africa-Europe-Interact Network, and the Welcome to Europe Network (W2EU). Migreurop is a Moving Beyond Borders

---

See: European Stability Initiative (ESI), 'Donors'.

220 Laub, 'Why the German-Turkish Migrant Plan Can Work'; European Stability Initiative (ESI), 'The Merkel-Samsom Plan — A proposal for the Syrian refugee crisis'. See also Volume II, chapter 7 for more information on the Merkel-Samsom plan and the ESI.

221 Barsky, 'An Essay on the Free Movement of Peoples', 86.

222 Boats4People (2011), http://www.boats4people.org/index.php/en/; Boats4People Facebook page, accessed September 2015, https://www.facebook.com/boats4people/info?tab=page_info.

project of the European Programme for Integration and Migration[223] and aims for 'a radical change in migration policies in order to make possible the freedom to go, to come and settle for everyone, freedom which is the necessary corollary of migrant rights'.[224] Africa-Europe-Interact Network is against the protection of EU's borders by Frontex (the European border management agency) and for a universal right of the free movement of peoples and 'flexible and non-regulated migration policies between Europe, North Africa and Africa south of the Sahara'.[225] The Welcome to Europe Network is a self-described 'antiracist network' that campaigns for the 'right of freely roaming the globe', but is especially focused on breaking down European external borders and its Dublin asylum system.[226] Although the Welcome to Europe Network state they neither encourage nor condemn illegal migration, they claim that 'freedom of movement is everybody's right', and they distribute pamphlets to illegal immigrants before they make their journey to clandestinely enter Europe via the Mediterranean Sea — those leaving from West Africa, North Africa, and Turkey — informing them of the 'risks, rights, and safety at sea' and what to do when landing illegally in Europe.[227] They have also distributed handbooks, written in Arabic, to would-be sea migrants that aid them in their illegal entry into Europe, including where they may get detained and screened so as to avoid these places.[228]

---

223 European Programme for Integration and Migration (EPIM), 'Project: Moving Beyond Borders' and 'About EPIM'. The European Programme for Integration and Migration (EPIM) is an initiative of the Network of European Foundations, which seeks to spread democracy and international development throughout the world. See: Network of European Foundations (NEF), 'NEF is the Network of European Foundations'.

224 Solennel, 'For freedom of movement'.

225 Afrique-europe-interact (æ act). https://afrique-europe-interact.net/38-1-Our-Network.html

226 W2eu.net, 'Solidarity with the crew of "Salamis"'.

227 W2eu.net, 'Safety at Sea'.

228 Samuels, 'Sky Finds "Handbook" For EU-Bound Migrants'.

Welcome to Europe Network is associated with the No Border Networks throughout the EU, which involve ultra-leftist militants protesting against the enforcement of national European borders (e.g. the UK border agency), external European borders (e.g. Frontex), and migration controls. A well-known chant they use on protest marches is 'Brick by brick, wall by wall, make this fortress Europe fall'.[229] In France, in the form of Calais Migrant Solidarity,[230] this group supports illegals trying to smuggle themselves into Britain. They also support 'antiracist' and 'antifascist' demonstrations, set up squats for illegal migrants, and help illegals organize protests and riots,[231] which have included blocking the Channel Tunnel, storming ferries, and stealing boats. They also train, organize, and incite mass-violence against police and other authorities, as well as vandalize and commit arson.[232] Behind their actions, lies this worldview:

> Borders create misery and death. They are a cruel fiction, a weapon of divide and rule. They serve the rich, who use them to protect the wealth hoarded by colonialism and capitalism, and to turn the rest of us against each other. Borders create an illusion of safety and control, while setting up poor migrants as a cheap labour force of "illegals", who can be easily exploited and easily made into scapegoats.[233]

The Open Society and open-border movements have developed a worldview like Sukant Chandan and other radical anti-European socialists and Third Worldists, that perceive Europe as a region of the world that has become rich by exploiting the resources and the poor

229 'Solidarian humanitarian #refugees convoy started to march to the #refugees kettled in spielfeld' YouTube video.

230 UNITED for Intercultural Action, 'Calais Migrant Solidarity'.

231 Vincent Wood, 'Calais chief'; Mulholland, 'Police arrest 35'; Julian Robinson, 'Knife fight in the Jungle'.

232 *Wikipedia*, s.v. 'No Border', retrieved June 2016, https://fr.wikipedia.org/wiki/No_Border.

233 Calais Migrant Solidarity, 'Who are we?'

peoples of the world, and has 'hoarded' this wealth behind borders, a wealth which ought to be shared by all the peoples of the world. They claim people are trying to access this wealth by illegally entering Europe, in the process of which some have died. Therefore, European wealth is the reason that there should be no borders because people attempt to reach that wealth and die trying. In other words, irregular migrants arriving in Europe from Africa, Asia, and the Middle East are not fleeing war or persecution, but instead are illegal migrants looking for economic opportunities in Europe. Yet no one forced people to travel across the Mediterranean Sea to enter Europe illegally; they were compelled by the lure of wealth. The attempts of open-border activists to pry open the borders of Europe to unlimited migration based on the idealistic notion of a one-world, has led to deaths, destabilized the EU, created economic, political, and security crises, severely affected the safety and well-being of Europeans, and may lead to civil conflicts and even war in the near future. Despite this, the Open or No Borders Network is associated with 'UNITED for Intercultural Action: European Network against Nationalism, Racism, Fascism and in Support of Migrants and Refugees' (and minority groups). This umbrella group has received 'financial backing' from more than 550 organisations since 1992, including the European Commission, the European Council, Home Office UK, the Rothschild Foundation, the Erasmus+ Programme of the European Union, and the Open Society Foundations.[234] Soros has also donated money to the US-based Migration Policy Institute and the Platform for International Cooperation on Undocumented Migrants, which are organizations that advocate for the resettlement of Muslims into Europe.

Another organisation that Soros funds is the Global Centre for Responsibility to Protect (R2P). This organisation promotes 'global governance' and redefines national sovereignty in a way that 'allow[s]

234 UNITED for Intercultural Action, 'Supported by'.

the international community to penetrate a nation-state's borders under certain conditions'.[235] Essentially, R2P enables the UN to militarily intervene in sovereign nations and force them to align with UN mandates on 'responsibility'. It also allows for the creation of 'No Fly Zones', which often unleash wars that devastate countries. The US-led wars in Syria, Libya, and Iraq for example, used No Fly Zones. These wars were backed by NGOs and humanitarian organisations, premised as they were on R2P and 'regime change' in these countries, yet they killed and maimed the peoples, destabilized and destroyed the societies, displaced millions, and created power vacuums filled by radical Islamists. General Carter Ham, former head of U.S. Africa Command (AFRICOM), stated that the creation of a 'No Fly Zone' in Syria

> entails *killing a lot of people* and destroying the Syrian air defenses and those people who are manning those systems. And then it entails destroying the Syrian air force, preferably on the ground, in the air if necessary. This is *a violent combat action that results in lots of casualties* and increased risk to our own personnel.[236]

And there is no mention of ISIS here. Organizations involved in the creation of the Syrian 'No Fly Zone' included: Avaaz, the White Helmets, The Syria Campaign, and Amnesty International.[237] Avaaz, an online lobby organization for global civic advocacy and democracy with the operational name of Global Engagement and Organizing Fund, had start-up funding from the OSF of Soros, which is also their foundation partner.[238] According to Rick Sterling, co-founder of the

---

235 Gareth Evans, 'The Limits of State Sovereignty'; Aaron Klein, 'Soros fingerprints'; Moran, 'Libya and the Soros'.

236 *CBS News*, 'Face the Nation Transcripts September 28, 2014: Blinken, Kaine, Flournoy' (my emphasis).

237 Sterling, 'Humanitarians for War on Syria'.

238 IN GAZA, '"Human Rights" front groups'; Avaaz, 'Libya: No-Fly Zone'; Avaaz, 'Safe zone for Syrians, now!'

Syria Solidarity Movement,[239] and Vanessa Beeley, an investigative journalist and peace activist, the White Helmets (also known as Syria Civil Defence), which is supposedly a human rights NGO, was founded in 2013 by America and Britain and only operates in areas controlled by the rebels (Nusra/al-Qaeda).[240] According to Brandon Turbeville writing for Global Research, the White Helmets are linked to Soros through Purpose Inc.,[241] which was set up by Jeremy Heimans, who is also co-founder of Avaaz.[242] Purpose Inc. is associated with BLM and the Syrian Campaign, the latter of which supports military intervention in Syria against Assad. Soros also funds Amnesty International and Human Rights Watch, both of which demonize Assad and bolster support for the war in Syria.[243]

US-led wars in the Muslim world are funded and armed by the West and based on global corporate interests that hide behind 'human rights', 'philanthropy', and 'liberal democracy'. These wars, which are supported by so-called humanitarian NGO's, lead to the mass migrations of peoples from these areas into Europe. American conservative Ron Paul notes that

> [t]he reason so many are fleeing places like Syria, Libya, Afghanistan, and Iraq is that US and European interventionist foreign policy has left these countries destabilized with no hopes of economic recovery. This mass migration from the Middle East and beyond is a direct result of the neocon foreign policy of regime change, invasion, and pushing "democracy" at the barrel of a gun.

---

239 Syria Solidarity Movement, 'Steering Committee'.

240 Sterling, 'Seven Steps'; *Sputnik News*, 'Soros-Sponsored NGO in Syria'.

241 Purpose, 'About'.

242 Turbeville, 'White Helmets NGO'; The Syria Campaign.

243 Engdahl, 'Soros Plays Both Ends in Syria Refugee Chaos'.

Paul suggests that 'the real solution to the refugee problem' is to 'stop meddling in the affairs of other countries'.[244] He is not wrong. What is staggering though, is that the very same Soros-funded NGOs that support wars in Muslim nations also support the refugee and migrant flows from these countries into Europe! Soros' Open Society Initiative for Europe and the International Migration Initiative support left-wing open-border, pro-immigration activists and NGOs in this endeavour. These organisations and activists direct African, Asian, and Middle Eastern migrants into Europe and helped facilitate the 2015/2016 European 'migrant crisis'. They, along with social media users[245] and twitter bots from outside of Europe,[246] lured both genuine

---

244 Paul, 'The Real Refugee Problem — And How To Solve It'. As an important note, a Pentagon report suggests that the US government knew that the opposition in Syria was being led by radical Islamists, those who have been involved in terrorist acts against the West, i.e. 'The Salafist, the Muslim Brotherhood, and AQI [al Qaeda in Iraq]', and fully supported them in order to 'isolate the Syrian regime'. They also knew that a 'Salafist principality in Eastern Syria' would be established, which was where ISI (Islamic State of Iraq) began setting up its Caliphate and became ISIS. Furthermore, Joe Biden, Vice President of the US at the time, spoke at Harvard in 2014, stating that '[t]he fact is, the ability to identify a moderate middle in Syria, um, was, uh — there was no moderate middle'. In other words, there are no 'moderate' rebel forces that exist in Syria and Iraq, despite the fact that the US and her allies have armed 'moderate' rebels against Assad and ISIS. Yet even ISIS, according to Biden and others, were inadvertently (or purposely) created by 'Obama's anti-ISIS coalition' which 'had armed, trained, and funded al Qaeda and ISIS to wage war on Assad'. See: JW v DOD and State 14–812, Pgs. 287–293 (291); Newman, 'U.S. Intel: Obama Coalition Supported Islamic State in Syria'.

245 Comes and Van de Walle, '#RefugeesWelcome'.

246 *Oriental Review*, 'Who is twitter-luring refugees to Germany?' According to Vladimir Shalak from the Russian Academy of Science (who developed the Internet Content-Analysis System for Twitter), the vast majority of welcoming tweets to migrants that suggested Germany and Austria were the most welcoming countries in the EU came from the USA and the UK, and many were 'galvanised' by netbots. Only 6.4% of '#RefugeesWelcome' Germany tweets came from Germany, whereas 19.2% came from the UK, 17% came from the US, and 5% came from Australia. In other words, non-Germans were

and bogus refugees to Europe by stressing the 'free movements of peoples' and informing the global public through social media of the very generous refugee policies offered by German Chancellor Angela Merkel and other European Union countries.[247] In response to the ensuing 'migrant crisis', Soros provided a solution to the problems he helped create, a solution that furthered his agenda. In his own words, he declared that Europe must accommodate new 'refugee arrivals' numbering 'between 300,000 and 500,000 per year'. Also included was less national sovereignty and more debt for Europeans (taxpayers provide money for non-European countries destabilized by the globalists as well as receiving large influxes of migrants from these same countries) and more dependency for Africans and Arabs (development of infrastructure, economic progress, democracy, rule of law, etc.). Put simply, more of the Western model of globalism in Europe and across the globe.[248] It is so-called 'humanitarian' groups like the OSF that create the problem and then provide the solution, a solution which furthers the goal of the open society agenda in Europe.

A Member of the European Parliament representing Ile-de-France, Jean-Luc Schaffhauser, said that Soros-funded humanitarian structures fostered the migrant crisis. He stated that 'the crisis was preceded by the almost simultaneous establishment of a series of pro-immigration associations, financed in particular by George Soros' "Open Society Foundations"', and that

> [w]e are faced with something we can no longer control, something that has been orchestrated behind our backs, on the one side because of the events, but on the other by putting in place the humanitarian infrastructure

---

the overwhelming majority of tweeters who were inviting migrants to go to Germany. See: Engdahl, 'Soros Plays Both Ends'; Fomin, 'Who is twitter-luring refugees'.

247 Morris, 'Sweden's asylum offer to refugees from Syria'.

248 Soros, 'Europe: A Better Plan for Refugees'.

> which dictates the way we should welcome those people, and thirdly by the collusion of organised crime with a certain number of states.[249]

Lew Rockwell, American libertarian author, editor, and founder of the Ludwig von Mises Institute, thinks that Soros

> is a caricature of an oligarch who thinks that he should be able to control other people's lives because he is wealthy… If he wants to pay for refugees, let him house them. He has got plenty of properties; let him put them in there. There is no right for welfare recipients to enter into Europe and be legally and financially privileged at the expense of European tax payers. This is destroying European civilization, which is why Soros, of course, has been promoting it. There is evidence that he was helping funding certain organizations that are promoting the flow of refugees. This wouldn't be happening if the US hadn't done its evil work along with Britain and others in Syria, but the answer is not to destroy European civilization.[250]

Daniel Friberg, CEO and co-founder of Arktos Media, and former chairman and editor of the think-tank *Right On*, stated that Soros is

> funding and encouraging the current migrant crisis by sponsoring movements that are helping so-called refugees, most of them aren't even refugees, to come into Europe illegally. What he is doing is illegal, immoral and it is none of his business.[251]

Serbian filmmaker Emir Kusturica said that 'Soros has helped spark Europe's migration crisis through his vocal support for freedom of movement'.[252] And according to Hungarian PM Viktor Orban, the European 'migrant crisis' was not a 'refugee crisis' but an uncontrolled flow of 'economic migrants, refugees, and foreign fighters'. He

---

249 Gotev, 'Nationalist MEP blames Soros for EU migration crisis'.

250 *RT News*, '"European nations should control their own borders & immigration policies" — Lew Rockwell'.

251 Friberg, 'Daniel Friberg: Interview with Russia Today'.

252 *Euronews*, 'Kusturica accuses Soros over migration, says EU leadership is soviet style'.

claims it was a 'planned invasion' that was 'driven, on the one hand, by people smugglers, and on the other by those (human rights) activists who support everything that weakens the nation-state', such as open borders, immigration, and multiculturalism.[253] Orban charges these activists for 'inadvertently' becoming part of the 'international human-smuggling network' and accuses Soros of 'drawing a living from the immigration crises'.[254]

In a speech at the European People's Party (EPP) Congress in Madrid on the 22nd of October, 2015, Orban declared that

> [w]e cannot hide the fact that the European left has a clear agenda. They are supportive to migration. They actually import future leftist voters to Europe hiding behind humanism. It is an old trick but I do not understand why we have to accept it. They consider registration and protection of borders bureaucratic, nationalist and against human rights. They have a dream about the politically constructed world society without religious traditions, without borders, without nations. They attack core values of our European identity: family, nation, subsidiarity and responsibility.[255]

In a May 2016 radio interview, Orban explained that 'a background power' exists, a power linked to 'the figure of George Soros'. Such 'background power' are the 'Hungarian organizations financed by George Soros', as well as other NGOs who have unelected 'political influence'. The objectives of these politically influential and Soros-funded organizations involve Europe (and Europeans) accepting 'millions or tens of millions of Muslims', a project that is justified by appealing to 'arguments based on human rights considerations'.[256] The

253 *Hungary Today*, 'PM Orbán: Europe's Peoples Are Beginning To Awake'; Hallett, 'Soros Admits Involvement'.

254 *RT News*, 'Hungarian PM blames Soros'; Kassam, 'Hungarian PM Slams Soros-Funded Advocacy Groups'.

255 Website of the Hungarian Government, 'Speech of Viktor Orbán at the EPP Congress'.

256 Website of the Hungarian Government, 'Interview with Prime Minister Viktor Orbán on the Kossuth Rádió programme "180 Minutes"'.

point of such importation is, according to Orban, 'to reshape the religious and cultural landscape of Europe, and to reengineer its ethnic foundations — thereby eliminating the last barrier to internationalism: the nation-states'.[257]

Similarly, István Hollik, an MP of the Christian Democrats in Hungary, said in early October 2015 that Soros and organisations associated with him, such as the Hungarian Helsinki Committee and the Civil Liberties Union (TASZ) or Migration Aid, will 'do everything to allow an unlimited number of immigrants to enter the country'.[258] Likewise, Hungarian mayor of the town of Ásotthalom (which is on the border with Serbia), László Toroczkai says that Soros and his OSF are funding illegal immigration into Europe, and laid criminal charges (human trafficking, incitement against a decree of authority, etc.) against several illegal left-wing organizations in Hungary.[259]

Not only is the abstract vision of a universal open society utopian at best, it is not representative of global developments towards exclusion and rejection of globalism, in both economic and liberal democratic forms. Global trends towards the 'unmixing' of populations since the advent of both decolonisation and globalism challenges the idea of one-worldism. They reveal that many non-Westerners and non-Western nations reject the universalism, ethnic mixing, and consequential ethnic impartiality of Westernization, and instead embrace, preserve, and promote their own unique cultural and ethnic heritages, their distinct national identities, and their particular indigenous histories and homeland territories. According to Weiner and Teitelbaum,

> [t]he current worldwide trend toward demographic unmixing runs counter to a prevailing view that the globalization process and global migration reduces the importance of borders and enables people to migrate more

257 'Orban's historic speech puts Hungary on war footing', YouTube video.

258 *Daily News*, 'Christian Democrats: Soros supports "unbridled" illegal migration'.

259 Custodela's Facebook page, (22 January 2016), accessed June 2016, https://www.facebook.com/custodela/.

> freely to areas of economic opportunity with little regard for differences in language, culture, or indeed citizenship.

They argue that new and old immigration countries, such as Western Europe (new) and the US, Canada, and Australia (old), which are governed by elites committed to a project of ethnic mixing and multi-racial and multi-cultural diversity ('destiny', as Timmermans et al. would say), starkly contrast with 'much of the world' where 'the demographic tendencies have been toward ethnic consolidation rather than diversification, and that the demographic processes of exodus and return have resulted in increasing homogeneity along religious, linguistic, and other ethnic lines'.[260] This re-indigenisation and 'unmixing' in the non-Western world is, in part, a reaction to the homogenizing influences of global capitalism and liberal universalism propounded by the West.

Of equal importance, EU integration has not always meant the sacrifice of national sovereignty to the centralisation of power. In May 2000, for instance, Joschka Fischer, the then German Foreign Minister and Vice-Chancellor of Germany, declared that Europe is 'full of different peoples, cultures, languages and histories' and that 'nation-states are realities that cannot simply be erased', especially in an age where 'globalization and Europeanization create superstructures and anonymous actors remote from the citizens'. He argued that European integration required that national 'institutions are not devalued or even made to disappear', and that 'the existing concept of a federal European state replacing the old nation-states and their democracies as the new sovereign power shows itself to be an artificial

260 Weiner and Teitelbaum, *Political Demography, Demographic Engineering*, 73; United Nations Expert Group Meeting on International Migration and Development 6—8 July 2005, 'International Migration Trends: 1960–2000'; Huntington, 'The Clash of Civilizations?'; Huntington, *The Clash of Civilizations and the Remaking of World Order*.

construct which ignores the established realities in Europe'.[261] Further, in January 2001, he made it quite clear that his version of a European federation would not be a superstate because its foundation would be centered on nation-states themselves.[262]

Just before Brexit, European Council President Donald Tusk declared that an integrated Europe without nation-states is not a vision shared amongst European indigenes. He stated that ordinary Europeans do not share the elitist vision of 'a utopia of Europe without nation-states, a utopia of Europe without conflicting interests and ambitions, a utopia of Europe imposing its own values on the external world, a utopia of Euro-Asian unity'.[263] He went on to say that in the face of reality these utopias show that elites are

> [o]bsessed with the idea of instant and total integration, we failed to notice that ordinary people, the citizens of Europe, do not share our Euro-enthusiasm. Disillusioned with the great visions of the future, they demand that we cope with the present reality better than we have been doing until now ... Euroscepticism (has) become an alternative to those illusions.[264]

Yet Soros and his army of no borders and leftist European elites are anti-national internationalists, a globalist force with an agenda for a denationalized, centralized, and cosmopolitan European Union and

---

261 Fischer, 'From Confederacy to Federation—Thoughts on the finality of European integration,' 9–10. However, Fischer is a previous leader of the Leftist 68er student revolts in Germany and is now German politician of the pro-immigration political group, the Alliance '90/The Greens. His friend, Daniel Cohn-Bendit, who was also a leader of the 68er revolts in France, is a French-German politician who co-chairs the Spinelli Group, which seeks to federalise Europe. Cohn-Bendit, was also co-chair of the pro-immigration European Greens–European Free Alliance in the European Parliament. See: Fuller, 'The Prospects for Philosophical Rhetoric,' 74.

262 Fischer, 'The future of Europe and the Franco-German partnership'.

263 Barber, 'Brexit: Haunted Europe'.

264 Alastair MacDonald, 'EU chief Tusk'; European Council, 'Speech by President Donald Tusk'.

a statist New World Order. Soros et al. seek to erode the remaining national sovereignty of European nation-states by cracking open the external borders of Europe and creating more supranational institutes empowered by the dis-powering of the nation-states. They have no concern about what Europeans want or what Europeans think about mass-immigration into their countries, or their rights as peoples to have sovereignty, autonomy, and self-determination, because the human rights of non-Europeans and the profits they can make from immigration (long term AAA bonds and furtherance of the global society[265]) are what matter to them.

In summary, due to the democratic principle of majority rule, Europeans becoming a demographic minority means that they must eventually hand over their collective right to govern their historic homelands to non-Europeans. This loss of homeland sovereignty is happening faster than ever due to majority rule increasingly coming to mean, via critical cosmopolitanism, a political rather than an ethnic majority. This means that the very foundations that provide the integrity, well-being, and longevity of Europeans as distinct ethnic peoples in Europe are being eroded. Radical leftists, cosmopolitan Eurocrats, Islamists, Third Wordlists, and NGOs like the Open Society Foundation who use migrants and non-White agitation as political weapons to engineer a fundamentally different Europe, to alter the traditional ethno-political compositions, identities, institutions, and power structures of European nations, are integral to and complicit in this destruction.

Soros uses his money to influence regime change and destabilize governments all over the world. More importantly, the 'prototype' for his utopian dream of an open global society is the European Union and is premised on the assumption that Europeans want such an open society, and that Europe can provide unlimited numbers of migrants with economic opportunities, which is just not the case. In fact,

265 Soros, 'The Case for Surge Funding'.

Europeans have never been given the opportunity to have their vote on mass-immigration acted upon, and their concerns about the radical transformation of the political, cultural, ethnic, and social aspects of their societies have never been addressed. One would think that the spending of enormous amounts of money on propaganda and regulations to promote mass-immigration and to stamp out indigenous resistance to it were obvious clues that Europeans do not want an open society.

But Soros presses on and makes crystal clear how unelected power through wealth effects established power structures in the West. The fact that Soros supports large-scale migration movements into Europe from the Third World, as well as regime change through military intervention in the MENA regions while at the same time supporting the resultant migrant flows from these areas into Europe, it can be argued that he is a non-state actor using demographic engineering as a political weapon to destabilize, subvert, and transform European nations to further his open society agenda. As he also funds anti-European radical leftists, Islamists, migrants, Third Worldists and other minority groups in Europe to agitate for change, to demolish European ethno-national and ethno-political cultural institutions and replace them with multi-ethnic Third-Worldist structures, he is also using these groups as political tools to achieve his goals. As his view of the 'open society' discredits European values and identities based on organic historical, religious, cultural, and traditional characteristics — identities and values that have been around for thousands of years and provide people with a sense of community, belonging, and understanding of right and wrong — and replaces them (imposingly) with an unrooted and unbounded secular, economic, open universal identity based on multi-ethnic individualism, abstract and impersonal rights, and an unsubstantiated value system, the OSF disregards people's right (and desire) to their particular and distinct collective identities, traditional values, and their right to self-determination. It is clear that as head of one of the most influential NGOs enacting

European transformation, Soros must be investigated for violating various rights of and for inciting a form of genocide against European indigenous peoples.

The transformative agendas of radical leftists, Islamists, Third Worldists, and NGOs like the OSF in Europe are in violation of numerous rights and laws that are meant to safeguard and enhance the foundations, territories, nations, identities, and institutions of native Europeans in Europe. We have already seen in Consequence One and throughout this chapter what rights and laws they have violated, so there is no need to repeat them here. However, it must be stated that the open borders movement is in defiance of established laws and procedures by promoting the freedom of movement of foreigners into sovereign European nations and the overthrow of EU border controls. Attempting to strip the right of countries to self-defence and security in terms of demanding the de-regulation of migration and border controls and helping to flood the shores of Europe with illegal migrants is simply criminal activity: human smuggling, violation of national sovereignty, incitement against decrees of authority, civilizational instability, and so on, and should be prosecuted as such. They may condemn the deaths of migrants at sea, but open-border/no-border activists themselves have contributed to these deaths by stressing the right of the free movement of peoples, which is an idea that fosters or incites them to travel rather than a right. They have also provoked civil unrest and riots, attempted to provide alternative illegal migrant routes into Europe that have proven fatal, profited human smuggling networks, and inadvertently helped criminals and terrorists to enter Europe who have unleashed crimes against European peoples: rape, sexual assault, structural damage, massive costs, and terrorist attacks.

16.3 Consequence Three: Declining Social Cohesion and the Risk of Civil Conflict

> '[H]omeland territories are imbued with historic significance and their boundedness allows communities of individuals to maintain distinct identities and cultures. These unique properties mean that people [nations] and states behave differently in conflicts over homeland territories.'[266]

The continuous settlement of large numbers of non-Europeans into European nation-states inevitably alters the ethnic compositions and balances of these countries, affects the distribution of political power and the relations between ethnic groups, and causes a variety of conflicts and problems. Demographic research has found that multiethnic states are 'the most violence-prone settlement pattern' for distinct ethnic groups and pluralistic or divided societies are often subject to genocidal conflict.[267] Political ethologist Frank Salter explains that 'ethnic diversity tends to increase social conflict and crime, undermine welfare, exacerbate ethnic inequality, racialize politics and erode civil liberties'.[268] In order to ensure stability and peace in multi-ethnic states ethnic balances are key, but social and political instability, violence, and civil war can result from a shift in these balances.[269] Such shifts can occur in countries with low fertility rates that

---

266 Johnson and Toft, 'Grounds for War: The Evolution of Territorial Conflict', 12–13.

267 Kuper, *Genocide: It's Political Use in the Twentieth Century*, 17; Toft, 'Indivisible territory, geographic concentration, and ethnic war', 82, 117; Salter, 'Germany's jeopardy: Could the immigrant influx "end European civilization"?', para. 10.

268 Salter, 'Germany's jeopardy: Could the immigrant influx "end European civilization"?', para. 5.

269 Salter, 'Germany's jeopardy: Could the immigrant influx "end European civilization"?', para. 12; Teitelbaum, 'The role of the state in international migration', 158; Toft, 'The State of the Field: Demography and War', 26; Weiner & Teitelbaum, *Political Demography, Demographic Engineering*, 32–33, 46.

also experience large-scale settlement immigration, 'deliberate state manipulation' and the purposeful mixing of different ethnicities, and the comparatively high fertility rates of particular ethnic immigrant groups.[270] Such countries undergo an erosion of national identity and sovereignty, and are prone to violent instability, 'radicalism, terrorism, religious fundamentalism, [and] environmental degradation'.[271] All of this can be exacerbated by ethnic tipping.

With the power transitions that occur as a result of ethnic tipping, influencing domestic and foreign policy, and the change from ethnic majority to political majority rule, the seeds of instability are sown. Just before, during, or after a power transition occurs, violence and civil wars are likely to break out between European indigenous minorities-to-be and non-European ethnic majorities-to-be, particularly if the latter are engaged in a war of opposition facilitated by leftist members of the European majority; power becomes contested and minorities-to-be fear their loss of power.[272] According to political scientist Tanja Ellingsen, 'wars are more likely to occur when the largest group is less than 80 percent'.[273] Consistent with demographic research that shows some European nations have foreign-born and migrant-background populations that already exceed 20 percent of the national population, as well as demographic projections that anticipate Europeans will become minorities within their own homelands in the latter half of this century, we can expect that European nations are likely to suffer from civil wars in the very near future.

If indigenous Europeans want to prevent the impending power transition from rapid ethnic and demographic changes in Europe

---

270 Toft, 'The State of the Field', 26; Weiner and Teitelbaum, *Political Demography, Demographic Engineering*, 32–33, 46.

271 Weiner & Russell, *Demography and National Security*, 1.

272 Toft, 'Population Shifts and Civil War: A Test of Power Transition Theory', 243–244, 248.

273 Ellingsen as cited by Toft, 'Indivisible territory, geographic concentration, and ethnic war', 247.

wrought by the colonization of their countries by foreign immigrants and induced by their own governments and influential non-state actors, if they wish to 'affect migratory movements', then they will need to have both 'coercive and organizational capacities' to do so.[274] These capacities are available to Europeans, but the political and economic interests of elites and the demands of non-European immigrants prevent them from affecting such change. Such interests involve those who 'benefit from immigration', i.e. employers who seek cheap labourers and want to keep wages low, liberal economists that want to increase the tax base, non-European 'co-ethnic' chain migrators, various political parties seeking to increase ethnic votes, and the diversity-promoters, cosmopolitanists, Third Worldists, Islamists, and cultural Marxists or leftists who seek to alter the ethnic composition and existing order of European nations. These actors who are invested in immigration and benefit from it politically, economically, or demographically are in 'contest' with European indigenes, who rightly perceive the ethnic transformation of Europe and their concurrent demographic and political decline as a threat to their survival in the long run.[275]

But European elites continue to justify immigration and consistently belittle European concerns. This is part of the logic of imposing regimes who engage in demographic engineering. They reject the fact that Europeans are indigenous to Europe and thus have sovereignty over their homelands and they dismiss the reality that immigrants can return to their 'other homes', their own homelands, whereas Europeans view Europe as their only home.[276] Instead, governments declare 'a counterposition' namely 'that in a multi-ethnic society people should be free to move to where economic opportunities are

274 Weiner & Teitelbaum, *Political Demography, Demographic Engineering*, 42.

275 Ibid, 43.

276 Weiner and Teitelbaum, *Political Demography, Demographic Engineering*, 121.

present'[277] or mass-immigration into Europe is part of inevitable global economic forces. However, this counter-position does not address the government-planned importation of foreigners and their settlement that rapidly created the multi-ethnic society in the first place, but only the consequence of such importation, i.e. multiethnic society. It also does not address the actions and campaigns of cosmopolitan and left-wing elites that gradually strip European natives of their political and territorial sovereignty and destroy their self-determination and identity, indeed their very existence as distinct peoples.

Weiner and Teitelbaum explain that in order for settlers and those that induce settlement to control an indigenous population, especially if it is in the majority, various coercive tactics need to be employed against the natives, such as the prevention of: 'secessionist and irredentist movements', 'protest movements', and 'political democratization'.[278] It is clear that coercive tactics have been used by EU establishment elites against their own protesting populations, including the use of massive propaganda campaigns that aim to alienate and crush populist opposition among native Europeans (the racist and Nazi paradigms) and the dismissal or lack of acknowledgment of the decades of polls and surveys that reveal European indigenes have wanted immigration levels to be reduced or stopped altogether.[279] It is very clear that EU elites have not and are not listening to the will of their peoples. By not listening to the will of the peoples of Europe, leading EU elites are defiling article 10 of the EU Treaty, which states that European nation-states and the EU are determined by the will of the people. They also violate article 21(3) of the UDHR, which states that the authority of the government must be based on the will of the people. By ignoring the will of the people, EU elites are also violating articles 18 and 19 of the *UN Declaration on the Rights of Indigenous Peoples*, which declare

277 Ibid, 74.

278 Weiner and Teitelbaum, *Political Demography, Demographic Engineering*, 61.

279 See Vol II, chapter 10.3.

that state actions that may affect the rights of indigenous peoples need to be approved by indigenes (Europeans) prior to their implementation. By not listening to the will of the people, EU elites are also in violation of article 1 of the ICCPR, which states that all peoples have self-determination. By extension, this means that European peoples have the right to re-determine the EU on a constant basis and the right to territorial integrity.

Another key part of the logic as to why the political apparatus of imposing regimes like the EU engage in demographic engineering while simultaneously demeaning and ignoring the concerns and will of their people is how they view territory.[280] Let us first look at how ethnic groups view territory. The ownership and defense of bounded territory and homelands is central to international laws that emerged in the era of decolonization and post WWII ethnic group independence movements that involved 'the gradual partitioning of the globe into self-determined territories'. According to evolutionary theory, territoriality or the 'partition' of 'living space' (a universal behavioural trait) and its defence (a conditional or contingent trait) is prevalent among both humans and the animal kingdom and can ensure relatively peaceful relations between distinct groups. The material resources of the territory such as 'water, food, and shelter', the 'human contents' of the territory such as 'the family, relatives, friends, allies, and ethnic group to which one belongs', and the immaterial or symbolic factor of territory, are 'key' to why 'territory [is] worth fighting over' for human ethnic groups.[281]

The symbolic or non-material factor of territoriality is the 'shared history' and attachment of ethnic groups to their historic and traditional land, seen as a common home or homeland, which provides 'in-group/out-group psychology' and group identity.[282] Toft explains

280 Toft, 'Indivisible Territory, Geographic Concentration, and Ethnic War', 84.

281 Johnson and Toft, 'Grounds for War: The Evolution of Territorial Conflict', 37, 8, 18, 31, 16.

282 Ibid, 16.

that a homeland is 'an indivisible attribute of group identity', it is 'inseparable from its past and vital to its continued existence as a distinct group' as it contains the very 'fundamentals of culture and identity' that have developed over millennia and cannot be exchanged for another homeland. Homelands are geographically 'bounded' and they sustain 'cultural boundaries'; such 'boundedness' is endangered by the 'other', by ethnically distinct immigrants who threaten the integrity, sovereignty, and security, the very survival of distinct ethnic groups in their homelands. As such, Toft clarifies that ethnic groups 'view territory as inextricably bound up with their identity and thus ultimately with their survival as a group'. They thus rationally view the right to control their homeland as a survival issue, regardless of a territory's objective value in terms of natural or man-made resources and will engage in fighting to protect and preserve control over their symbolic territories and thus secure their collective group identities. Losing control over a homeland means the 'dilution of the national group, its loss of power, and consequent diminution of national identity', as well as a loss of control over the distribution of 'economic and political resources', immigration, and the cultural content of the society.[283] According to Toft and Dominic D. P. Johnson[284] almost three quarters of all ethnic wars between 1940 and 2000 were about the control of territory.[285]

This deep connection between homeland and the survival of distinct ethnic group identity is not shared by states. For states, power and survival are seen in terms of control over material and physical territories and resources, not in symbolic terms. Although a central duty of the state is the protection and survival of its citizens in the long-term, their focus on their own survival may trump the survival

---

283 Toft, 'Indivisible Territory, Geographic Concentration, and Ethnic War', 84—90.

284 Johnson is Professor of International Relations in the department of Politics and International Relations at Oxford University.

285 Johnson and Toft, 'Grounds for War: The Evolution of Territorial Conflict', 15.

of distinct indigenous groups. This difference in territorial control for survival between states and ethnic groups can result in violent conflicts.[286] For example, European states may rationally calculate that their survival, in terms of the preservation and enhancement of economic and political power at the global level, depends on the mass-importation of foreign migrants as a 'replacement population'. But large inflows of foreign migrants leading to the creation of multiethnic cosmopolitan states based on multicultural immigrant rights and an ethnically neutral abstract European identity is not conducive to the long-term survival and sovereignty of indigenous Europeans who inhabit the European nation-states as homelands. In other words, European state survival at the global level overrides indigenous European survival at the national homeland level. As such, because they are engaged in non-European in-migration, in the decoupling of European ethnic identity from political power, and in propaganda campaigns that aim to belittle European concerns and discredit their distinct identities and sovereignty over their traditional homelands (projects that have defined various leftist-socialist EU integration models since the time of Kalergi), they may be perceived as hostile to European indigenous peoples and thus represent illegitimate political power. They no longer represent the interests, provide secure homelands, or protect the survival of distinct and indigenous European peoples. In this situation, along with ethnic tipping and impending power transitions, indigenous ethnic groups may 'rationally calculate' to enter into conflicts, including political struggles and violent conflicts leading to civil war with both immigrant-settler ethnic groups and the state.[287]

---

286 Toft, 'Indivisible Territory, Geographic Concentration, and Ethnic War', 87, 84, 88.

287 Toft, 'Indivisible Territory, Geographic Concentration, and Ethnic War', 114; Weiner and Teitelbaum, *Political Demography, Demographic Engineering*, 61–64.

Polls and surveys not only demonstrate that Europeans are tired of endless mass-immigration into their countries, they also show that Europeans are not happy with the EU and its institutions either. In a Pew Research survey released in May 2014 with the subtitle 'EU Favorability Rises, but Majorities say their Voice is not Heard in Brussels', it was found that 48 percent of Europeans were not in favor of the European Union, 64 percent were not in favour of the European Parliament, 66 percent were not in favour of the European Commission, and 70 percent were not in favour of the European Central Bank.[288] In a Eurobarometer survey conducted by the European Commission, it was found that in August 2014 less than two fifths of Europeans trusted the EU and 53 percent thought their voice didn't count.[289] By 2018/19, the mood had improved somewhat, with 62 percent having favourable views of the European Union. But some 54 percent thought the EU was 'inefficient', 51 percent thought it was 'intrusive', and 62 percent thought that it 'does not understand the needs of its citizens'. Further, around fifty percent viewed the European Parliament and European Commission negatively.[290] In 2020/2021, almost 40 percent did not trust the European Parliament or the European Commission, almost 40 percent did not trust the European Council, and over 40 percent did not trust the European Union.[291]

What is striking, is that although public support for the EU and its institutions is low, influential 'non-state actors', EU establishment elites, and national elites themselves demand that the leaders of

288 Pew Research Center, *A Fragile Rebound for EU Image on Eve of European Parliament Elections*, 6.

289 European Commission, 'Public Opinion in the European Union, First results', 6–9.

290 Wike, Fetterolf, and Fagan, 'Europeans Credit EU With Promoting Peace and Prosperity, but Say Brussels Is Out of Touch with Its Citizens'.

291 European Commission, 'Public opinion in the European Union Report', 94, 101, 135.

European nations should listen even less to their peoples, the public outcry, for the sake of the European project. George Soros, for example, said in a December 2015 interview with Gregor Peter Schmitz of the German magazine *WirtschaftsWoche* that Angela Merkel should 'change public opinion instead of following it' because 'national sovereignty' needs to become subordinate 'to a supranational, European order'.[292] In May 2016, Jean-Claude Juncker, the president of the EU commission, complained that national political elites listen too much to their voters: 'Too many politicians are listening exclusively to their national opinion. And if you are listening to your national opinion you are not developing what should be a common European sense and a feeling of the need to put together efforts'.[293] In June 2016, German President Joachim Gauck said, 'The elites are not the problem; the population is at the moment the problem.'[294] Kieron O'Hara, associate professor at the University of Southampton where he specializes in the politics, philosophy, and epistemology of technology, rightly complains that

> [f]or many years, the architects of European Union have tacitly assumed that they know the political and economic interests of the people of Europe better than they do themselves. This is a symptom of the so-called democratic deficit in the EU, and one reason why whenever people are directly consulted they tend to reject the project, only to be ignored. European Parliamentary elections receive ever-lower turnouts. These setbacks are seen as regrettable, but not important. There is actually nothing wrong with that if Eurocrats wish to assert (and risk) their own authority and political legitimacy; what is wrong is to give the impression of consultation without really consulting at all. Genuine consultation involves not only collecting and listening to heterodox opinion: it also means acting upon it.[295]

292 Soros and Schmitz, '"The EU Is on the Verge of Collapse" — An Interview'.

293 Holehouse, 'Prime Ministers listen too much to voters, complains EU's Juncker'.

294 'German president Gauck', YouTube video.

295 O'Hara, *Conservatism*, 43–44.

The prime minister of Hungary, Viktor Orban, captured the gist of the democratic deficit and leftist demographic engineering project of the EU quite well on several occasions. In a speech at the European People's Party (EPP) Congress in Madrid on the 22nd of October, 2015, he declared that

> [w]e are the European People's Party — Partie Populaire, Volkspartei, Partido Popular, Party of the People — our responsibility is towards the people. Listen to the people. Let's be determined, let's defend Europe. Do not let the leftist mess up and reconstruct Europe! And do not let them oust the soul of Europe! Do not let liberals and socialists take away Europe from the people![296]

In a May 2016 radio interview, Orban stated that the 'bureaucratic Brussels elite is [sic] quite clearly acting against the will of the European peoples'.[297] In regards to the 'migrant crisis' and EU imposed mandatory refugee quotas, he asked 'When and who voted for admitting millions of people who entered illegally, and distributing them among EU member states? What's happening lacks democratic foundations'[298] and that '[n]obody has voted for what is going on, so the quality of European democracy is in question'.[299] In a speech he gave on March 15th, 2016, it was already clear what Orban understood about the migrant crisis in Europe. He stated that 'Europe is not free. Because freedom begins with speaking the truth. Today in Europe it is forbidden to speak the truth', such as stating 'that those arriving are not refugees', that 'Europe is threatened by migration', that 'immigration brings crime and terror to our countries', and that 'the masses

---

296 Website of the Hungarian Government, 'Speech of Viktor Orbán at the EPP Congress'.

297 Website of the Hungarian Government, 'Interview with Prime Minister Viktor Orbán on the Kossuth Rádió programme "180 Minutes"'.

298 *RT News*, 'Hungarian PM blames Soros for fueling refugee crisis in Europe'.

299 Hallett, 'Orban: Multiculturalism Endangers Christian Europe, Leads To "Parallel Societies"'.

arriving from other civilizations endanger our way of life, our culture, our customs, and our Christian traditions'. Most importantly, Orban declared that Europeans are

> forbidden to point out that this [migrant crisis] is not an accidental and unintentional chain of consequences but a preplanned and orchestrated operation; a mass of people directed towards us [and that] the purpose of settling people here is to reshape the religious and cultural landscape of Europe, and to reengineer its ethnic foundations — thereby eliminating the last barrier to internationalism: the nation-states.

And he didn't mince his words. He stated that Brussels 'is now stealthily devouring more and more slices of our national sovereignty'. He knows well that attacks on sovereign nation-states by bureaucrats and their lackeys, such as the 'media's artillery bombardments, denunciations, threats, and blackmail', are 'a set of tools to force us' to submit to the plan of 'a United States of Europe — for which no-one has ever given authorisation'.[300]

It is no wonder that there is widespread anti-immigration, anti-Eurabian, and anti-Eurafrican sentiments throughout Europe. This is a legitimate response of native Europeans to the rapid transformation of their societies and their demographic and political marginalisation by the constant arrival and settlement of millions of dissimilar peoples into their homelands. Such opposition is reinforced when confronted by anti-European Third Worldists and Islamists who foster 'ancient hatreds'[301] towards Europeans and openly declare their aims to colonize, subjugate, conquer, and even genocide Europeans. According to Weiner and Teitelbaum, native ethnic groups may feel that the rapid arrival and settlement of non-co-ethnic foreigners 'represents a conquering power'. A settler population may be the indigenes 'nemesis — a long-standing rival or enemy whose presence in the territory constitutes a threat to one's culture, social structure, and perhaps even

300 'Orban's historic speech puts Hungary on war footing', YouTube video.

301 Toft, 'Indivisible Territory, Geographic Concentration, and Ethnic War', 82–84.

to one's safety'. Indigenous resistance to immigration and Islam in Europe can be understood therefore as a legitimate reaction to the settler nature of current immigration practices and part of the historically hostile relations and incommensurable cultures between peoples. Contentious relations between ethnic minorities and indigenous Europeans are due, in part, to cultural and ethnic differences and past and present grievances as discussed elsewhere in this work. In fact, European elites are importing a religious group that has historical and current relations with Europeans characterized by 'tensions' and 'conflicts over land, power, security and expressions of group identity, such as language, religion and culture'; as such, they are putting Europeans at risk of genocide (category 1 of the OSAPG). Such realities further complicate the state of affairs in Europe. It is likely that any form of integration and 'tipping' will be resisted. Resistance comes in the form of the 'will to difference', which is also strong in the settler populations. The native 'will to difference' involves a shared perception of the settler population as a 'conquering power' that imposes itself, occupies their lands, and attempts to oppress and humiliate them. Natives will demand 'autonomy, independence, self-determination, and other measures' to rectify this situation and restore their control over their homelands and their very selves.[302]

Europe has witnessed a rapid rise of populist anti-immigration and anti-Islamist political parties and social and political movements over the last few decades, parties and movements that are resisting the state and migrant settlement, and seek to regain sovereign control over their nations.[303] There are also numerous authors, political figures,

---

302 Weiner and Teitelbaum, *Political Demography, Demographic Engineering*, 104, 61.

303 Freedom Party in Austria; Flemish Bloc in Belgium; the British National Party, Liberty GB, and UKIP in Britain; the Progress Party in Denmark; the National Front in France; the Party for Freedom in the Netherlands; the Alternative for Germany; the Progress Party in Norway; the National Socialist Front in Sweden; the People's Party in Switzerland; and Golden Dawn in Greece; as

and influential elites that have declared that immigration, political correctness, multiculturalism, and universalism are leading to the death of European countries. Historian Michael O'Meara, in his book *New Culture, New Right* (2004), views multiculturalism as insisting upon 'the presence of other cultures' and the 'mixing of populations' (multiracialism) so as to 'impose a system in which Europeans are to be turned into an indifferent multiracial multitude, without roots or collective memories — programmed simply to consume'.[304] Likewise, cultural anthropologist Dr. Mark Dyal, writing the foreword for *Babel Inc: Multiculturalism, Globalisation, and the New World Order* (2013) by Kerry Bolton, considers multiculturalism a 'moral regime' that 'condemn[s] pride in one's particularity' (i.e. European indigenous particularity), and is used by the State 'at the bidding of the capitalist oligarchs… to spread a monolithic culture of liberal politics, feminism, anti-racism, and identity-based hyper-consumption'.[305] In these contexts, there have been growing debates about European countries suffering from an 'identity crisis'[306] (if not a civilizational crisis) and anti-White racism or Caucasophobia,[307] as well as concerns about the 'end of Europe',[308] 'White genocide',[309] the Islamization of Europe, and the creation of 'Eurabia'.[310]

---

well as PEGIDA, Stop the Islamification of Europe, Generation Identitaire, the European New Right, and so on.

304 O'Meara, *New Culture, New Right: Anti-Liberalism in Postmodern Europe*, 101.

305 Dyal, foreword to *Babel Inc: Multiculturalism, Globalisation, and the New World Order*, by Kerry Bolton, vi–vii; Bolton, *Babel Inc: Multiculturalism, Globalisation, and the New World Order*, 101. Bolton is a Fellow of the Academy of Social and Political Research (Athens) and the Institute for Higher Studies on Geopolitics and Auxiliary Sciences (Lisbon).

306 Fukuyama, 'The Challenges for European Identity'.

307 Fjordman, 'Caucasophobia — the Accepted Racism'.

308 'The End of Europe — Mark Steyn (1 of 5)', YouTube video (Heritage Foundation).

309 Christian Miller, 'The White Genocide Evidence Project'; Christian Miller, 'None Dare Call It White Genocide'.

310 Such as Bat Ye'or, Melanie Phillips, Bruce Bawer and many others.

In 2010, Thilo Sarrazin, former member of the Executive Board of the Deutsche Bundesbank and former senator of finance for the State of Berlin, published one of the most widely read and controversial books ever published in Germany, *Deutschland schafft sich ab* (*Germany Abolishes Itself*). In this work he argued that 'Islamic immigrants threaten Germany's freedom and prosperity because they are unwilling to integrate and rely overwhelmingly on welfare benefits'.[311] He has also said of Islam:

> No other religion in Europe makes so many demands. No immigrant group other than Muslims is so strongly connected with claims on the welfare state and crime. No group emphasizes their differences so strongly in public, especially through women's clothing. In no other religion is the transition to violence, dictatorship and terrorism so fluid.[312]

Although condemned by leading elites in Germany, 89 percent of German readers of the *Bild* newspaper said they would choose to elect a party headed by Sarrazin and a poll by Emnid found that a fifth of Germans would vote for his party.[313] In France Éric Zemmour, a conservative French journalist, published *Le Suicide Français* (*The French Suicide*) in 2014. This book broke many sales records and elite reactions have been similar to those towards Sarrazin.[314] In his work, Zemmour argues that 'the policies of the French political elite are destroying the country' and that

> France is being destroyed by immigrants who refuse to assimilate; by political correctness that stifles freedom of speech and by supranational organizations, such as the European Union (EU), which are undermining the French nation state and the French economy.[315]

311 Peter Martino, 'Will Germany Abolish Itself and France Commit Suicide?'

312 Sarrazin, 'Bei keiner anderen Religion ist der Übergang zu Gewalt und Terrorismus so fließend'.

313 Solms-Laubach, 'Würden Sie eine Sarrazin-Partei wählen?'

314 Benbassa, 'Zemmour: le bouffon du populisme-roi'.

315 Peter Martino, 'Will Germany Abolish Itself and France Commit Suicide?'

In Belgium, a well-known Flemish politician, Filip Dewinter, has argued that Islam will colonize and replace Europe. He said that

> mass-immigration and multiculturalism have become the Trojan horse of Islamisation. Millions of Muslims and their families come to live in Europe and multiculturalism encourages Islam and under the guise of freedom of religion put it on equal terms with European religions. Europe will be colonised by Islam.

Dewinter has also said that the West is persecuted and stupefied with guilt complexes, namely 'racism, violence, anti-Semitism, slavery, colonialism, and xenophobia', and which are liberally heaped upon Europeans by leftist-Islamist-Third World-neoconservative agents.[316]

In Sweden, the chief of the Swedish army, General Anders Brännström, told his troops in 2016 to prepare for a war in Europe and defend Sweden against skilled opponents that were expected 'within a few years'.[317] In Norway, Army Chief Odin Johannessen remarked that Europe 'must be prepared to fight, both with words, actions — and if necessary weapons — to preserve the land and the values we have in common' against the threat posed by radical Islam.[318] In Switzerland, in reaction to the 'migrant crisis' in Europe, Roger Köppel, Swiss People's Party (SVP) member of parliament, stated that 'Europe is about to abolish itself' due to a 'megalomaniac' open-border policy, and such 'overconfidence is at the root of all evil'. He further declared that 'The basic problem today is Islam' and that 'It is an illusion to believe that politics can cope with this mass migration'.[319]

But the crisis situation in Europe is not just about Islam and Muslims and the protection of European cultural values; it is also

---

316 Dewinter, 'The Colonisation of Europe: How Europe Will Become Eurabia'.

317 Lane, 'Sweden's Army Chief Warns Of WORLD WAR 3 Inside Europe "Within a Few Years"'.

318 *Dagens Nærinsliv*, 'Hærsjefen: Vi må være beredt til å kjempe'.

319 Köppel, 'Terrorismus und Migration: Wir produzieren Heerscharen von Entwurzelten und Unzufriedenen'.

about the deliberate transformation of ethnic European homelands into multi-ethnic cosmopolitan states by the importation of non-European immigrants, a situation that is hostile to European indigenous peoples. What is really at stake in Europe is the actual survival of European indigenous peoples as distinct ethnic groups and the preservation of a European Europe, the historic homeland of Europeans.

Demographic engineering, the deliberate mixing of the ethnic, cultural, and political compositions of nations through immigration, is making indigenous Europeans become ethnic and political minorities within their own nations. What began almost a century ago as an elite socialist and cosmopolitan movement that was initiated by Kalergi and focused on the cultural, economic, and political integration of Europe, the creation of a new type of European without ethnonational identity, and the establishment of the Pan-European Union and Eurafrica, has now become an anti-European Third World/New World open society project. Economically and politically motivated demographic engineering in Europe involving large scale non-European replacement migration, anti-European propaganda campaigns, the Habermasian/Soros/leftist cosmopolitan EU project, the globalism and monoculturalism of the liberal Right, and the Islamism and Third Worldism of non-Europeans is gradually stripping native Europeans of their cultural integrity, ethnic identity, popular power, historical memory, birthright, and the right to dissent, creating a new type of European that is deracinated, abstract, and obedient to the dictates of global accumulation. These processes are undermining many rights of European peoples, especially their 'essential foundations', and are leading to unprecedented power transitions, possibly civil war, and certainly the end of distinct ethnic legacies in Europe.

As the socialist-capitalist global alliance continues to engineer the EU into a cosmopolitan society, high levels of Third World (Muslim and non-Muslim) immigration into Europe will persist and the 'long march through the institutions' will continue to undermine the demographic and political existence of European peoples. Therefore, the left-liberal EU cosmopolitan project raises some very serious questions as to the short- and long-term well-being, territorial and political sovereignty, and survival of indigenous Europeans in their ancestral homelands.

INDEX

I

J

K

L

M

N

O

BIBLIOGRAPHY

1994/45. Draft United Nations declaration on the rights of indigenous peoples. The Sub-Commission on Prevention of Discrimination and Protection of Minorities, August 26, 1994. United Nations: E/CN.4/Sub.2/1994/. http://www.un-documents.net/c4s29445.htm.

'37 000 year old European DNA Identical to Modern Day Europeans'. Youtube video, 0:49. Posted by Faces of Ancient Europe ~ ArianrhodJelena, February 2, 2016. https://www.youtube.com/watch?v=GkgYBbECwBs.

Abelson, Richard. 'Muslim Brotherhood Front Group calls EU Counter-Terrorism Programs to Stamp Out Violent Extremism "Racist" and "Islamophobic"'. *The Spectator.* March 31, 2021. https://thespectator.info/2021/03/31/muslim-brotherhood-front-group-calls-eu-counter-terrorism-programs-to-stamp-out-violent-extremism-racist-and-islamophobic/.

Afrique-europe-interact (æ act). https://afrique-europe-interact.net/.

Al-Qadhafi, Mu'ammar. 'Europe and the US Should Agree to Become Islamic or Declare War on Muslims'. *The Middle East Media Research Institute (MEMRI)*, April 10, 2006. http://www.memritv.org/clip/en/1121.

Alcock, Leslie. *Arthur's Britain: History and Archaeology AD 367–634*. Penguin Books, 1973.

Alexiev, Alex. *The Wages of Extremism: Radical Islam's Threat to the West and the Muslim World.* Hudson Institute: Security and Foreign Affairs, March 2011. http://www.hudson.org/content/researchattachments/attachment/875/aalexievwagesofextremism032011.pdf.

Alibhai-Brown, Y. 'Don't blame migrants—the West helped to create their plight'. *Independent.* May 24, 2015. http://www.independent.co.uk/voices/comment/don-t-blame-migrants-the-west-helped-to-create-their-plight-10273545.html.

American Foreign Policy Council. *The World Almanac of Islamism.* Lanham, Maryland; Plymouth: Rowman and Littlefield, 2014.

Androuët, Mathilde. 'Subject: Is funding for the ENAR in line with EU values?' Question for written answer. E-002743/2020 to the Commission. Rule 138. European Parliament. Parliamentary Questions. May 5, 2020. https://www.europarl.europa.eu/doceo/document/E-9-2020-002743_EN.html.

Archdiocese of Vienna. 'Schönborn: Christliches Erbe Europas erneuern!' [Schönborn: renew the Christian heritage of Europe!]. *Erzdiözese Wien.* September 11, 2016. http://www.erzdioezese-wien.at/site/home/nachrichten/article/52118.html.

Avaaz. 'Libya: No-Fly Zone'. https://secure.avaaz.org/en/libya_no_fly_zone_1/?rc=fb.

——— . 'Safe zone for Syrians, now!' Updated June 18, 2015. https://secure.avaaz.org/en/syria_safe_zone_loc/?pv=194&rc=fb.

Baas, Timo and Silvia Maja Melzer. 'The Macroeconomic Impact of Remittances: A sending country perspective'. Norface Migration: Discussion Paper No. 2012–21. April 12, 2012. http://www.norface-migration.org/publ_uploads/NDP_21_12.pdf.

Bahlul, Raja. 'Democracy Without Secularism? Reflections on the Idea of Islamic Democracy'. Chap. 5 in *Islam, Judaism, and the Political Role of Religions in the Middle East*, edited by J. Bunzl. Florida: University of Florida Press, 2004.

'Barbara Lerner Spectre Calls for Destruction of Christian European Ethnic Societies'. YouTube video (IBA News), 01:17. Posted by GeneralTitus70AD, May 2012. https://www.youtube.com/watch?v=MFEoqAiofMQ.

Barber, Tony. 'Brexit: Haunted Europe'. *Financial Times*, June 26, 2016. https://www.ft.com/content/7cf0fd82-3b80-11e6-9f2c-36b487ebd80a.

Barron, J.B. *Palestine: Report and General Abstracts of the Census of 1922 Taken on 23rd October, 1922*. Jerusalem: Government of Palestine, 1922.

Barsky, Robert F. 'An Essay on the Free Movement of Peoples'. *Refuge* 19, no. 4 (2001): 84–93. Available from: http://refuge.journals.yorku.ca/index.php/refuge/article/view/21218/19889.

Bastié, Eugénie. 'L'universitaire Gilles Kepel ravive la fracture à gauche sur l'islam'. *Le Figaro*. November 8, 2016. https://www.lefigaro.fr/actualite-france/2016/11/08/01016-20161108ARTFIG00271-l-universitaire-gilles-kepel-ravive-la-fracture-a-gauche-sur-l-islam.php.

Baumgartner, Falko. 'The Africanization of France…as of 2014'. Council of European Canadians. October 20, 2014. https://www.eurocanadians.ca/2014/10/the-africanization-of-france-2014.html.

Bawer, Bruce. *While Europe Slept: How Radical Islam is Destroying the West from Within*. New York: Anchor Books, 2006.

BBC News. 'Study: US is an Oligarchy, Not a Democracy'. *BBC*, April 17, 2014. http://www.bbc.com/news/blogs-echochambers-27074746.

'BE DEUTSCH! [Achtung! Germans on the rise!] | NEO MAGAZIN ROYALE mit Jan Böhmermann — ZDFneo'. YouTube video (Neo Magazin Royale), 04:38. Posted by Neo Magazin Royale, March 31, 2016. https://www.youtube.com/watch?v=HMQkV5cTuoY.

Be the Change Network. http://bethechangenetwork.tumblr.com/network.

Benbassa, Esther. 'Zemmour: le bouffon du populisme-roi'. *Huffington Post*, October 21, 2014. http://www.huffingtonpost.fr/esther-benbassa/zemmour-le-bouffon-du-populisme-roi_b_6015500.html.

Bernstein, Leandra. 'George Soros: The Forced-Open Society'. *Executive Intelligence Review* 35, no. 26 (July 4, 2008): 71–75. http://www.larouchepub.com/eiw/public/2008/2008_20-29/2008-27/pdf/71-75_3526.pdf.

Bershidsky, Leonid. 'Europe Doesn't Have Enough Immigrants'. *Bloomberg*, September 3, 2015. https://www.bloomberg.com/view/articles/2015-09-03/europe-doesn-t-have-enough-immigrants.

Bilan D'activité. Association Française pour le Dépistage et la Prévention des Handicaps de l'Enfant. AFDPHE 2015. https://www.yumpu.com/fr/document/read/56590552/bilan-afdphe-2015.

Bild. 'So denken die Deutschen wirklich über den Islam'. *Bild*, May 4, 2016. https://www.bild.de/politik/inland/umfrage/so-denken-die-deutschen-ueber-den-islam-45606118,var=x.bild.html?jsRedirect.

Bird, Karen, Thomas Saalfeld, and Andreas M. Wüst (eds.). *The Political Representation of Immigrants and Minorities: Voters, Parties and Parliaments in Liberal Democracies.* Oxon; New York: Routledge/ECPR Studies in European Political Science, 2011.

Birmingham City Council. Census 2011: Birmingham Population and Migration Topic Report. October 2013. https://www.birmingham.gov.uk/downloads/file/208/census_2011_birmingham_population_and_migration_topic_report.

Bolton, Kerry. *Babel Inc: Multiculturalism, Globalisation, and the New World Order.* London: Black House Publishing, 2013.

Bremmer, Paul. 'Soros-funded group promises even more anti-Trump protests'. *WND*, March 15, 2016. http://www.wnd.com/2016/03/soros-funded-group-promises-even-more-anti-trump-protests/.

Brenner, Yermi. 'A Family Reunification Dilemma for the EU'. *Global Government Forum*, March 23, 2016. http://www.globalgovernmentforum.com/family-reunification-dilemma-for-eu/.

Browne, Anthony. 'The last days of a white world'. *Guardian*, September 3, 2000. https://www.theguardian.com/uk/2000/sep/03/race.world.

———. *The Retreat of Reason: Political Correctness and the Corruption of Public Debate in Modern Britain.* London: Civitas, 2006.

Bryne, Peter. 'Panama Papers reveal George Soros' deep money ties to secretive weapons, intel investment firm'. *Fox News*, May 16, 2016. http://www.foxnews.com/world/2016/05/16/panama-papers-reveal-george-soros-deep-money-ties-to-secretive-weapons-intel-firm.html.

Buchanan, Patrick. *The Death of the West: How Dying Populations and Immigrant Invasions Imperil Our Country and Civilization.* New York: Thomas Dunne Books, 2002.

Bundesamt für Verfassungsschutz. 'Salafist efforts'. N.d. https://www.verfassungsschutz.de/en/fields-of-work/islamism-and-islamist-terrorism/what-is-islamism/salafist-efforts.

Bures, Oldrich. *EU Counterterrorism Policy. A Paper Tiger?* New York: Routledge, (2011), 2016.

Butko, Thomas. 'Revelation or Revolution: A Gramscian Approach to the Rise of Political Islam'. *British Journal of Middle Eastern Studies* 31, no. 1 (May 2004): 41–62.

———. 'Terrorism Redefined'. *Peace Review* 18, no. 1 (August 2006): 145–151.

Calais Migrant Solidarity. 'Who are we?' https://calaismigrantsolidarity.wordpress.com/who-are-we-%d9%85%d9%88%d9%86%da%96-%da%85%d9%88%da%a9-%db%8c%d9%88-%d8%9f-%d9%85%d8%a7-%da%a9%db%8c-%d9%87%d8%b3%d8%aa%db%8c%d9%85-%d8%9f/.

Camarota, Steven A. and Karen Zeigler. 'The Declining Fertility of Immigrants and Natives'. *Centre for Immigration Studies*, March 2015. http://cis.org/declining-fertility.

Cassese, Antonio. *Self-Determination of Peoples: A Legal Reappraisal.* Cambridge: Cambridge University Press, 1995.

CBS News. 'Face the Nation Transcripts September 28, 2014: Blinken, Kaine, Flournoy'. *Cbsnews.com*, September 28, 2014. http://www.cbsnews.com/news/face-the-nation-transcripts-september-28-2014-blinken-kaine-flournoy/.

Central European University. 'George Soros's Open Society University Network: "The power to transform global higher education"'. January 24, 2020. https://www.ceu.edu/article/2020-01-24/george-soross-open-society-university-network-power-transform-global-higher.

Chandan, Sukant. 'Introducing the Malcolm X Movement: Building towards a new wave of Global South decolonial anti-imperialist Resistance in Britain'. *Dissident Voice*. February 24, 2015. http://dissidentvoice.org/2015/02/introducing-the-malcolm-x-movement/.

———. 'Taking Over the West'. *Monthly Review*, April 9, 2011. http://mrzine.monthlyreview.org/2011/chandan090411.html.

Chandler, David. 'Critiquing Liberal Cosmopolitanism? The Limits of the Biopolitical Approach'. *International Political Sociology* 3 (2009): 53–70.

Cheah, Pheng. 'Cosmopolitanism'. *Theory, Culture and Society* 23, no. 2–3 (May 2006): 486–496.

———. *Inhuman Conditions: On Cosmopolitanism and Human Rights*. Cambridge; London: Harvard University Press, 2006.

Chengu, Garikai. 'America Created Al-Qaeda and the ISIS Terror Group'. *Global Research*, September 19, 2014, updated August 27, 2016. http://www.globalresearch.ca/america-created-al-qaeda-and-the-isis-terror-group/5402881.

Christmann, Kris. *Preventing Religious Radicalisation and Violent Extremism: A Systematic Review of the Research Evidence*. Youth Justice Board for England and Wales, 2012. https://www.gov.uk/government/uploads/system/uploads/attachment_data/file/396030/preventing-violent-extremism-systematic-review.pdf.

Citrin, Jack and John Sides. 'European Immigration in the People's Court'. Chap. 13 in *Immigration and the Transformation of Europe*, edited by Craig A. Parsons and Timothy M. Smeeding. Cambridge: Cambridge University Press, 2006.

Clark, Neil. 'NS Profile—George Soros'. *New Statesman*, June 2, 2003. http://www.newstatesman.com/economics/economics/2014/04/ns-profile-george-soros.

Clavero, Bartolomé. Genocide or Ethnocide, 1933–2007: How to Make, Unmake, and Remake Law with Words. Milan: Giuffrè Editore, 2008.

Coleman, David. 'Divergent Patterns in the Ethnic Transformation of Societies'. *Population and Development Review* 35, no. 3 (September 2009): 449–478. doi:10.1111/j.1728-4457.2009.00293.x.

———. 'Immigration and ethnic change in low fertility countries: A third demographic transition'. *Population and Development Review* 32, no. 3 (September 2006): 401–446. doi:10.1111/j.1728-4457.2006.00131.x.

———. *Immigration, Population, and Ethnicity: The UK in International Perspective*. April 17, 2013. Migration Observatory, University of Oxford. https://www.spi.ox.ac.uk/fileadmin/documents/PDF/131030_Briefing_-_Immigration_Population_and_Ethnicity_0.pdf.

———. 'Projections of the Ethnic Minority Populations of the United Kingdom 2006–2056'. *Population and Development Review* 36, no. 3 (September 2010): 441–486.

———. '"Replacement Migration," or why everyone's going to have to live in Korea: A fable for our times from the United Nations'. *The Royal Society B* 357, (2002): 583–598. doi:10.1098/rstb.2001.1034.

Colonialism Reparation. 'France: reparation is possible'. June 6, 2013. https://www.colonialismreparation.org/en/france-reparation-is-possible.html.

Comes, Tina and Bartle Van de Walle. '#RefugeesWelcome: How Smartphones and Social Media Empower Refugees and EU Citizens and Bring Change to European Refugee Policies'. ATHA: Harvard Humanitarian Initiative, October 2, 2015. http://atha.se/blog/refugeeswelcome-smartphones-and-social-media-empower-refugees-and-citizens.

Commission of the European Communities. 'Meeting social needs in an ageing society'. Working Document, SEC 2911. Brussels. 2008. http://www.igfse.pt/upload/docs/gabdoc/2008/11-Nov/Demography2008_exec_summary.pdf.

Convention on the Prevention and Punishment of the Crime of Genocide—the Secretariat and Ad Hoc Committee Drafts. May 1947. April and May 1948. Available at http://www.preventgenocide.org/law/convention/drafts/.

Convention on the Prevention and Punishment of the Crime of Genocide. December 9, 1948. Available at http://www.ohchr.org/EN/ProfessionalInterest/Pages/CrimeOfGenocide.aspx.

Conversi, Daniele. 'Genocide, Ethnic Cleansing and Nationalism'. The SAGE Handbook of Nations and Nationalism, edited by Gerard Delanty and Krishan Kumar. London; Thousand Oaks; New Delhi: SAGE Publications, 2006.

Corcoran, Kieran. 'Billionaire George Soros spent $33MILLION bankrolling Ferguson demonstrators to create "echo chamber" and drive national protests'. *Daily Mail*, January 16, 2015. http://www.dailymail.co.uk/news/article-2913625/Billionaire-George-Soros-spent-33MILLION-bankrolling-Ferguson-demonstrators-create-echo-chamber-drive-national-protests.html.

Courtois, Gerard. 'Les crispations alarmantes de la société française'. *Le Monde*, January 25, 2013. http://www.lemonde.fr/politique/article/2013/01/24/les-crispations-alarmantes-de-la-societe-francaise_1821655_823448.html.

Crawley, Heaven. 'Evidence and Attitudes to Asylum and Immigration: What We Know, Don't Know, and Need to Know'. Working Paper no. 23, 2005. *Centre on Migration, Policy and Society (COMPAS)*, University of Oxford. https://www.compas.ox.ac.uk/fileadmin/files/Publications/working_papers/WP_2005/Heaven%20Crawley %20WP0523.pdf.

Dagens Nærinsliv. 'Hærsjefen: Vi må være beredt til å kjempe'. *Dn.no*, February 1, 2016. http://www.dn.no/nyheter/politikkSamfunn/2016/02/01/1834/hrsjefen-vi-m-vre-beredt-til--kjempe.

Daily News. 'Christian Democrats: Soros supports "unbridled" illegal migration'. *Dailynewshungary.com*, October 11, 2015. http://dailynewshungary.com/fidesz-soros-supports-unbridled-illegal-migration/.

Dashefsky, Arnold and Ira Sheskin (eds.). *American Jewish Year Book 2014: The Annual Record of the North American Jewish Communities*. London; Springer, 2015.

Decker, Oliver, Johannes Kiess, and Elmar Brähler. *Die enthemmte Mitte: Autoritäre und Rechtsextreme Einstellung in Deutschland*. Die Leipziger Mitte—Studie 2016. https://www.boell.de/sites/default/files/2016-06-mitte_studie_uni_leipzig.pdf.

De la Bédoyère, Guy. *Eagles Over Britannia: The Roman Army in Britain*. Tempus, 2001.

De Lima, P., S.Bernabè, R.L. Bubbico, S. Leonardo, and C. Weiss. 'Migration and the EU: Challenges, opportunities, the role of EIB'. European Investment Bank (EIB), Economics Department. March 2016. http://www.eib.org/attachments/migration_and_the_eu_en.pdf.

Denning, Stephanie. 'Why Jeff Bezos Bought The Washington Post'. *Forbes*, September 19, 2018. https://www.forbes.com/sites/stephaniedenning/2018/09/19/why-jeff-bezos-bought-the-washington-post/?sh=3ca270603aab.

Der Spiegel. 'The World from Berlin: "Should Muslims Be Treated on an Equal Footing?"' Spiegel.de, October 8, 2010. http://www.spiegel.de/international/germany/the-world-from-berlin-should-muslims-be-treated-on-an-equal-footing-a-722065.html.

Destatis. 'Births| Live births by citizenship of mother'. 2020. https://www.destatis.de/EN/Themes/Society-Environment/Population/Births/Tables/live-birth-citizenship.html.

Deutsche Welle. 'Germany: Intelligence agency labels Pegida "anti-constitutional"'. May 7, 2021. https://www.dw.com/en/germany-intelligence-agency-labels-pegida-anti-constitutional/a-57461336.

———. 'German population of migrant background rises to 21 million'. *DW*. July 28, 2020. https://www.dw.com/en/german-population-of-migrant-background-rises-to-21-million/a-54356773.

Deutscher Bundestag. *Islamische Organisationen in Deutschland. Organisationsstruktur, Vernetzungen und Positionen zur Stellung der Frau sowie zur Religionsfreiheit.* Wissenschaftliche Dienste. Deutscher Bundestag. WD 1—3000—004/15. 2015.

Deutschland. 'Germany needs more immigrants'. *Deutschland.de*, December 23, 2014. https://www.deutschland.de/es/node/6210.

Devlin, Hannah. 'Genetic study reveals 30% of white British DNA has German ancestry'. *Guardian*, March 18, 2015. https://www.theguardian.com/science/2015/mar/18/genetic-study-30-percent-white-british-dna-german-ancestry.

de Waal, Joel Rogers. 'Western/MENA attitudes to religion portray a lack of faith in common values'. YouGov. February 13, 2019. https://yougov.co.uk/topics/international/articles-reports/2019/02/03/westernmena-attitudes-religion-portray-lack-faith.

Dewinter, Filip. 'The Colonization of Europe: How Europe Could Become Eurabia'. *American Renaissance* 22, no. 4 (April 2011). http://www.amren.com/ar/2011/04/index.html.

Dias, Timon. 'Erdogan the Tyrant and his EU Accomplices'. *The Jerusalem Post*, July 1, 2013, http://www.jpost.com/ Opinion/Op-Ed-Contributors/Erdogan-the-tyrant-and-his-EU-accomplices-318361.

Die Welt. 'Europa wird Islamisch' [Europe is becoming Islamic]. *Die Welt.* April 19, 2006. https://www.welt.de/print-welt/article211310/Europa-wird-islamisch.html.

Dilanian, Ken. 'Taliban Control of Afghanistan Highest Since U.S. Invasion'. *NBC News*, January 29, 2016. http://www.nbcnews.com/news/us-news/taliban-control-afghanistan-highest-u-s-invasion-n507031.

Discover The Networks. 'Organizations Funded Directly by George Soros and his Open Society Foundations'. Discoverthenetworks.org, n.d. http://www.discoverthenetworks.org/viewSubCategory.asp?id=1237.

Duchesne, Ricardo. 'Will Kymlicka and the Disappearing Dominion'. *The Quarterly Review* (April 22, 2014). http://www.quarterly-review.org/?p=2513.

Durch, William J. 'Keepers of the Gates: National Militaries in an Age of International Population Movement'. Chap. 4 in *Demography and National Security*, edited by Myron Weiner and Sharon Stanton Russell. New York; Oxford: Berghahn Books, 2001.

Durocher, Guillaume. 'How Fast Is France's Muslim Population Growing?' The UNZ Review. October 16, 2020. https://www.unz.com/gdurocher/how-fast-is-frances-muslim-population-growing/.

Dworkin, Anthony. 'Europe's New Counter-Terror Wars'. European Council on Foreign Relations. October 21, 2016. https://ecfr.eu/publication/europes_new_counter_terror_wars7155/.

———. 'Europe's War on Terror'. European Council on Foreign Relations. June 23, 2017. https://ecfr.eu/article/essay_europes_war_on_terror/.

Dyal, Mark. Foreword to *Babel Inc: Multiculturalism, Globalisation, and the New World Order*, by Kerry Bolton, v-ix. London: Black House Publishing, 2013.

Electronic Immigration Network. 'Demos: Almost Half of Ethnic Minority Population Now Live in Majority Non-white Areas'. May 5, 2013. https://www.ein.org.uk/news/demos-almost-half-ethnic-minority-population-now-live-majority-non-white-areas.

Elghossain, Anthony. 'The Enduring Power of Neoconservatism'. *New Republic.* April 3, 2019 https://newrepublic.com/article/153450/enduring-power-neoconservatism.

ENAR. 'About Us. Our theory of change'. https://www.enar-eu.org/Our-theory-of-change-1526.

———. Annual Report 2019. ENAR Europe. https://www.enar-eu.org/IMG/pdf/annualreport_2019_final_lr-2.pdf.

ENAR Extraordinary General Assembly 2021. October 8, 2021. ENAR blog. https://www.enar-eu.org/ENAR-Extraordinary-General-Assembly-2021.

Engdahl, F. William. 'Soros Plays Both Ends in Syria Refugee Chaos'. *New Eastern Outlook (NEO)*, December 18, 2015. http://m.journal-neo.org/2015/12/18/soros-plays-both-ends-in-syria-refugee-chaos/.

Erlanger, Steven. 'A Quandary for Europe: Fighting a War on ISIS Within Its Borders'. *New York Times*, March 23, 2016. http://www.nytimes.com/2016/03/24/world/europe/a-quandary-for-europe-fighting-a-war-on-isis-within-its-borders.html?_r=2.

Esipova, Neli, Anita Pugliese, and Julie Ray. 'Europeans Most Negative Toward Immigration'. Gallup, October 16, 2015. http://www.gallup.com/poll/186209/europeans-negative-toward-immigration.aspx.

EUR-Lex. Consolidated versions of the Treaty on European Union and the Treaty on the Functioning of the European Union. *Official Journal of the European Communities*, C 326 (October 26, 2012): 1–390. http://eur-lex.europa.eu/legalcontent/EN/NOT/?uri=CELEX:12012E/TXT.

———. Council Directive 2003/86/EC of September 22, 2003 on the Right to Family Reunification. *Official Journal of the European Communities*, L 251 (October 3, 2003): 12–18. http://data.europa.eu/eli/dir/2003/86/oj.

———. Directive 2011/95/EU of the European Parliament and of the Council of December 13, 2011. *Official Journal of the European Union*, L 337 (December 20, 2011): 9–26. https://eur-lex.europa.eu/legal-content/EN/TXT/HTML/?uri=CELEX:32011L0095&from=EN.

Euro-Islam. 'Muslims in European politics'. N.d. http://www.euro-islam.info/key-issues/political-representation/.

Euronews. 'Kusturica accuses Soros over migration, says EU leadership is soviet style'. *Euronews.com*, April 15, 2016. http://www.euronews.com/2016/04/15/kusturica-accuses-soros-over-migration-says-eu-leadership-is-soviet-style.

Europa. 'Family Reunification'. Migration and Home Affairs. Last updated September 21, 2016. http://ec.europa.eu/dgs/home-affairs/what-we-do/policies/legal-migration/family-reunification/index_en.htm.

———. 'Living in the EU'. https://europa.eu/european-union/about-eu/figures/living_en#goto_1 (accessed June 2016).

'Europe will be diverse, or war! — Frans Timmermans'. YouTube video, 1:31. Posted by divpolitics, March 29, 2016. https://www.youtube.com/watch?v=q94syUDDhxA.

European Commission. 'Opening remarks of First Vice-President Frans Timmermans at the First Annual Colloquium on Fundamental Rights'. October 1, 2015. http://europa.eu/rapid/press-release_SPEECH-15-5754_en.htm.

———. 'Public Opinion in the European Union, First results'. Standard Eurobarometer 82, Autumn 2014, 7256. http://ec.europa.eu/public_opinion/archives/eb/eb82/eb82_first_en.pdf.

———. Standard Eurobarometer 94. 'Public opinion in the European Union Report'. Winter 2020 — 2021. Fieldwork: February–March 2021. doi:10.2775/841401.

European Council. 'Speech by President Donald Tusk at the event marking the 40th anniversary of European People Party (EPP)'. *Europa*, May 30, 2016. http://www.consilium.europa.eu/en/press/press-releases/2016/05/30-pec-speech-epp/.

European Council on Foreign Relations (ECFR). ECFR Internship Rome, 2012. http://www.ecfr.eu/page/-/ECFRinternshipRome.pdf.

European Court of Human Rights. *Annual Report 2003*. http://www.echr.coe.int/Documents/Annual_report_2003_ENG.pdf.

———. *European Convention on Human Rights.* Council of Europe, June 1, 2010. http://www.echr.coe.int/Documents/Convention_ENG.pdf.

European Programme for Integration and Migration (EPIM). 'About EPIM'. http://www.epim.info/.

———. 'Project: Moving Beyond Borders — Protect undocumented migrants on either side of the European borders'. Migreurop. http://www.epim.info/migreurop/.

European Stability Initiative (ESI). 'Donors'. *ESI.* http://www.esiweb.org/index.php?lang=en&id=65.

———. Gerald Knaus. *ESI.* http://www.esiweb.org/index.php?lang=en&id=279&person_ID=1.

———. Gerald Knaus. *ESI*, September 2, 2009. http://www.esiweb.org/rumeliobserver/about-the-author/.

———. 'The Merkel Plan'. *ESI*, October 4, 2015. http://www.esiweb.org/pdf/ESI%20-%20The%20Merkel%20Plan%20-%20Compassion%20and%20Control%20-%204%20October%202015.pdf.

———. 'The Merkel-Samsom Plan — A proposal for the Syrian refugee crisis'. *ESI*, 2016. http://www.esiweb.org/index.php?lang=en&id=597.

European Union External Action. 'Federica Mogherini's remarks at "Call to Europe V: Islam in Europe", FEPS conference'. *EEAS*, June 25, 2015. 150625_07. https://eeas.europa.eu/headquarters/headquarters-homepage/6332_en.

Eurostat. 'All Valid Permits by Reason on 31 December of Each Year'. 2008–2015. [tps00171] http://ec.europa.eu/eurostat/tgm/refreshTableAction.do?tab=table&plugin=1&pcode=tps00171&language=en.

———. 'First Population Estimates'. 124/2015 — July 10, 2015. http://ec.europa.eu/eurostat/documents/2995521/6903510/3-10072015-AP-EN.pdf/d2bfb01f-6ac5-4775-8a7e-7b104c1146d0.

———. 'Foreign-born Population by Country of Birth, January 1, 2014'. *Statistics Explained*, updated July 1, 2015. http://ec.europa.eu/eurostat/statistics-explained/index.php/File:Foreign-born_population_by_country_of_birth,_1_January_2014_%28%C2%B9%29_YB15.png.

———. 'Foreign-born Population by Country of Birth, January 1, 2015'. *Statistics Explained*, updated May 31, 2016. http://ec.europa.eu/eurostat/statistics-explained/index.php/File:Foreign-born_population_by_country_of_birth,_1_January_2015_(%C2%B9)_YB16.png.

———. 'Migration and Migration Population Statistics'. *Statistics Explained*, May 2016 http://ec.europa.eu/eurostat/statistics-explained/index.php/Migration_and_migrant_population_statistics.

Evans, Gareth. 'The Limits of State Sovereignty: The Responsibility to Protect in the 21st Century'. Eighth Neelam Tiruchelvam Memorial Lecture by Gareth Evans, President, International Crisis Group, International Centre for Ethnic Studies (ICES), Colombo, July 29, 2007. http://www.gevans.org/speeches/speech232.html.

Event Chronicle, The. 'Organizations Funded Directly by George Soros and his Open Society Institute'. *Theeventchronicle.com*, November 13, 2015. http://www.theeventchronicle.com/study/george-soros-funded-organizations/#.

EVS. 'European Values Study 1999'. Integrated Dataset. GESIS Data Archive, Cologne, 2011. ZA3811 Data File Version 3.0.0, doi:10.4232/1.10789.

Feldman, Matthew (ed.). *A Fascist Century: Essays by Roger Griffin.* Hampshire; New York: Palgrave MacMillan, 2008.

FEMYSO. 'FEMYSO — Annual Report 2014'. 2014. Available from https://www.scribd.com/document/260745472/FEMYSO-Annual-Report-2014.

———. 'Islamophobia Monitoring & Action Network'. https://femyso.org/campaigns/past/iman/.

———. 'We are FEMYSO'. https://femyso.org/we-are-femyso/.

Fernandez-Morera, Dario. *The Myth of the Andalusian Paradise: Muslims, Christians, and Jews under Islamic Rule in Medieval Spain*. Intercollegiate Studies Institute. 2016.

Fischer, Joschka. 'From Confederacy to Federation — Thoughts on the finality of European integration'. Speech at the Humboldt University, Berlin, May 12, 2000. Available from http://ec.europa.eu/dorie/fileDownload.do?docId=192161&cardId=192161.

———. 'The future of Europe and the Franco-German partnership'. Address given by Joschka Fischer, Federal Minister for Foreign Affairs, on January 30, 2001 at the French Cultural Center of the University of Freiburg. http://www.cvce.eu/en/obj/address_given_by_joschka_fischer_on_the_future_of_europe_and_the_franco_german_partnership_freiburg_30_january_2001-en-19480146-ae28-4934-bf58-87a2f7a4fe67.html.

Fjordman. 'Caucasophobia — the Accepted Racism'. *Gates of Vienna* (blog), October 23, 2006. http://gatesofvienna.blogspot.ca/2006/10/caucasophobia-accepted-racism.html.

Fria Tider. 'Muslimer mest vänstervridna' [Muslims most leftist]. January 11, 2012. http://www.friatider.se/muslimer_mest_vanstervridna.

———. '93% av franska muslimer röstade på Hollande' [93% of French Muslims voted for Hollande]. May 9, 2012. http://www.friatider.se/93-av-franska-muslimer-rostade-pa-hollande.

Friberg, Daniel. 'Daniel Friberg: Interview with Russia Today'. *Right On*, April 15, 2016. https://www.righton.net/2016/04/15/interview-with-russia-today/.

Friedman, Victoria. 'Soros Pledges Renewed Fight Against "Dominant Ideology" of Nationalism, Says EU "on Verge of Breakdown"'. *Breitbart*. January 15, 2018. https://www.breitbart.com/europe/2018/01/15/soros-dominant-ideology-nationalism-eu-verge-breakdown/.

Fukuyama, Francis. 'The Challenges for European Identity'. *The Global Journal*, January 11, 2012. http://theglobal journal.net/article/view/469/.

Fuller, Steve. 'The Prospects for Philosophical Rhetoric'. Chap. 5 in *Reengaging the Prospects of Rhetoric: Current Conversations and Contemporary Challenges*, edited by Mark J. Porrovecchio. New York and London: Routledge, 2010.

Garbaye, R. 'Birmingham: Conventional Politics as the Main Channel for Political Incorporation'. In *Multicultural Policies and Modes of Citizenship in European Cities*, edited by A. Rogers and J. Tillie. Ashgate; Aldershot, 2001.

Gellately, Robert and Ben Kiernan. *The Specter of Genocide: Mass Murder in Historical Perspective*. Cambridge: Cambridge University Press, 2003.

'George Soros Interview 60 Minutes [FULL]'. YouTube video (ReasonReport), 13:27. Posted by ReasonReport, November 17, 2016. https://www.youtube.com/watch?v=QSyczwuTQfo.

'German president Gauk'. YouTube video, 00:34. Posted by Vlad Tepesblog, June 22, 2016. https://www.youtube.com/watch?v=9hX6LPqOFf8.

'Germanistan — Diversity is our future!' YouTube video, 00:47. Posted by Rabbi Steinberg, June 20, 2016. https://www.youtube.com/watch?v=te9EGCwCWoc.

Global News. 'ISIS'. http://globalnews.ca/tag/isis/.

Glover, Julian. 'Most Europeans see themselves as liberal, Guardian poll shows'. *Guardian*, March 13, 2011. https://www.theguardian.com/world/2011/mar/13/european-union-immigration-survey.

Goodwin, Matthew, Thomas Raines, and David Cutts. 'What Do Europeans Think About Muslim Immigration?' Chatham House, February 7, 2017. https://www.chathamhouse.org/expert/comment/what-do-europeans-think-about-muslim-immigration.

Gotev, Georgi. 'Nationalist MEP blames Soros for EU migration crisis'. *Euractiv*, June 22, 2016. https://www.euractiv.com/section/global-europe/news/nationalist-mep-blames-soros-for-eu-migration-crisis/.

Gottfried, Paul. 'Murdoch is Daddy Warbucks to The Neocons'. *The American Conservative.* July 27, 2011. https://www.theamericanconservative.com/murdoch-is-daddy-war-bucks-to-the-neocons/.

Gottheil, Fred M. 'The Smoking Gun: Arab Immigration into Palestine, 1922–1931'. *Middle East Quarterly* 10, no. 1 (Winter 2003): 53–64.

Gramsci, Antonio. *Selections from the Prison Notebooks of Antonio Gramsci.* Edited and translated by Quentin Hoare and Geoffrey Nowell Smith. London: Elec. Book, 1999. http://courses.justice.eku.edu/PLS330_Louis/docs/gramsci-prison-notebooks-vol1.pdf.

Gray, John. *Black Mass: How Religion Led the World into Crisis.* Anchor Canada, 2008.

'Green politician Dr. v. Berg: Good thing that Germans will be a minority in "supercultural" society'. YouTube video, 00:55. Posted by Face of a dying Nation, November 23, 2015. https://www.youtube.com/watch?v=4F-bv9zTpo.

Greenhill, Kelly. 'Strategic Engineered Migration as a Weapon of War'. *Civil Wars* 10, no. 1 (March 2008): 6–21.

Greep, Monica. 'Revealed: The most popular baby names of 2021 so far'. *MailOnline.* June 14, 2021. https://www.msn.com/en-us/lifestyle/lifestyle-buzz/revealed-the-most-popular-baby-names-of-2021-so-far/ar-AAL1Bps.

Guardian. 'Angela Merkel Issues New Year's Warning over Right-Wing Pegida Group'. December 30, 2014, http://www.theguardian.com/world/2014/dec/30/angela-merkel-criticises-pegida-far-right-group-germany.

Guardian (datablog). 'Guardian/ICM Europe poll'. *Theguardian.com,* (2011). https://www.theguardian.com/news/datablog/2011/mar/14/europe-poll-icm#data.

Guidetti, Debora and Clara Grosset. 'Slavery and Reparation in France'. Open Society Foundations. May 9, 2013. https://www.opensocietyfoundations.org/voices/slavery-and-reparation-france.

Hale, Virginia. 'EU Elections: Soros Foundation Spent $6 Million to Destroy Populism'. *Breitbart.* August 18, 2016. https://www.breitbart.com/europe/2016/08/18/eu-elections-soros-populism/.

Hall, J. '"How is democracy treating you guys?" ISIS militants take to social media to encourage Ferguson protesters to embrace Islamic extremism'. *Daily Mail.* August 19, 2014. http://www.dailymail.co.uk/news/article-2728624/How-democracy-treating-guys-ISIS-militants-social-media-encourage-Ferguson-protesters-embrace-Islamic-extremism.html.

Hallett, Nick. 'Orban: Multiculturalism Endangers Christian Europe, Leads To "Parallel Societies"'. *Breitbart,* October 24, 2015. http://www.breitbart.com/london/2015/10/24/orban-multiculturalism-endangers-christian-europe-leads-parallel-societies/.

———. 'Soros Admits Involvement In Migrant Crisis: "National Borders Are The Obstacle"'. *Breitbart,* November 2, 2015. http://www.breitbart.com/london/2015/11/02/soros-admits-involvement-in-migrant-crisis-national-borders-are-the-obstacle/.

Harley, Nicky. 'French "Islamist pharmacy" charity CCIF is forced to close'. *The National,* December 2, 2020. https://www.thenationalnews.com/world/french-islamist-pharmacy-charity-ccif-is-forced-to-close-1.1121828.

Harvey, Oliver. 'March of the Pinstripe Right'. *Sun*, January 6, 2015. https://www.thesun.co.uk/archives/news/5527/march-of-the-pinstripe-right/.

Hashmi, Taj. *Global Jihad and America: The Hundred-Year War Beyond Iraq and Afghanistan*. California; London: Sage Publications, 2014.

Heilbrunn, Jacob. 'The Neocons Strike Back'. *New Republic*, January 23, 2020. https://newrepublic.com/article/156266/neocons-strike-back.

Hermanin, Costanza, Debora Guidetti, and Eefje de Kroon. 'Racism in Europe and what to do about it'. New York: Open Society Foundations. December 3, 2012. https://www.opensocietyfoundations.org/voices/racism-europe-and-what-do-about-it.

Hickley, Matthew. 'Only two in three babies born in England and Wales are white British'. *Mail Online*, August 30, 2008. http://www.dailymail.co.uk/news/article-1050593/Only-babies-born-England-Wales-white-British.html.

Hochschild, Jennifer L. and John Mollenkopf. *The Complexities of Immigration: Why Western Countries Struggle with Immigration Politics and Policies*. Transatlantic Council on Migration: A Project of the Migration Policy Institute, 2008.

Hoft, Jim. '"Massive Scandal"—EU pays Muslim Brotherhood €36,5 Million to "Subjugate Europe"'. Gateway Pundit. August 5, 2020'. https://www.thegatewaypundit.com/2020/08/massive-scandal-eu-pays-muslim-brotherhood-e365-million-subjugate-europe/.

Holehouse, Matthew. 'Prime Ministers listen too much to voters, complains EU's Juncker'. *Telegraph*, May 5, 2016. http://www.telegraph.co.uk/news/2016/05/05/prime-ministers-listen-too-much-to-voters-complains-eus-juncker/.

Hollifield, James F. 'The Emerging Migration State'. *International Migration Review* 38, no. 3 (Fall 2004): 885–912. doi:10.1111/j.1747-7379.2004.tb00223.x.

Howson, Richard. *Challenging Hegemonic Masculinity*. London: Taylor and Francis Group, 2005.

Hubinette, Tobias. *Creol*, no. 1/1996. Wikiquote. https://sv.m.wikiquote.org/wiki/Tobias_H%C3%BCbinette.

Hungary Today. 'PM Orbán: Europe's Peoples Are Beginning To Awake'. *Hungarytoday.hu*, October 30, 2015. http://hungarytoday.hu/news/pm-orban-europes-peoples-beginning-awake-91035.

Huntington, Samuel P. 'The Clash of Civilizations?' *Foreign Affairs* 72, no. 3 (Summer 1993): 22–49.

———. *The Clash of Civilizations and the Remaking of World Order*. New York: Simon & Schuster Paperbacks, 1996.

Ifop. *Comparative survey France /Germany on Islam*. Ifop for Le Monde, December 13, 2010. http://www.ifop.com/media/poll/1365-2-study_file.pdf.

———. *Le regard des Européens sur l' I slam*. Ifop, 2012. http://www.ifop.fr/media/pressdocument/410-1-document_file.pdf.

Ignatius, David. 'Tension of the Times'. *Washington Times*, June 18, 2004. Page A29. https://www.washingtonpost.com/wp-dyn/articles/A50909-2004Jun17.html.

IN GAZA. '"Human Rights" front groups ("Humanitarian Interventionalists") warring on Syria'. https://ingaza.wordpress.com/syria/human-rights-front-groups-humanitarian-interventionalists-warring-on-syria/.

'Insight—Migrant Crisis: ISIS & The Security Threat to Europe'. YouTube video (Red Ice Insight), 17:22. Posted by Red Ice Radio, November 25, 2015. https://www.youtube.com/watch?v=oDoBT9kqXxI.

International Organization for Migration. *Compendium of Migrant Integration Policies and Practices*. IOM, Summer 2009. https://www.iom.int/jahia/webdav/shared/shared/mainsite/activities/facilitating/mi_compendium_ver_feb2010.pdf.

Ipsos. *Global Views on Immigration*. Global @dvisor Wave 22. August 2011. http://www.ipsos-na.com/download/pr.aspx?id=10883> (March 2012).

Islamic Human Rights Commission. 'Year long course: Counter-racism'. November 21, 2013. http://www.ihrc.org.uk/events/10793-year-long-course-counter-racism.

Israeli, Raphael. *Muslim Minorities in Modern States: The Challenge of Assimilation*. London: Transaction Publishers, 2009.

Jenkins, Philip. 'Demographics, Religion, and the Future of Europe'. *Orbis* 50, no. 3, (Summer 2006): 519–539.

Jenkins, Simon. 'Germany's "Pinstripe Nazis" Show the Immigration Debate is Overheated'. *Guardian*, December 16, 2014, http://www.theguardian.com/commentisfree/2014/dec/16/germany-pinstripe-nazis-temperature-immigration-debate-reduced.

Johnson, Dominic D. P. and Monica Duffy Toft. 'Grounds for War: The Evolution of Territorial Conflict'. *International Security* 38, no. 3 (Winter 2013/2014): 7–38.

Johnson, Paul. *Offshore Islanders: From Roman Occupation to European Entry*. Littlehampton Book Services Ltd., 1972.

Judgements on the merits delivered by the Grand Chamber. *Case of Refah Partisi (The Welfare Party) and Others v. Turkey*. Nos. 41340/98, 41342/98, 41343/98 and 41344/98, ECHR 2003-II.

Judis, John B. 'A Kind Word About Neoconservatism'. *New Republic*, August 2, 2013. https://newrepublic.com/article/114142/danger-neo-conservatism.

JW v DOD and State 14–812. *Judicial Watch*, May 18, 2015. Pgs. 287–293 (291). http://www.judicialwatch.org/document-archive/pgs-287-293-291-jw-v-dod-and-state-14-812-2/.

Kassam, Raheem. 'Hungarian PM Slams Soros-Funded Advocacy Groups: They "Are Drawing A Living From The Immigration Crisis"'. *Breitbart*, September 15, 2015. http://www.breitbart.com/london/2015/09/15/hungarian-pm-slams-soros-funded-advocacy-groups-they-are-drawing-a-living-from-the-immigration-crisis/.

Kaufmann, Eric. 'A Comparative-Historical Perspective on the United States and European Union'. *Global Society* 17, no. 4 (2003): 359–383.

Kemp, Arthur. Four Flags: The Indigenous People of Great Britain. Deeside: Excalibur Books, 2010.

Kent, Simon. 'UN Migration Envoy Believes EU Should "Undermine" National Homogeneity'. *Breitbart*, September 25, 2015. http://www.breitbart.com/london/2015/09/25/un-migration-envoy-believes-eu-should-undermine-national-homogeneity/.

Kern, Soeren. 'European Concerns Over Muslim Immigration Go Mainstream'. *Gatestone Institute*, August 15, 2011. http://www.gatestoneinstitute.org/2349/european-concerns-over-muslim-immigration.

Kettani, Houssain. 'Muslim Population in Europe: 1950–2020'. *Internet Journal of Environmental Science and Development* 1, no. 2 (June 2010): 154–164. http://www.ijesd.org/papers/29-D438.pdf.

Kilpatrick, William. 'Islam, revolution, and Black Lives Matter'. *Crisis Magazine*, July 14, 2016. http://www.crisismagazine.com/2016/islam-revolution-black-lives-matter.

Klein, Aaron. 'Hacked Soros memo: $650,000 to Black Lives Matter'. *Breitbart*, August 16, 2016. http://www.breitbart.com/big-government/2016/08/16/hacked-soros-memo-baltimore-riots-provide-unique-opportunity-reform-police/.

———. 'Soros fingerprints on Libya bombing'. *WND*, March 23, 2011. http://www.wnd.com/2011/03/278685/.

Kofman, Eleonore, Madalina Rogoz, and Florence Lévy. *Family Migration Policies in France*. International Center for Migration Policy Development, January 2010. http://research.icmpd.org/fileadmin/Research-Website/Project_material/NODE/FR_Policy_Report_formatted7May.pdf.

Köppel, Roger. 'Terrorismus und Migration: Wir produzieren Heerscharen von Entwurzelten und Unzufriedenen'. *Die Weltwoche*, August 13, 2016. http://www.weltwoche.ch/ausgaben/2016-13/artikel/islam-die-weltwoche-ausgabe-132016.html.

Kovács, Adorján F. 'Wahrheiten zur Flüchtlingskrise'. *The European*, December 28, 2015. http://www.theeuropean.de/adorjan-f-kovacs/10622-einwanderung-oder-zuflucht.

Kovacs, Stéphane. 'Islamophobie : la campagne qui derange'. *Le Figaro*, November 14, 2012. https://www.lefigaro.fr/actualite-france/2012/11/14/01016-20121114ARTFIG00746-islamophobie-la-campagne-qui-derange.php.

Krebs, Ronald R. and Jack S. Levy. 'Demographic Change and the Sources of International Conflict'. Chap. 3 in *Demography and National Security*, edited by Myron Weiner and Sharon Stanton Russell. New York; Oxford: Berghahn Books, 2001.

Krogull, Ute and Michael Stifter. 'Prognose: Zugewanderte sind in Augsburg bald in der Mehrheit'. *Augsburger Allgemeine*, April 19, 2016. http://www.augsburger-allgemeine.de/politik/Prognose-Zugewanderte-sind-in-Augsburg-bald-in-der-Mehrheit-id37523202.html.

Kuper, L. *Genocide: It's Political Use in the Twentieth Century*. New Haven and London: Yale University Press, 1982.

Kurth, James. 'Western Civilization: Our Tradition'. *The Intercollegiate Review* 39, no. 1–2 (Fall 2003/Spring 2004): 5–13.

Laing, Lloyd Robert and Jennifer Laing. *Anglo-Saxon England. Britain before the Conquest*. London: Routledge & Kegan Paul, 1979.

Lambton, John. 'The Great Replacement—Part I'. *Right On*, December 10, 2015. https://www.righton.net/2015/12/10/the-great-replacement-part-i/.

Lane, Oliver JJ. 'Sweden's Army Chief Warns Of WORLD WAR 3 Inside Europe "Within a Few Years"'. *Breitbart*, January 26, 2016. http://www.breitbart.com/london/2016/01/26/swedens-army-chief-warns-the-country-will-be-at-war/.

Lanzieri, Giampaolo. 'Fewer, older and multicultural? Projections of the EU populations by foreign/ national background'. Eurostat: Methodologies and Working Papers. 2011. doi:10.2785/17529.

Laub, Zachary. 'The Taliban in Afghanistan'. *Council on Foreign Relations*, July 4, 2014. http://www.cfr.org/afghanistan/taliban-afghanistan/p10551.

———. 'Why the German-Turkish Migrant Plan Can Work'. Interview: Gerald Knaus. *Council on Foreign Relations*, March 16, 2016. http://www.cfr.org/europe/why-german-turkish-migrant-plan-can-work/p37660.

Laurence, Jonathan. 'Islam and Social Democrats: Integrating Europe's Muslim minority'. *Dissent*. Fall 2013. https://www.dissentmagazine.org/article/islam-and-social-democrats.

Lavelle, Peter. 'Human Tidal Wave'. RT News CrossTalk Video, 28:20. CrossTalking with Chris Bambery, Sukant Chandan, and Catherine Shakdam. February 19, 2016. https://www.rt.com/shows/crosstalk/332964-refugee-crisis-record-numbers/.

Law, John. 'The European Race Evolved in the European Continent — Relatively Recently'. *Council of European Canadians*, June 12, 2015. http://www.eurocanadian.ca/2015/06/european-race-evolved-in-europe.html.

Leeden, Michael A. *The War Against the Terror Masters: Why It Happened. Where We Are Now. How'll We Win*. New York: Macmillan, 2003/2007.

Legrain, Phillippe. *Immigrants: Your Country Needs Them*. Princeton and Oxford: Princeton University Press, 2006/2007.

Lemkin, Raphael. *Axis Rule in Occupied Europe: Laws of Occupation, Analysis of Government, Proposals for Redress*. New Jersey: The Lawbook Exchange Ltd., 2004 (1944).

Leslie, Stephen, Bruce Winney, Garrett Hellenthal, Dan Davison, Abdelhamid Boumertit, Tammy Day, Katarzyna Hutnik, Ellen C. Royrvik, Barry Cunliffe, Wellcome Trust Case Control Consortium, International Multiple Sclerosis Genetics Consortium, Daniel J. Lawson, Daniel Falush, Colin Freeman, Matti Pirinen, Simon Myers, Mark Robinson, Peter Donnelly and Walter Bodmer. 'The Fine-Scale Genetic Structure of the British Population'. *Nature* 519, no. 7543 (March 19, 2015): 309–314.

Lester, Anthony. 'Multiculturalism and Free Speech'. Presentation at De Montfort University, Leicester, UK, June 10, 2009. Available from Blackstone Chambers, https://www.blackstonechambers.com/news/analysis-multiculturalism/.

Liddle, Rod. 'Fabricant was WRONG... but his target is thick, bigoted and hysterical'. *Sun*, June 23, 2014. https://www.thesun.co.uk/archives/news/924258/fabricant-was-wrong-but-his-target-is-thick-bigoted-and-hysterical/.

Lipka, Michael. 'The continuing decline of Europe's Jewish population'. *Pew Research Center*, February 9, 2015. http://www.pewresearch.org/fact-tank/2015/02/09/europes-jewish-population/.

Litterick, David. 'Billionaire who broke the Bank of England'. *The Telegraph*, September 13, 2002. https://www.telegraph.co.uk/finance/2773265/Billionaire-who-broke-the-Bank-of-England.html.

Local, The. 'Government in a twist over "pinstriped Nazis"'. *Thelocal.de*, December 12, 2014. https://www.thelocal.de/20141212/government-in-a-twist-over-pinstriped-nazis.

MacDonald, Alastair. 'EU chief Tusk slams utopian "illusions" of united Europe'. *Reuters*, May 31, 2016. http://af.reuters.com/article/worldNews/idAFKCN0YL1UL.

MacDonald, Kevin. 'Going Against the Tide: Ricardo Duchesne's Intellectual Defense of the West'. *The Occidental Quarterly* 11, no. 3 (Fall 2011). http://www.kevinmacdonald.net/duchesne-review.pdf.

Macleod, Alan. 'With Bezos at the Helm, Democracy Dies at the Washington Post Editorial Board'. *Mint Press News*, June 18, 2021. https://stage.mintpressnews.com/jeff-bezos-at-helm-democracy-dies-at-washington-post-editorial-board/277738/.

Malcolm X Movement. In *Facebook* [BlackLivesMatter vs BlackLiberation]. 2016. Retrieved January 2017 from https://www.facebook.com/events/637404226432816/.

———. In *Facebook* [2016: Year of the Panther & the Black Panther research project]. January 1, 2016. Retrieved January 2017 from https://www.facebook.com/MalcolmXMovement/posts/514606782053022.

Marcuse, Herbert. *The New Left and the 1960s: Collected Papers of Herbert Marcuse*. Vol. 3. Edited and introduction by Douglas Kellner. New York: Routledge, 2005.

Martine. 'Drépanocytose: la carte du grand remplacement mise à jour + projection sur 35 ans (rediff)'.

Fdesouche, February 5, 2015. http://www.fdesouche.com/481589-drepanocytose-la-carte-de-france-du-grand-remplacement#.

Martino, Peter. 'Will Germany Abolish Itself and France Commit Suicide?' *Gatestone Institute*, December 3, 2014. https://www.gatestoneinstitute.org/4921/germany-france-suicide.

Matthews, Warren. *World Religions*. Seventh edition. Wadsworth: Cengage Learning, 2007.

McNamara, Thomas E. 'Despite Divisions, Europe and the United States Are Fighting Terrorism.

Together'. *European Affairs* 4, no. 2 (Spring 2003). The European Institute. http://www.europeaninstitute.org/index.php/30-european-affairs/spring-2003/350-despite-divisions-europe-and-the-united-states-are-fighting-terrorism-together.

McWhinney, Edward. *Self-Determination of Peoples and Plural-Ethnic States in Contemporary International Law: Failed States, Nation Building and the Alternative, Federal Option*. Leiden; Boston: Martinus Nijhoff Publishers, 2007.

Merritt, Giles. 'The refugee crisis: Europe needs more migrants, not fewer'. *Europe's World*, October 26, 2015. http://europesworld.org/2015/10/26/the-refugee-crisis-europe-needs-more-migrants-not-fewer/#.WAaXaiT3jpt.

Mertens, Thomas. 'Cosmopolitanism and Citizenship: Kant Against Habermas'. *European Journal of Philosophy* 4, no. 3, (1996): 328–347.

Messina, Anthony M. *The Logics of Politics of Post-WWII Migration to Western Europe*. Cambridge University Press, 2007.

Middle East Media Research Institute (MEMRI), The. 'Belgian Islamist Sheik Abu Imran with Al-Qaeda flag opposite the Atomium monument in Brussels: Our flag will soon be flying on top of all the palaces in Europe until we reach the White House'. Video file. Clip #3234. December 10, 2011. https://www.memri.org/tv/belgian-islamist-sheik-abu-imran-al-qaeda-flag-opposite-atomium-monument-brussels-our-flag-will.

———. 'Egyptian cleric Ali Abu Al-Hasan: In several decades, "Europe will become a single Islamic state"'. Video file. Clip #3259. January 5, 2012. https://www.memri.org/tv/egyptian-cleric-ali-abu-al-hasan-several-decades-europe-will-become-single-islamic-state.

Miller, Christian. 'None Dare Call It White Genocide'. *Counter-currents*, February 7, 2011. http://www.counter-currents.com/2011/02/none-dare-call-it-white-genocide/.

———. 'The White Genocide Evidence Project'. *MajorityRights.com* (blog), 2011. http://majorityrights.com/weblog/comments/the_white_genocide_evidence_project/.

Moran, Rick. 'Libya and the Soros Doctrine'. *Frontpage Mag*, March 27, 2011. http://www.frontpagemag.com/fpm/89019/libya-and-soros-doctrine-rick-moran.

Morris, Chris. 'Sweden's asylum offer to refugees from Syria'. *BBC News*, October 23, 2013. http://www.bbc.com/news/world-europe-24635791.

Movement for Black Lives, The. (n.d.). 'Platform'. https://policy.m4bl.org/.

Mulholland, Rory. 'French police break up riot in migrant camp in Calais'. *Telegraph*, May 25, 2015. http://www.telegraph.co.uk/news/worldnews/europe/france/11628507/French-police-break-up-riot-in-migrant-camp-in-Calais.html.

———. 'Police arrest 35 after migrants stormed ferry temporarily closing Port of Calais'. *Telegraph*, January 23, 2016. http://www.telegraph.co.uk/news/worldnews/europe/france/12117793/Port-of-Calais-closed-as-migrants-storm-ferry.html.

Murray Web Works. 'Open Secularism — Required for Democracy'. SCS Nexus, April 29, 2012. http://www.secularconnexion.ca/open-secularism-required-for-democracy/.

Network of European Foundations (NEF). 'NEF is the Network of European Foundations'. http://www.nef-europe.org/.

New Urban Collective. http://nucnet.nl/.

New World Encyclopedia contributors. 'The Washington Post'. *New World Encyclopedia*, December 28, 2021 https://www.newworldencyclopedia.org/entry/Washington_Times#cite_ref-25.

Newenham, Pamela. 'Peter Sutherland to retire as Goldman Sachs chairman'. *Irish Times*, May 20, 2015. http://www.irishtimes.com/business/financial-services/peter-sutherland-to-retire-as-goldman-sachs-chairman-1.2219623.

Newman, Alex. 'U.S. Intel: Obama Coalition Supported Islamic State in Syria'. *New Statesman*, May 26, 2015. http://www.thenewamerican.com/world-news/asia/item/20943-u-s-intel-obama-coalition-supported-islamic-state-in-syria.

'"No more blue Eyes & blonde Hair!"- Islam Researcher who taught ISIS fighters applauded on German TV'. YouTube video, 0:28. Posted by Face of a dying Nation — Backup, May 15, 2016. https://www.youtube.com/watch?v=Qb9QAUsUA98.

Noack, Rick. 'Anti-Islam Protestors March in Dresden, Germany'. *CNN*, January 13, 2015, http://edition.cnn.com/ 2015/01/12/europe/germany-anti-islam-marches/.

Office for National Statistics. *2011 Census: Key Statistics and Quick Statistics for Local Authorities in the United Kingdom*. ONS, October 11, 2013. http://www.ons.gov.uk/peoplepopulationandcommunity/populationandmigration/populationestimates/bulletins/keystatisticsandquickstatisticsforlocalauthoritiesintheunitedkingdom/2013-10-11.

———. 'Births and infant mortality by ethnicity, England and Wales (2007–2019)'. ONS Dataset. May 26, 2021. https://www.ons.gov.uk/peoplepopulationandcommunity/healthandsocialcare/childhealth/datasets/birthsandinfantmortalitybyethnicityenglandandwales.

———. 'Ethnicity and national identity in England and Wales: 2011'. December 11, 2012. https://www.ons.gov.uk/peoplepopulationandcommunity/culturalidentity/ethnicity/articles/ ethnicityandnationalidentityinenglandandwales/2012–12–11.

———. 'Muslim population in the UK'. August 2, 2018. https://www.ons.gov.uk/aboutus/transparencyandgovernance/freedomofinformationfoi/muslimpopulationintheuk.

———. 'Population estimates by ethnic group and religion, England and Wales: 2019'. December 16, 2021. https://www.ons.gov.uk/peoplepopulationandcommunity/populationandmigration/populationestimates/articles/populationestimatesbyethnicgroupandreligionenglandandwales/2019.

———. 'Population of the UK by country of birth and nationality: 2019'. May 21, 2020. https://www.ons.gov.uk/peoplepopulationandcommunity/populationandmigration/internationalmigration/bulletins/ukpopulationbycountryofbirthandnationality/2019 .

———. 'Population of the UK by country of birth and nationality: year ending June 2021'. November 25, 2021. https://www.ons.gov.uk/peoplepopulationandcommunity/populationandmigration/internationalmigration/bulletins/ukpopulationbycountryofbirthandnationality/yearendingjune2021.

———. 'Table KS201EW: 2011 Census: Ethnic group, Local Authorities in England and Wales'. In *2011 Census: Key Statistics for England and Wales, March 2011*. ONS, December 11, 2012. http://www.ons.gov.uk/peoplepopulationandcommunity/populationandmigration/populationestimates/bulletins/2011censuskeystatisticsforenglandandwales/2012-12-11.

Office of the UN Special Adviser on the Prevention of Genocide (OSAPG). 'Analysis Framework'. Available at https://www.un.org/ar/preventgenocide/adviser/pdf/osapg_analysis_framework.pdf.

O'Hara, Kieron. *Conservatism*. London: Reaktion Books, 2011.

Olney, William W. 'Remittances and the Wage Impact of Immigration'. 2011/2014. Available from: http://web.williams.edu/Economics/wp/OlneyRemittancesAndWages.pdf.

O'Meara, Michael. *New Culture, New Right: Anti-Liberalism in Postmodern Europe*. London: Arktos, 2011.

Open Society Foundations. 'Awarded Grants: ENAR'. https://www.opensocietyfoundations.org/grants/past?filter_keyword=ENAR.

———. 'Contributions to JEKHUTNO and Work on Roma. From OSF Unit Proposed Strategies 2014 — 2017'. 2013. Available from Scribd: 'Jekhutno From May 31 Unit Strategies

1'. Uploaded by Peter Hasson. https://www.scribd.com/document/343846279/Jekhutno-From-May-31-Unit-Strategies-1?secret_password=Smyuo4URrunN72orKZMr.

———. 'George Soros'. Founder/Chair. https://www.opensocietyfoundations.org/george-soros.

———. 'International Migration Initiative'. https://www.opensocietyfoundations.org/about/programs/international-migration-initiative.

———. 'Open Society Initiative for Europe'. https://www.opensocietyfoundations.org/about/programs/open-society-initiative-europe.

———. 'OSI Announces New Fund to Protect Immigrants' Rights'. January 29, 2004. https://www.opensocietyfoundations.org/press-releases/osi-announces-new-fund-protect-immigrants-rights.

Open Society Initiative for Europe (OSIFE). 'List of European Elections 2014 Projects'. 2014. Available from Scribd. '-European Election-Portfolio Review-Annex i Ee14 Project List of All Elections Related Grants (3)'. Uploaded by Peter Hasson. https://www.scribd.com/document/343846323/European-Election-Portfolio-Review-Annex-i-Ee14-Project-List-of-All-Elections-Related-Grants-3?secret_password=m3V6G7QksxsGSFvjnXa4#from_embed.

'Orban's historic speech puts Hungary on war footing'. YouTube video, 13:01. Posted by Vlad Tepesblog, March 18, 2016. https://www.youtube.com/watch?v=EbINrdyAXlE.

Organisation of Islamic Cooperation. 'Cairo Declaration of Human Rights in Islam'. OIC, 1990. http://www.oic-oci.org/english/article/human.htm.

Oriental Review. 'Who is twitter-luring refugees to Germany?' *Orientalreview.org*, September 21, 2015. http://orientalreview.org/2015/09/21/who-is-twitter-luring-refugees-to-germany/.

P. Magazine. '32,1 procent van de Belgen is geen "Belgische Belg"' [32.1 percent of Belgians are not "Belgian Belgians"]. *P. Magazine.be*, January 13, 2021. https://pnws.be/321-procent-van-de-belgen-is-geen-belgische-belg/.

Passel, Jeffrey S., Gretchen Livingston, and D'Vera Cohn. 'Explaining Why Minority Births Now Outnumber White Births'. *Pew Research Center*, May 17, 2012. http://www.pewsocialtrends.org/2012/05/17/explaining-why-minority-births-now-outnumber-white-births/.

Paul, Ron. 'The Real Refugee Problem — And How To Solve It'. *Ron Paul Institute*, September 6, 2015. http://www.ronpaulinstitute.org/archives/featured-articles/2015/september/06/the-real-refugee-problem-and-how-to-solve-it/.

Paz, Reuven. 'Middle East Islamism in the European Arena'. *Middle East Review of International Affairs* 6, no. 3 (September 2002): 67–76.

PEGIDA. 'Programm'. https://www.pegida.de/.

'Peter Sutherland: Global agenda, nationalism & migration'. YouTube video, 04:24. Posted by Invandring Sverige, August 10, 2015. https://www.youtube.com/watch?t=85&v=RgSsM3MGLuk.

Pew Research Center. *A Fragile Rebound for EU Image on Eve of European Parliament Elections*. Global Attitudes Project, May 12, 2014. http://www.pewglobal.org/files/2014/05/2014-05-12_Pew-Global-Attitudes-European-Union.pdf.

Phares, Walid, Lorenzo Vidino, and Amr Hamzawy. *Political Islam in Europe and the Mediterranean: Three Contributions*. Centre for European Studies, 2011. http://www.martenscentre.eu/sites/default/files/publication-files/political_islam_in_europe_and_the_mediterranean.pdf.

Phillips, Melanie. *Londonistan*. New York: Encounter Books, 2006.

———. *The World Turned Upside Down: The Battle over God, Truth, and Power.* New York: Encounter Books, 2010.

Pickles, Kate. 'Imam tells Muslim migrants to "breed children" with Europeans to "conquer their Countries" and vows: "We will trample them underfoot, Allah willing"'. *Mail Online*, September 18, 2015. http://www.dailymail.co.uk/news/article-3240295/Imam-tells-Muslim-migrants-breed-children-Europeans-conquer-countries-vows-trample-underfoot-Allah-willing.html.

Pierce, Andrew. 'Nutters, Nick Clegg? They're closer than you think'. *Mail on Sunday*, April 26, 2010. http://www.dailymail.co.uk/debate/election/article-1268826/General-Election-2010-Nutters-Nick-Clegg-Theyre-closer-think.html.

Piketty, Thomas. 'For an open Europe'. *Fusion*, September 9, 2015. http://fusion.net/story/195478/for-an-open-europe/.

Pollack, Detlef. *Wahrnehmung und Akzeptanz Religiöser Vielfalt.* Exzellenzcluster: Religion und Politik, Westfälischen Wilhelms—Universit ät Münster (WWU), 2010. http://www.uni-muenster.de/imperia/md/content/religion_und_politik/aktuelles/2010/12_2010/studie_wahrnehmung_und_akzeptanz_religioeser_vielfalt.pdf.

Portes, Jonathan. 'Immigration Is Good for Economic Growth. If Europe Gets It Right, Refugees Can Be Too'. *WorldPost*, September 15, 2015. http://www.huffingtonpost.com/jonathan-portes/economic-europe-refugees_b_8128288.html.

Press TV. 'Turkish diaspora in Europe should have at least 5 children: Erdogan'. March 17, 2017. Retrieved from http://www.presstv.ir/Detail/2017/03/17/514742/Turkey-Erdogan-EU-Eskisehir-refugee-deal.

'Pro-Israel American Conservative: Thank God for ISIS...US Will be in Middle East Forever'. YouTube video (Horowitz Freedom Center TV), 02:38. Posted by Eretz Zen, December 13, 2014. https://www.youtube.com/watch?v=7cTTr9TufKs.

Puppinck, Grégor. 'ECHR: Conflicts of Interest Between Judges and NGOs'. European Centre for Law and Justice (ECLJ). January 2020. https://eclj.org/geopolitics/echr/conflits-d-interets-entre-juges-et-ong.

Purpose. 'About'. https://www.purpose.com/about/.

Ravnbak, Thorleif. 'Muslimerne i Danmark stemmer rødt' [Muslims in Denmark vote red]. *Danish Broadcasting Corporation* (DR), April 23, 2009. http://www.dr.dk/nyheder/indland/muslimerne-i-danmark-stemmer-roedt.

Rayne, Sierra. 'Whites already "visible minorities" in two of Canada's three largest cities, nationally by 2045'. *American Thinker* (blog), March 22, 2016. http://www.americanthinker.com/blog/2016/03/whites_already_visible_minorities_in_two_of_canadas_three_largest_cities_nationally_by_2045.html.

Raza, Hamzah. 'Why Muslims must support #BlackLivesMatter'. *Huffington Post* [Blog], December 31, 2015. http://www.huffingtonpost.com/hamzah-raza/muslims-must-support-blacklivesmatter_b_8899156.html.

Reference re Secession of Quebec [1998] 2 S.C.R. 217, 1998 SCC 25506. http://www.lib.sfu.ca/help/cite-write/citation-style-guides/gov-docs-chicago#CaseLaw.

Reid, Sue. 'It's time to confront this taboo: First cousin marriages in Muslim communities are putting hundreds of children at risk'. *Mail on Sunday*, June 3, 2011. http://www.dailymail.co.uk/news/article-1394119/Its-time-confront-taboo-First-cousin-marriages-Muslim-communities-putting-hundreds-children-risk.html.

ReMix News staff. 'Mohamed races ahead as most common boy name in Brussels last year'. *ReMix News*, January 12, 2022. https://rmx.news/article/mohamed-races-ahead-as-most-common-boy-name-in-brussels-last-year/.

Richardson, Valerie. 'Black Lives Matter cashes in with $100 million from liberal foundations'. *Washington Times*, August 16, 2016. http://www.washingtontimes.com/news/2016/aug/16/black-lives-matter-cashes-100-million-liberal-foun/.

Riddell, Kelly. 'George Soros funds Ferguson protests, hopes to spur civil action'. *Washington Times*, January 14, 2015. http://www.washingtontimes.com/news/2015/jan/14/george-soros-funds-ferguson-protests-hopes-to-spur/.

R.K. 'Attentat de Christchurch : des plaintes déposées en France, notamment pour « apologie du terrorisme »' [Christchurch attack: complaints filed in France, in particular for 'glorifying terrorism']. *Le Parisien*, March 18, 2019. https://www.leparisien.fr/faits-divers/attentat-de-christchurch-des-plaintes-deposees-en-france-notamment-pour-apologie-du-terrorisme-18-03-2019-8034903.php.

Robinson, Julian. 'Knife fight in the Jungle: Terrifying moment migrant is stabbed by blade-wielding attacker as Calais governor reveals British anarchists are fuelling violence in the camp'. *Mail Online*, March 2, 2016. http://www.dailymail.co.uk/news/article-3473141/Knife-fight-Jungle-Terrifying-moment-migrant-flees-blade-wielding-attacker-Calais-governor-reveals-British-anarchists-fuelling-violence-camp.html.

Rossi, Nicola. 'Managed Diversity'. Chap. 5 in *The Progressive Manifesto, New Ideas for the Centre-Left*, edited by Anthony Giddens. Oxford: Polity Press, 2003.

Rowlatt, Justin. 'The risks of cousin marriage'. *BBC Newsnight*, November 16, 2005. http://news.bbc.co.uk/2/hi/programmes/newsnight/4442010.stm.

RT News. '"European nations should control their own borders & immigration policies" — Lew Rockwell'. *Rt.com*, April 14, 2016. http://on.rt.com/7a0b.

———. 'Germany needs 500,000 migrants a year until 2050 — study'. *Rt.com*, March 28, 2015. http://on.rt.com/fsnwpu.

———. 'Hungarian PM blames Soros for fueling refugee crisis in Europe'. *Rt.com*, October 30, 2015. http://on.rt.com/6v28.

———. 'Islam does not belong in Germany, 60% agree with AfD'. *Rt.com*, May 5, 2016. https://www.rt.com/news/341888-islam-germany-poll-afd/.

Salter, Frank. 'Germany's Jeopardy: Could the Immigrant Influx "End European Civilization"?' *Council of European Canadians*, January 15, 2016. http://www.eurocanadian.ca/2016/01/germanys-jeopardy-could-immigrant-influx-end-european-civilization.html.

Samuels, Jonathan. 'Sky Finds "Handbook" For EU-Bound Migrants'. *Sky News*, September 13, 2015. http://news.sky.com/story/sky-finds-handbook-for-eu-bound-migrants-10346437.

Sanchez, Raf. 'Erdogan calls on Turkish families in Europe to have five children to protect against "injustices"'. *Telegraph*, March 17, 2017. http://www.telegraph.co.uk/news/2017/03/17/erdogan-calls-turkish-families-have-five-children-bulwark-against/.

Sarrazin, Thilo. 'Bei keiner anderen Religion ist der Übergang zu Gewalt und Terrorismus so fließend'. *Bild*, August 26, 2010. http://www.bild.de/politik/2010/spd-politiker-schreibt-in-seinem-neuen-buch-ueber-den-islam-13749562.bild.html.

Schabas, William. Genocide in International Law: The Crime of Crimes. Cambridge; New York: Cambridge University Press, 2000.

Schröter, S. 'Salafism and Jihadism: An introduction'. Frankfurt: Frankfurter Forschungszentrum Globaler Islam. February 2015. http://www.ffgi.net/en/files/dossier/dossier-intro-schroeter_en.pdf.

Seguin-Orlando, Andaine, Thorfinn S. Korneliussen, Martin Sikora, Anna-Sapfo Malaspinas, Andrea Manica, Ida Moltke, Anders Albrechtsen, Amy Ko, Ashot Margaryan, Vyacheslav Moiseyev, Ted Goebel, Michael Westaway, David Lambert, Valeri

Khartanovich, Jeffrey D. Wall, Philip R. Nigst, Robert A. Foley, Marta Mirazon Lahr, Rasmus Nielsen, Ludovic Orlando, and Eske Willerslev. 'Genomic Structure in Europeans Dating Back at Least 36,200 years'. *Science 346*, no. 6213 (November 28, 2014): 1113–1118.

Shaw, Martin. What is Genocide. Cambridge: Polity Press, 2007.

Shoichet, Catherine E. and Josh Levs. 'Al Qaeda Branch Claims Charlie Hebdo Attack Was Years in the Making'. *CNN*, January 21, 2015, http://edition.cnn.com/2015/01/14/europe/charlie-hebdo-france-attacks/.

Simmons, Alan. *Immigration and Canada: Global and Transnational Perspectives*. Toronto: Canadian Scholars' Press, 2010.

Simpson, James. 'Reds exploiting Blacks: The roots of Black Lives Matter'. *Accuracy in Media*, January 12, 2016. http://www.aim.org/special-report/reds-exploiting-blacks-the-roots-of-black-lives-matter/.

SITE Intelligence Group: Jihadist Threat. https://news.siteintelgroup.com/.

Smith, Anthony D. *National Identity*. New York; London: University of Nevada Press, 1991.

Solennel, Appel. 'For freedom of movement'. *Migreurop: observatoire des frontieres*, December 18, 2013. http://www.migreurop.org/article2396.html?lang=fr.

'Solidarian humanitarian #refugees convoy started to march to the #refugees kettled in spielfeld'. YouTube video, 01:47. Posted by Kanal uporabnika Prisotnoststeje, October 31, 2015. https://www.youtube.com/watch?v=SpQv215LmHE.

Solms-Laubach, Franz. 'Würden Sie eine Sarrazin-Partei wählen?' *Bild*, September 6, 2010. http://www.bild.de/politik/2010/hatte-eine-sarrazin-partei-13869414.bild.html.

Somerville, Will, Dhananjayan Sriskandarajah and Maria Latorre. *United Kingdom: A Reluctant Country of Immigration*. Migration Policy Institute, July 21, 2009. http://www.migrationpolicy.org/article/united-kingdom-reluctant-country-immigration.

Sondage OpinionWay— Fiducial pour Le Figaro. 'Sondage jour du vote au second tour Présidentielle 2012' [Poll of the vote in the second Presidential round 2012]. *Le Figaro*, May 6, 2012. http://opinionlab.opinion-way.com/dokumenty/Sondage_jour_de_vote_T2_SOCIOLOGIE_DU_VOTE_2_1.pdf.

Soros, George. 'The Capitalist Threat'. *The Atlantic Monthly* 279, No. 2 (February 1997): 45–58. Available from: http://www.theatlantic.com/magazine/archive/1997/02/the-capitalist-threat/376773/.

———. 'The Case for Surge Funding'. *Project Syndicate*, February 17, 2016. https://www.project-syndicate.org/commentary/refugee-crisis-surge-funding-most-effective-approach-by-george-soros-2016-02?barrier=true.

———. *The Crisis of Global Capitalism: Open Society Endangered*. New York: Public Affairs, 1998.

———. 'Europe: A Better Plan for Refugees'. *The New York Review of Books*. April 2016. https://www.georgesoros.com/2016/04/09/europe-a-better-plan-for-refugees/.

Soros, George and Gregor Peter Schmitz. '"The EU Is on the Verge of Collapse"—An Interview'. *New York Review of Books*, February 11, 2016. http://www.nybooks.com/articles/2016/02/11/europe-verge-collapse-interview/.

Southern Poverty Law Center. 'Nation of Islam'. N.d. https://www.splcenter.org/fighting-hate/extremist-files/group/nation-islam.

Sputnik News. 'Soros-Sponsored NGO in Syria Aims at Ousting Assad, Not Saving Civilians'. *Sputnik*, September 8, 2015. http://sptnkne.ws/c3QP.

Statista. 'Distribution of the population* in Germany in 2020, by migration background'. October 2021. https://www.statista.com/statistics/891809/german-population-by-migration-background/.

Statista Research Department. 'Islam in the UK — Statistics & Facts'. August 5, 2021. https://www.statista.com/topics/4765/islam-in-the-united-kingdom-uk/#dossierKeyfigures.

Statistics Canada. 'Immigration and diversity: Population projections for Canada and its regions, 2011 to 2036'. Demosim team. Catalogue no. 91–551-X. Issue no. 2017001. January 25, 2017. http://www.statcan.gc.ca/pub/91-551-x/91-551-x2017001-eng.htm.

Statistics Sweden. 'Children per woman by country of birth 1970–2020 and projection 2021–2070'. https://www.scb.se/en/finding-statistics/statistics-by-subject-area/population/population-projections/population-projections/pong/tables-and-graphs/children-per-woman-by-country-of-birth-and-projection/.

———. Demographic Reports: *The future population of Sweden 2012–2060*. 2012. http://www.scb.se/statistik/_publikationer/BE0401_2012I60_BR_BE51BR1202ENG.pdf.

———. Demographic Reports: *The future population of Sweden 2015–2060*. 2015:2. http://www.scb.se/Statistik/_Publikationer/BE0401_2015I60_BR_BE51BR1502.pdf.

———. 'Population in Sweden by Country/Region of Birth, Citizenship and Swedish/Foreign background, December 31, 2019 and 2020'. https://www.scb.se/en/finding-statistics/statistics-by-subject-area/population/population-composition/population-statistics/pong/tables-and-graphs/yearly-statistics--the-whole-country/population-in-sweden-by-countryregion-of-birth-citizenship-and-swedishforeign-background-31-december-2020/.

———. 'Sveriges befolkning, kommunala jämförelsetal, December 31, 2020' [Swedish population, municipal comparative figures, December 31, 2020]. https://www.scb.se/hitta-statistik/statistik-efter-amne/befolkning/befolkningens-sammansattning/befolkningsstatistik/.

Staub, Ervin. *The Roots of Evil: The Origins of Genocide and Other Group Violence*. Cambridge: Cambridge University Press, 1989/2002.

Sterling, Rick. 'Humanitarians for War on Syria'. *CounterPunch*, March 31, 2015. http://www.counterpunch.org/2015/03/31/humanitarians-for-war-on-syria/.

———. 'Seven Steps of Highly Effective Manipulators'. *Dissident Voice*, April 9, 2015. http://dissidentvoice.org/2015/04/seven-steps-of-highly-effective-manipulators/.

Svirsky, M. 'Cruz proposes bill to label Brotherhood, CAIR as terror orgs'. *Clarion Project*, November 4, 2015. https://clarionproject.org/cruz-proposes-bill-label-brotherhood-cair-terror-orgs/.

'Sweden: Leading Social Democrat "The White Majority is the Problem"'. YouTube video (SSU), 01:23. Posted by Kokytus Antenora, March 20, 2013. https://www.youtube.com/watch?NR=1&feature=endscreen&v=1HNcLKj_USE.

Swinford, Steven. 'First cousin marriages in Pakistani communities leading to "appalling" disabilities among children'. *Telegraph*, July 7, 2015. http://www.telegraph.co.uk/news/health/children/11723308/First-cousin-marriages-in-Pakistani-communities-leading-to-appalling-disabilities-among-children.html.

Syria Campaign, The. https://thesyriacampaign.org/.

Syria Solidarity Movement. 'Steering Committee'. http://www.syriasolidaritymovement.org/about/steering-committee/.

Tadmouri, Ghazi O., Pratibha Nair, Tasneem Obeid, Mahmoud T. Al Ali, Najib Al Khaja and Hanan A. Hamamy. 'Consanguinity and Reproductive Health Among Arabs'. *Reproductive Health* 6, no. 17 (October 8, 2009): 9 pages.

Tarmann, Allison. 'The Flap Over Replacement Migration'. *Population Reference Bureau*, June 2000. http://www.prb.org/Publications/Articles/2000/TheFlapOverReplacementMigration.aspx.

Teitelbaum, Michael S. 'The Role of the State in International Migration'. *The Brown Journal of World Affairs* VIII, no. 2 (Winter 2002): 157–167.

'The End of Europe—Mark Steyn (1 of 5)'. YouTube video (Heritage Foundation), 09:56. Posted by Catholic2cortex, July 4, 2008. http://www.youtube.com/watch?v=xlkEYoKCkA.

Tibi, Bassam. 'Europeanisation, Not Islamisation'. *SignandSight.com*, March 22, 2007. http://www.signandsight.com/features/1258.html.

———. 'International Relations and the Study of Islam and World Politics in the Age of Global Jihad'. *Ankara Papers* 16, no. 1 (Summer 2005): 7–12.

———. 'Introduction'. *Ankara Papers* 16, no. 1 (Summer 2005): 1–6.

———. 'The Totalitarianism of Jihadist Islamism and its Challenge to Europe and to Islam'. *Totalitarian Movements and Political Religions* 8, no. 1 (2007): 35–54.

Toft, Monica Duffy. 'Indivisible Territory, Geographic Concentration, and Ethnic War'. *Security Studies* 12, no. 2, (Winter 2002/2003): 82–119.

———. 'Population Shifts and Civil War: A Test of Power Transition Theory'. *International Interactions* 33, no. 3 (July 2007): 243–269.

———. 'Territory and War'. *Journal of Peace Research* 51, no. 2 (March 2014): 185–198.

———. 'The State of the Field: Demography and War'. *ECSP Report*, no. 11 (2005): 25–28. Available from: https://www.wilsoncenter.org/sites/default/files/Toft.pdf.

Tomlin, Gregory. 'Cardinal: Islam's goal is to conquer Europe by faith and "birth rate"'. *Christian Examiner*, November 9, 2015. http://www.christianexaminer.com/article/cardinal-islams-goal-is-to-conquer-europe-by-faith-and-birth-rate/49759.htm.

Tomlinson, Chris. 'Islamic scholar: Europe may be heading toward civil war'. *Breitbart*, September 11, 2016. http://www.breitbart.com/london/2016/09/11/islam-scholar-europe-may-heading-toward-civil-war/.

Tribalat, Michèle. 'Une estimation des populations d'origine étrangère en France en 2011' [An estimate of populations of foreign origin in France in 2011]. Espace populations sociétés, 2015/1–2|2015. https://doi.org/10.4000/eps.6073.

Turbeville, Brandon. 'White Helmets NGO: A "Rescue and Assist" Operation under Guise of Human Rights'. *Global Research*, May 13, 2016. http://www.globalresearch.ca/white-helmets-ngo-a-rescue-and-assist-operation-under-guise-of-human-rights/5524928.

Turkiye Cumhuriyeti Cumhurbaskanligi. 'İstanbul'un Yüreğinde 562 Yıldır Yanan Fetih Işığını Söndürmek İsteyenlere Asla İzin Vermeyeceğiz'. Tccb.gov.tr, May 30, 2015. http://www.tccb.gov.tr/haberler/410/32500/istanbulun-yureginde-562-yildir-yanan-fetih-isigini-sondurmek-isteyenlere-asla-izin-vermeyecegiz.html.

UNITED for Intercultural Action. 'Calais Migrant Solidarity'. July 13, 2012. http://www.unitedagainstracism.org/addressbook/calais-migrant-solidarity/.

United Nations. *Declaration on the Rights of Indigenous Peoples*. 07-58781, March 2008. http://www.un.org/esa/socdev/unpfii/documents/DRIPS_en.pdf.

———. 'New Report on Replacement Migration Issued by UN Population Division'. Press Release DEV/2234, POP/735. March 17, 2000. http://www.un.org/press/en/2000/20000317.dev2234.doc.html.

———. *Replacement Migration: Is it a Solution to Declining and Ageing Population?* Population Division. Department of Economic and Social Affairs. ST/ESA/SER.A/206. 2001. Available at http://www.un.org/esa/population/publications/migration/migration.htm.

———. 'Status of Palestine in the United Nations'. General Assembly. Sixty-seventh session. Agenda item 37. Question of Palestine. A/67/L.28, November 26, 2012. https://unispal.un.org/unispal.nsf/0080ef30efce525585256c38006eacae/181c72112f4d0e0685257ac500515c6c?OpenDocument.

——— . *Universal Declaration of Human Rights*. Paris, December 10, 1948. http://www.un.org/en/universal-declaration-human-rights/.

United Nations Expert Group Meeting on International Migration and Development July 6–8, 2005. 'International Migration Trends: 1960–2000'. Population Division/DESA United Nations. http://www.un.org/esa/population/meetings/ittmigdev2005/PopulationDivI_pp.pdf.

United Nations General Assembly Security Council. *Protracted conflicts in the GUAM area and their implications for international peace, security and development: The situation in the occupied territories of Azerbaijan*. A/63/664-S/2008/823. December 29, 2008. https://web.archive.org/web/20120120120717/http:/www.un.int/azerbaijan/pdf/unrep1.pdf.

United Nations Human Rights Office of the High Commissioner (OHCHR). *Convention on the Rights of the Child*. November 2, 1990. http://www.ohchr.org/en/professionalinterest/pages/crc.aspx.

——— . *International Covenant on Civil and Political Rights*. December 16, 1966/March 23, 1976. http://www.ohchr.org/EN/ProfessionalInterest/Pages/CCPR.aspx.

United Nations Permanent Forum on Indigenous Issues. 'Who are Indigenous Peoples?' Indigenous Peoples, Indigenous Voices: Factsheet. N.d. http://www.un.org/esa/socdev/unpfii/documents/5session_factsheet1.pdf.

United Nations Security Council. *Resolution 242 (1967) of 22 November 1967*. https://unispal.un.org/DPA/DPR/unispal.nsf/0/7D35E1F729DF491C85256EE700686136.

——— . *Resolution 1373. Threats to international peace and security caused by terrorist acts*. S/RES/1373. December 28, 2001. http://unscr.com/en/resolutions/1373.

University of California. 'Migration and Refugee Crisis in Europe'. UC Davis: Gifford Center for Population Studies. Last updated August 22, 2016. http://gifford.ucdavis.edu/workshop/past/migration-and-refugee-crisis-europe/.

Van der Brug, Wouter, Sara B. Hobolt, and Claes Hubert. 'Religion and Party choice in Europe'. *West Europe Politics* 32, no. 6 (November 2009): 1266–1283. doi:10.1080/01402380903230694.

Van der Vyver, Johan D. 'Self-determination of the Peoples of Quebec under International Law'. *Journal of International Law and Policy* 10, no. 1 (Fall 2003): 1–38. Available at http://tamilnation.co/selfdetermination/countrystudies/quebec/quebec.pdf.

Vasileva, Katya. 'Nearly two-thirds of the foreigners living in EU Member States are citizens of countries outside the EU-27'. *Statistics in Focus* 31/2012. Eurostat: Population and Social Conditions. http://ec.europa.eu/eurostat/documents/3433488/5584984/KS-SF-12-031-EN.PDF/be48f08f-41c1-4748-a8a5-5d92ebe848f2.

Vazquez, Joseph. 'George Soros is spending billions to fund social justice-focused "global" university network'. *Lifesite News*, January 12, 2022. https://www.lifesitenews.com/opinion/george-soros-is-spending-billions-on-global-university-network-to-bend-direction-of-history/.

Vidino, Lorenzo. 'A Dagger in the Soft Heart'. Part I in *Al Qaeda in Europe: The New Battleground of International Jihad*. Buffalo, NY: Prometheus, 2005.

———. 'Aims and Methods of Europe's Muslim Brotherhood'. *Current Trends in Islamist Ideology* 4, (November 1, 2006): 22–44. Center on Islam, Democracy, and the Future of the Muslim World: Hudson Institute. http://www.hudson.org/research/9776-aims-and-methods-of-europe-s-muslim-brotherhood.

———. 'Islamism in Europe'. World Watch Monitor. https://www.worldwatchmonitor.org/research/3215322.

———. 'Political Islam in Europe'. In *Political Islam in Europe and the Mediterranean: Three Contributions*, by Walid Phares, Lorenzo Vidino, and Amr Hamzawy. Centre for European Studies, 2011. http://www.martenscentre.eu/sites/default/files/publication-files/political_islam_in_europe_and_the_mediterranean.pdf.

———. 'The Tripartite Threat of Radical Islam to Europe'. *InFocus Quarterly* 1, (Winter 2007). http://www.jewishpolicycenter.org/91/the-tripartite-threat-of-radical-islam-to-europe.

Vidino, Lorenzo and Sergio Altuna. *The Muslim Brotherhood's Pan-European Structure.* Study Report. February 2021. Published by the Austrian Fund for the Documentation of Religiously Motivated Extremism (Documentation Centre Political Islam) October 2021. https://www.academia.edu/60867490/The_Muslim_Brotherhood_s_Pan_European_Structure.

Vltchek, Andre. 'Refugee crisis: Brought to you by Western imperialism'. *RT: Op-Edge*, September 20, 2015. https://www.rt.com/op-edge/316022-refugees-somalia-congo-eu/.

Vogel, Kenneth P. and Sarah Wheaton. 'Major donors consider funding Black Lives Matter'. *Politico*, November 13, 2015. http://www.politico.com/story/2015/11/major-donors-consider-funding-black-lives-matter-215814.

W2eu.net. 'Solidarity with the crew of "Salamis," who rescued 102 boatpeople and are blocked on open sea by Maltese maritime forces'. August 6, 2013. http://w2eu.net/.

———. 'Safety at Sea'. http://www.w2eu.info/seasafety.en.html.

Website of the Hungarian Government. 'Interview with Prime Minister Viktor Orbán on the Kossuth Rádió programme "180 Minutes"'. *Kormany.hu*, May 22, 2016. http://www.kormany.hu/en/the-prime-minister/the-prime-minister-s-speeches/interview-with-prime-minister-viktor-orban-on-the-kossuth-radio-programme-180-minutes-20160520.

———. 'Speech of Viktor Orbán at the EPP Congress'. *Kormany.hu*, October 26, 2015. http://www.kormany.hu/en/the-prime-minister/the-prime-minister-s-speeches/speech-of-viktor-orban-at-the-epp-congress20151024.

Weiderud, P. 'Hjälp troende att rösta vänster' [Help believers to vote left]. Analysis 100802. *Aktuellt i politiken*. N.d. http://www.aip.nu/default.aspx?page=3&ideologi=84.

Weiner, Myron and Sharon Stanton Russell (eds.). *Demography and National Security*. New York; Oxford: Berghahn Books, 2001.

Weiner, Myron and Michael S. Teitelbaum. *Political Demography, Demographic Engineering*. New York; Oxford: Berghahn Books, 2001.

Wheeler, Brian. 'EU should "undermine national homogeneity" says UN migration chief'. *BBC News*, June 21, 2012. http://www.bbc.com/news/uk-politics-18519395.

Whitehead, Tom. 'Illegal immigrants granted permanent residence by staying hidden'. *Telegraph*, May 16, 2011. http://www.telegraph.co.uk/news/uknews/immigration/8514882/Illegal-immigrants-granted-permanent-residence-by-staying-hidden.html.

Wike, Richard, Janell Fetterolf and Moira Fagan. 'Europeans Credit EU With Promoting Peace and Prosperity, but Say Brussels Is Out of Touch With Its Citizens'. Pew Research Center, March 19, 2019. https://www.pewresearch.org/global/wp-content/uploads/sites/2/2019/03/Pew-Research-Center_Views-of-EU-Report_2019-03-19.pdf.

Winsor, Morgan. 'Black Lives Matter protests go global, from Ireland to South Africa'. *ABC News*, July 13, 2016. http://abcnews.go.com/International/black-lives-matter-protests-global-ireland-south-africa/story?id=40546549.

Withnall, Adam. 'Dresden march: Germans warned not to heed "Nazis in pinstripes" as 10,000 turn out for "anti-Islam" protest'. *Independent*, December 16, 2014. http://www.independent.co.uk/news/world/europe/

dresden-march-germans-warned-not-to-heed-nazis-in-pinstripes-as-10000-turn-out-for-anti-islam-9928176.html.

Wood, Vincent. 'Calais chief says BRITISH hard-left activists causing migrant chaos should be "kicked Out"'. *Express*, January 16, 2016. http://www.express.co.uk/news/world/635206/Calais-chief-hard-left-activists-should-be-kicked-out.

Wren, Christopher C. 'Moscow Angrily Denying Role in Arab Oil Embargo'. *The New York Times*, December 6, 1973.

Wright, Oliver. 'Baroness Warsi: Fewer than one in four people believe Islam is compatible with British way of life'. *Independent*, January 23, 2013. http://www.independent.co.uk/news/uk/home-news/baroness-warsi-fewer-than-one-in-four-people-believe-islam-is-compatible-with-british-way-of-life-8464026.html.

Wulff, Christian. 'Valuing Diversity—Fostering Cohesion'. Speech by Christian Wulff, President of the Federal Republic of Germany, to mark the twentieth anniversary of German Unity on October 3, 2010 in Bremen. Bundespräsidialamt. http://www.bundespraesident.de/SharedDocs/Reden/DE/Christian-Wulff/Reden/2010/10/20101003_Rede.html.

X, M. and Haley, A. 'The Playboy interview'. Malcolm-x.org, May 1963. http://www.malcolm-x.org/docs/int_playb.htm.

Ye'or, Bat. *Eurabia: The Euro-Arab Axis*. Maryland/Plymouth: Fairleigh Dickinson University Press, 2005/2011.

Zeit Online. 'Afrika wird unser Problem sein'. *Zeit.de*, June 8, 2016. http://www.zeit.de/politik/deutschland/2016-06/wolfgang-schaeuble-aussenpolitik-wandel-afrika-arabische-welt.

Zeusse, Eric. 'Jeff Bezos's Politics'. *Strategic Culture Foundation*, August 24, 2019. https://www.strategic-culture.org/news/2019/08/24/jeff-bezoss-politics/.

OTHER BOOKS PUBLISHED BY ARKTOS

Virginia Abernethy	*Born Abroad*
Sri Dharma Pravartaka Acharya	*The Dharma Manifesto*
Joakim Andersen	*Rising from the Ruins*
Winston C. Banks	*Excessive Immigration*
Stephen Baskerville	*Who Lost America?*
Alfred Baeumler	*Nietzsche: Philosopher and Politician*
Matt Battaglioli	*The Consequences of Equality*
Alain de Benoist	*Beyond Human Rights* *Carl Schmitt Today* *The Ideology of Sameness* *The Indo-Europeans* *Manifesto for a European Renaissance* *On the Brink of the Abyss* *The Problem of Democracy* *Runes and the Origins of Writing* *View from the Right* (vol. 1–3)
Armand Berger	*Tolkien, Europe, and Tradition*
Pawel Bielawski	*European Apostasy*
Arthur Moeller van den Bruck	*Germany's Third Empire*
Kerry Bolton	*The Perversion of Normality* *Revolution from Above* *Yockey: A Fascist Odyssey*
Isac Boman	*Money Power*
Daniel Branco	*The Absolute Philosopher*
Charles William Dailey	*The Serpent Symbol in Tradition*
Antoine Dresse	*Political Realism*
Ricardo Duchesne	*Faustian Man in a Multicultural Age*
Alexander Dugin	*Ethnos and Society* *Ethnosociology* *Eurasian Mission* *The Fourth Political Theory* *The Great Awakening vs the Great Reset* *Last War of the World-Island* *Politica Aeterna* *Political Platonism* *Putin vs Putin* *The Rise of the Fourth Political Theory* *The Trump Revolution* *Templars of the Proletariat* *The Theory of a Multipolar World*
Daria Dugina	*A Theory of Europe*
Edward Dutton	*Race Differences in Ethnocentrism*
Mark Dyal	*Hated and Proud*
Clare Ellis	*The Blackening of Europe*
Koenraad Elst	*Return of the Swastika*
Julius Evola	*The Bow and the Club* *Fascism Viewed from the Right* *A Handbook for Right-Wing Youth* *Metaphysics of Power* *Metaphysics of War* *The Myth of the Blood*

OTHER BOOKS PUBLISHED BY ARKTOS

	Notes on the Third Reich *Pagan Imperialism* *Recognitions* *A Traditionalist Confronts Fascism*
Guillaume Faye	*Archeofuturism* *Archeofuturism 2.0* *The Colonisation of Europe* *Convergence of Catastrophes* *Ethnic Apocalypse* *A Global Coup* *Prelude to War* *Sex and Deviance* *Understanding Islam* *Why We Fight*
Daniel S. Forrest	*Suprahumanism*
Andrew Fraser	*Dissident Dispatches* *Reinventing Aristocracy in the Age of Woke Capital* *The WASP Question*
Génération Identitaire	*We are Generation Identity*
Peter Goodchild	*The Taxi Driver from Baghdad* *The Western Path*
Paul Gottfried	*War and Democracy*
Petr Hampl	*Breached Enclosure*
Porus Homi Havewala	*The Saga of the Aryan Race*
Constantin von Hoffmeister	*Esoteric Trumpism* *MULTIPOLARITY!*
Richard Houck	*Liberalism Unmasked*
A. J. Illingworth	*Political Justice*
Institut Iliade	*For a European Awakening* *Guardians of Heritage*
Alexander Jacob	*De Naturae Natura*
Jason Reza Jorjani	*Artemis Unveiled* *Closer Encounters* *Erosophia* *Faustian Futurist* *Iranian Leviathan* *Lovers of Sophia* *Metapolemos* *Novel Folklore* *Philosophy of the Future* *Prometheism* *Promethean Pirate* *Prometheus and Atlas* *Psychotron* *Uber Man* *World State of Emergency*
Henrik Jonasson	*Sigmund*
Edgar Julius Jung	*The Significance of the German Revolution*
Ruuben Kaalep & August Meister	*Rebirth of Europe*
James Kirkpatrick	*Conservatism Inc.*
Ludwig Klages	*The Biocentric Worldview* *Cosmogonic Reflections*

OTHER BOOKS PUBLISHED BY ARKTOS

	The Science of Character
Andrew Korybko	*Hybrid Wars*
Pierre Krebs	*Guillaume Faye: Truths & Tributes*
	Fighting for the Essence
Julien Langella	*Catholic and Identitarian*
Henri Levavasseur	*Identity: The Foundation of the City*
John Bruce Leonard	*The New Prometheans*
Diana Panchenko	*The Inevitable*
Jean-Yves Le Gallou	*The Propaganda Society*
Stephen Pax Leonard	*The Ideology of Failure*
	Travels in Cultural Nihilism
William S. Lind	*Reforging Excalibur*
	Retroculture
Pentti Linkola	*Can Life Prevail?*
Giorgio Locchi	*Definitions*
H. P. Lovecraft	*The Conservative*
Norman Lowell	*Imperium Europa*
Richard Lynn	*Sex Differences in Intelligence*
	A Tribute to Helmut Nyborg (ed.)
John MacLugash	*The Return of the Solar King*
Charles Maurras	*The Future of the Intelligentsia & For a French Awakening*
Graeme Maxton	*The Follies of the Western Mind*
John Harmon McElroy	*Agitprop in America*
Michael O'Meara	*Guillaume Faye and the Battle of Europe*
	New Culture, New Right
Michael Millerman	*Beginning with Heidegger*
Dmitry Moiseev	*The Philosophy of Italian Fascism*
Maurice Muret	*The Greatness of Elites*
Brian Anse Patrick	*The NRA and the Media*
	Rise of the Anti-Media
	The Ten Commandments of Propaganda
	Zombology
Tito Perdue	*The Bent Pyramid*
	Journey to a Location
	Lee
	Morning Crafts
	Philip
	The Sweet-Scented Manuscript
	William's House (vol. 1–4)
John K. Press	*The True West vs the Zombie Apocalypse*
Raido	*A Handbook of Traditional Living* (vol. 1–2)
P R Reddall	*Towards Awakening*
Claire Rae Randall	*The War on Gender*
Steven J. Rosen	*The Agni and the Ecstasy*
	The Jedi in the Lotus
Nicholas Rooney	*Talking to the Wolf*

OTHER BOOKS PUBLISHED BY ARKTOS

Richard Rudgley	*Barbarians* *Essential Substances* *Wildest Dreams*
Ernst von Salomon	*It Cannot Be Stormed* *The Outlaws*
Werner Sombart	*Traders and Heroes*
Piero San Giorgio	*Giuseppe* *Survive the Economic Collapse* *Surviving the Next Catastrophe*
Sri Sri Ravi Shankar	*Celebrating Silence* *Know Your Child* *Management Mantras* *Patanjali Yoga Sutras* *Secrets of Relationships*
Oswald Spengler	*The Decline of the West* *Man and Technics*
Richard Storey	*The Uniqueness of Western Law*
J. R. Sommer	*The New Colossus*
Tomislav Sunic	*Against Democracy and Equality* *Homo Americanus* *Postmortem Report* *Titans are in Town*
Askr Svarte	*Gods in the Abyss*
Hans-Jürgen Syberberg	*On the Fortunes and Misfortunes of Art in Post-War Germany*
Abir Taha	*Defining Terrorism* *The Epic of Arya* (2nd ed.) *Nietzsche is Coming God, or the Redemption of the Divine* *Verses of Light*
Jean Thiriart	*Europe: An Empire of 400 Million*
Bal Gangadhar Tilak	*The Arctic Home in the Vedas*
Dominique Venner	*Ernst Jünger: A Different European Destiny* *For a Positive Critique* *The Shock of History*
Hans Vogel	*How Europe Became American*
Markus Willinger	*A Europe of Nations* *Generation Identity*
Alexander Wolfheze	*Alba Rosa* *Globus Horribilis* *Rupes Nigra*

www.ingramcontent.com/pod-product-compliance
Lightning Source LLC
Chambersburg PA
CBHW020607270326
41927CB00005B/217

9781917646789